1 YEAR UPGRADE
BUYER PROTECTION PLAN

Nokia NETWORK
Security

Solutions Handbook

Doug Maxwell
Cherie Amon

KEY	SERIAL NUMBER
001	GYF7M3UV43
002	Q2CVPK9H7F
003	N7T65TAUX3
004	Z8J9HFU29Y
005	U8MB76NH3S
006	4ES8PT5R36
007	G8DX6B7NC4
008	PQ2AKJ6RD7
009	SW9BKMV6FH
010	5BVE4KP79Z

PUBLISHED BY
Syngress Publishing, Inc.
800 Hingham Street
Rockland, MA 02370

Nokia Network Security Solutions Handbook

Printed in the United States of America

2 3 4 5 6 7 8 9 0

ISBN: 1-931836-70-1

Technical Editors: Doug Maxwell and Cherie Amon   Cover Designer: Michael Kavish
Technical Reviewer: Doug Maxwell   Page Layout and Art by: Shannon Tozier
Acquisitions Editor: Jonathan Babcock   Copy Editor: Darlene Bordwell
                                                    Indexer: J. Edmund Rush

Distributed by Publishers Group West in the United States and Jaguar Book Group in Canada.

Acknowledgments

We would like to acknowledge the following people for their kindness and support in making this book possible.

Karen Cross, Lance Tilford, Meaghan Cunningham, Kim Wylie, Harry Kirchner, Kevin Votel, Kent Anderson, Frida Yara, Jon Mayes, John Mesjak, Peg O'Donnell, Sandra Patterson, Betty Redmond, Roy Remer, Ron Shapiro, Patricia Kelly, Andrea Tetrick, Jennifer Pascal, Doug Reil, David Dahl, Janis Carpenter, and Susan Fryer of Publishers Group West for sharing their incredible marketing experience and expertise.

Duncan Enright, AnnHelen Lindeholm, David Burton, Febea Marinetti, and Rosie Moss of Elsevier Science for making certain that our vision remains worldwide in scope.

David Buckland, Wendi Wong, Daniel Loh, Marie Chieng, Lucy Chong, Leslie Lim, Audrey Gan, and Joseph Chan of Transquest Publishers for the enthusiasm with which they receive our books.

Kwon Sung June at Acorn Publishing for his support.

Jackie Gross, Gayle Voycey, Alexia Penny, Anik Robitaille, Craig Siddall, Darlene Morrow, Iolanda Miller, Jane Mackay, and Marie Skelly at Jackie Gross & Associates for all their help and enthusiasm representing our product in Canada.

Lois Fraser, Connie McMenemy, Shannon Russell, and the rest of the great folks at Jaguar Book Group for their help with distribution of Syngress books in Canada.

David Scott, Annette Scott, Delta Sams, Geoff Ebbs, Hedley Partis, and Tricia Herbert of Woodslane for distributing our books throughout Australia, New Zealand, Papua New Guinea, Fiji Tonga, Solomon Islands, and the Cook Islands.

Winston Lim of Global Publishing for his help and support with distribution of Syngress books in the Philippines.

Contributors

Kyle X. Hourihan (NSA) is the Senior Technical Trainer and Course Developer for Nokia Internet Communications in Mountain View, CA. He designs, writes and teaches Nokia Internet Division's internal and external training material. He conducts Train-the-Trainer sessions for Nokia Authorized Training Partners as well as high-end training for Nokia's internal R&D and TACs (Telephone Assistance Centers). Kyle has been working in network security since 1999, and previously worked for 3Com as a Senior Instructor and Developer for their Carrier Systems Division (Commworks). He started off his career working as a programmer, writing code for Cisco IOS, implementing minor routing protocols, and performing software QA on their routers. Kyle earned a bachelor's of Science degree in Computer Science from the University of Maryland, College Park. He is also a co-author of Freesoft.org (www.freesoft.org), a comprehensive source of Internet engineering information. Kyle resides in Palo Alto, CA.

Daniel Kligerman (Check Point CCSA, CCSE, Extreme Networks GSE, LE) is a Consulting Analyst with TELUS. As a member of TELUS Enterprise Solutions Inc., he specializes in routing, switching, load balancing, and network security in an Internet hosting environment. Daniel was a contributing author for *Check Point NG Security Administration* (Syngress Publishing, ISBN: 1-928994-74-1). A University of Toronto graduate, Daniel holds an honors bachelor's of Science degree in Computer Science, Statistics, and English. Daniel currently resides in Toronto, Canada, and would like to thank Robert, Anne, Lorne, and Merita for their support.

Tony Bautts is a Senior Security Consultant with AsTech Consulting. He currently provides security advice and architecture for clients in the San Francisco Bay area. His specialties include wireless security and deployment, intrusion detection systems, firewall design and integration, post-intrusion forensics, bastion hosting, and secure infrastructure design.

Tony's security experience has led him to work with Fortune 500 companies in the United States as well as two years of security consulting in Japan. He is co-author of *Hack Proofing Your Wirless Network* (Syngress Publishing, ISBN: 1-928994-59-8) and Technical Reviewer for *Configuring IPv6 for Cisco IOS* (Syngress Publishing, ISBN: 1-928994-84-9).

Robert J. Shimonski (Sniffer SCP, Cisco CCDP, CCNP, Nortel NNCSS, MCSE, MCP+I, Master CNE, CIP, CIBS, CWP, CIW, GSEC, GCIH, Server+, Network+, Inet+, A+, eBiz+, TICSA, SPS) is the Lead Network Engineer and Security Analyst for a leading manufacturer and provider of linear motion products and engineering. One of Robert's primary responsibilities is to use multiple network analysis tools on a daily basis to monitor, baseline, and troubleshoot an enterprise network comprised of a plethora of protocols and media technologies. In Robert's many years of performing high and low level network design and analysis, he has been able to utilize a methodology of troubleshooting and analysis for not only large enterprises, but also for small to medium sized companies looking to optimize their WANs, LANs, and security infrastructure.

Robert has contributed to many articles, study guides, certification preparation software, Web sites, and organizations worldwide, including *MCP Magazine*, Techtarget.com, Brainbuzz.com, and SANS.Org. Robert's background includes positions as a Network Architect at Avis Rent A Car and Cendant Information Technology. Robert holds a bachelor's degree from SUNY, NY, and is a part time Licensed Technical Instructor for Computer Career Center in Garden City, NY teaching Windows-based and networking technologies. Robert is also a contributing author for *Configuring & Troubleshooting Windows XP Professional* (Syngress Publishing, ISBN: 1-928994-80-6) and *BizTalk Server 2000 Developer's Guide for .NET* (Syngress Publishing, ISBN: 1-928994-40-7), and was the Technical Editor and contributing author for *Sniffer Pro Network Optimization and Troubleshooting Handbook* (Syngress Publishing, ISBN: 1-931836-57-4).

Kevin Greene is a Senior Security Consultant leading technical risk assessments, managing security projects, and implementing security solutions for clients. Kevin has over six years experience in information security. His focus is on network security, security architectures and perimeter security. Kevin's focus is on Check Point Firewall-1 firewall software on Nokia platforms, Cisco PIX, NetScreen firewalls, and Intrusion Detection (overall threat management). Kevin conducts large-scale threat and vulnerability assessments using numerous vulnerability assessments and detection tools including commercial products and non-commercial (freeware) products. Kevin holds a bachelor's of Science in Management Information Systems and a master's of Science in Information Systems from the New Jersey Institute of Technology. He is a Check Point Firewall-1 Certified Systems Administrator and Systems Engineer (CCSA/CCSE). He has co-authored *CCNP CISCO Internetworking Troubleshooting 4.0 Study Guide (Exam 640-440)* and was a contributing author to the *Cisco Newsletter* in 2001.

Technical Editors and Contributors

Doug Maxwell (CCSI, NSA) is a Senior Professional Services Engineer with Integralis in East Hartford, CT. He primarily designs and implements the integration of Nokia and other Check Point firewalls, as well as IDS solutions into enterprise networks, and teaches Nokia Security Administration and Check Point NG to clients. He is also the Lead Engineer for the Integralis-US S3 team, which provides network security auditing, penetration testing, and computer forensic services. His specialties include UNIX network security and firewall/IDS network integration. Doug holds a bachelor's of Science degree in Computer Science from the University of Massachusetts at Amherst, and is a member of the Association for Computing Machinery (ACM), USENIX, and SAGE, the System Administrator's Guild. Doug was a contributing author for *Check Point NG Security Administration*, (Syngress Publishing, ISBN: 1-928994-74-1). He happily resides in Ellington, CT with his wife and two-year-old son.

Cherie Amon (CCSI, Nokia Certified Security Instructor) is a Senior Professional Security Engineer for Integralis. She is both a Check Point and Nokia Certified Security Instructor and has been installing, configuring and supporting Check Point products since 1997. Cherie teaches at the Integralis training center in East Hartford, CT and operates as a third-tier engineer in the technical support division. Cherie is also the Technical Editor and co-author of *Check Point NG Security Administration* (Syngress Publishing, ISBN: 1-928994-74-1). As a member of USENIX and SAGE, she enjoys attending technical conferences. A resident of Tampa, FL, she is currently attending college at the University of South Florida pursuing a math degree. Cherie thanks her husband, Kyle, and father, Jerry Earnest, for sparking her interest in computers and technology.

Contents

Foreword

Security and convenience seldom go together. All too often, security is sacrificed for user or administrator convenience. It is becoming increasingly apparent that this all-too-human attitude is causing trouble in today's connected world.

Many of the reasons for this situation include things that are out of your control, things that intrude on an already overworked network administrator's precious time and that were not always seen as necessary in the past. Keeping track of operating system security patches, software versions and upgrades, system backups, and the myriad other tasks dependent on administrators sometimes makes the work involved in securing basic systems overwhelming. Every day, security and vulnerability disclosure mailing lists contain exploits found in commercial or open-source software, some of which have a huge impact because of the wide use of that software. What can you do to keep up with this barrage of information and make time for the real task of updating your systems? At the most fundamental level, you can attempt to simplify and really *focus* on what exactly is needed to produce a secure, maintainable firewall or routing platform.

That is exactly what Nokia did when it designed the IPSO operating system and bundled it on hardware appliances made of common but reliable components that were easily replaceable. With IPSO, Nokia took a solid, time-tested UNIX base and redesigned it from the bottom up with security in mind. Readers who have UNIX or network security experience will notice this redesign immediately in some of the small features that are present in IPSO—things such as a read-only root partition or a lack of compilers or other development tools. But Nokia realized that the hardening of its core operating system was not enough; the system also had to be *maintainable* once it was installed. Nokia provides this maintainability with the Voyager Web interface and a system that is configured out of the box to be accessible and configurable via a serial console. This system enables once-difficult (or impossible, on some operating systems) tasks such as remotely rebuilding or upgrading your operating system—and easily so, but with security in mind. Tasks that are easy but time-consuming on other operating systems, such as log maintenance or system backups, are both easy and *fast* in IPSO. (Some of these tasks are done for you, without your intervention.) In fact, Nokia has brought the two disparate worlds of security and convenience much closer together than was once possible, enabling you to concentrate on your network without worrying so much about one part of its security.

This book was written with the network and firewall administrator in mind. Throughout, we have tried to concentrate on the day-to-day tasks that administrators must perform and to give the book a practical focus. Our hope is that you find this book useful enough to keep a dog-eared copy on your shelf to refer to as the need arises. Where it is appropriate and enhances understanding, we explain underlying concepts so that perhaps the reference will become less necessary with time. Although an understanding of UNIX is helpful as you read this book, it is not necessary; to help you get up to speed, Appendix A presents a gentle introduction to the concepts and tools involved. The contents of this appendix should be all you need to make the most out of the chapters that stray from the Voyager interface and into the command line.

We begin in Chapter 1 by describing in detail each member of the Nokia enterprise security platform: the IP series of devices. We discuss each model's hardware specifications and features and why one particular model might suit your needs more than another. We discuss things such as how much memory each model has, how many network interfaces it can support, and what kinds of carrier-class features you can expect from the high-end Nokia models.

Chapter 2 gives you an overview of the IPSO operating system, the workhorse that powers all the IP series appliances. We discuss IPSO's history and how it was engineered with security in mind from the bottom up. We also talk about the IPSO file system structure and the user and group structure, and we briefly discuss the configuration interface called *Voyager* that can be used to perform almost everything you need to do as an administrator, from initial configuration to ongoing maintenance and troubleshooting. The specific version of IPSO discussed in this book is 3.6 FCS3, which was released in August 2002, although most of what we discuss applies to most recent IPSO versions. Where we discuss new features available only in IPSO 3.6, we point that out to you.

Chapter 3 describes how to perform the initial, out-of-the-box configuration of your Nokia appliance. We talk about the physical equipment that is required, exactly what information you need to prepare for first-time configuration, and how to prepare your network connections for the actual configuration process. We describe the options available to you for first-time setup, including console-only, Web-based, or DHCP.

Chapter 4 continues where Chapter 3 left off and describes how to configure your Nokia appliance once you have established a network connection to it. This chapter introduces you to use of the Voyager Web interface and discusses things essential to getting your IP series device up and running as a firewall or router with as little pain as possible. We talk about things such as configuring network access and services, determining interface settings (such as IP addressing, speed, and duplex), setting a default gateway, setting your time zone and system clock, and adding host entries to your system's hosts file. Particular emphasis is placed on security, so we show you how to enable and use Secure Shell (SSH, preferred over Telnet and FTP) for remote access and file transfers and how to require HTTPS access for future Voyager configuration sessions.

In Chapter 5, the topic of basic system administration is covered quite thoroughly. Again, almost anything you need to do with regard to administering your system on a day-to-day basis is possible through Voyager. Where appropriate, we show you other options available for making required system configuration changes, including the console-based Web browser, lynx, and the new command-line shell, CLISH. Particular topics discussed in this chapter include managing software packages and IPSO images (including new installation, removal, and upgrades), user and group administration, and system backup and restore. We also tell you how to add, remove, and change static routes, how to manage syslog and perform other logging configuration, and how to schedule repetitive tasks with *cron*.

Chapter 6 focuses on setting up and using Check Point's FireWall-1 software, probably the reason for which most administrators purchase and use Nokia appliances. We show you how to install, enable, and initially configure the bundled FireWall-1 software; then we talk about upgrading and applying hot fixes to ensure smooth operation of your firewall. We even walk you step by step through an upgrade from v4.1 SP-6 to NG FP2 so that you can follow the same procedure on your Nokia. In case something goes awry, we show you how to downgrade or back out your FireWall-1 installation or service pack. Check Point NG is the focus of Chapter 6, although the procedures apply to any Check Point firewall releases.

System monitoring is a good way to be proactive about your Nokia appliance's overall health, and Voyager gives you plenty of options where monitoring, reporting, and system logging are concerned. Chapter 7 talks about using Voyager's static and dynamic monitoring features to give you access to such information as disk space, memory and swap resources, system load averages, and process CPU utilization. Proper routing configuration is always the core of a smoothly running network, and we show you Voyager's ability to peer into your static and dynamic routing setup as well as how to get real-time information about the way routing protocols are functioning. Finally in Chapter 7, we describe the use of *Iclid*, Nokia's Cisco-like command shell for displaying real-time routing statistics.

Chapter 8 ventures into the topic of advanced system administration, where we leave behind the Voyager GUI interface and concentrate on what you must or can do from the IPSO command line. We first talk about the IPSO boot manager and show you how this tool can be useful in repairing your system or performing factory-default installs. We then delve into CLISH, the new command-line shell introduced in IPSO 3.6, from which you can do anything possible from Voyager. The last part of Chapter 8 concentrates on troubleshooting; we show you how to search through and display various system logs, how to automate secure log transfers with SCP, and how to use the excellent packet sniffer *tcpdump*. Finding information in the event of a problem is paramount to resolving it, either on your own or with Nokia support, so we continue the troubleshooting theme by talking about two information-gathering tools: *ipsoinfo* and *dmesg*. Finally, we finish Chapter 8 by discussing tools to monitor memory and processes on a running system. We even give you a short but useful shell script that you can use to automate the collection of memory usage data.

In Chapter 9, we go back to the world of Voyager and show you how you can configure the most commonly used dynamic routing protocols through its convenient interface. IPSO, after all, was designed to be a highly efficient routing appliance, complementing nicely its common use as a firewall. In Voyager, Nokia has provided a way to completely configure all the various routing protocols it supports. With that in mind, we discuss all the configuration screens and parameters for RIP, OSPF, and BGP. One section is devoted to the logging of these and the other dynamic routing protocols supported in IPSO, where you will see the extremely fine-grained logs that can be produced with a few clicks of your mouse. Chapter 9 finishes with a discussion of VLAN-aware routing, another new feature that was introduced in IPSO 3.5.

We build on the previous chapters in this book in Chapter 10, where we discuss in detail how to set up and maintain multiple Nokia appliances in high-availability configurations, specifically referring to the Virtual Router Redundancy Protocol, or VRRP. VRRP provides a simple, cost-effective, and reliable failover method that will keep your network up and protected if one Nokia firewall in a high-availability pair should fail for some reason. We show you how to configure VRRP within Voyager, and we discuss Nokia's useful extension to VRRP, called *monitored circuit*. Routing and FireWall-1 considerations such as default gateways, allowing connections to virtual IP addresses, and state synchronization are discussed as well, to make sure you have all you need to set up highly available configurations with a minimum of fuss.

IPSO is a UNIX-based operating system, and although it is certainly possible to perform most if not all of your setup and maintenance through Voyager, an understanding of UNIX concepts still comes in handy at times. With that in mind, Appendix A talks about UNIX basics—things such as UNIX file system concepts, user and group permissions and how they operate to provide system security, and use of the command shell, including the commands you need to perform basic file system upkeep. Appendix A finishes with a section on using the *Vi* editor.

For network and system administrators who have UNIX experience, Appendix B shows you how to obtain some tools from Nokia that you can use on other platforms on a daily basis—things such as alternate command shells (Bash or ksh, for example), Perl, and netcat. The throughput-monitoring and reporting tool MRTG is also available for IPSO; Appendix B discusses where to get it and how to configure and run it. Appendix B finishes with a discussion of the other shell utilities available from Nokia, such as ktrace, fstat, and ncftp.

—Doug Maxwell and Cherie Amon,
Technical Editors and Contributors

## Chapter 1

Overview of the Nokia Security Platform

Solutions in this chapter:

- Introducing the Nokia IP Series Appliances
- Administration Made Easy

☑ Summary

☑ Solutions Fast Track

☑ Frequently Asked Questions

Introduction

In today's world, ensuring security and stability of the corporate network infrastructure is no longer an option. In a global economy, businesses demand 24 x 7 uptime and expect that communication with their peers will be both swift and secure. Previously, when contending with these requirements, network administrators were forced to install third-party firewall software (such as Check Point's FireWall-1) on standalone PCs or proprietary hardware. This necessity forced administrators to deal with details such as hardware selection, operating system configuration, and software installation and provided for inconsistent stability and security, even within the same organization. Even a formal, standardized corporate policy that specifies all of the above may be forced to differ in implementation by hardware vendors or will be implemented in slightly different ways by different administrators. Is the default installation of your operating system secure enough? (Probably not.) Is the hardware adequate for the task at hand? Is the hardware optimized for high performance under conditions common to firewalls? Is secure, remote access or troubleshooting possible? Are remote operating system or firewall software upgrades possible?

Enter the Nokia Security Platform (NSP), a group of UNIX-based appliances that provide easy, integrated access to third-party software such as FireWall-1 or Internet Security Systems' (ISS) RealSecure intrusion detection platform. NSP's applications provide a resounding "Yes" answer to all the questions we just asked. All the models have standardized on a common Web interface, called the Voyager, through which you can remotely administer and configure almost any aspect of the operating system or firewall. Serial console access is standard. The NSP consists of eight different hardware models, all part of the IP series. Two are for small office/home office (SOHO) implementations; the other six are for enterprise rollouts.

In this chapter, we discuss the enterprise IP series models, showing the hardware specifics of each and discussing where each would be appropriate in a business environment. Then we present an overview of the Voyager Web-based administrative interface and briefly discuss how Nokia has made the administrator's life easier in various ways. Detailed specifics on using Voyager and administering your NSP can be found in Chapters 4, 7, and 8.

Introducing the Nokia IP Series Appliances

In this chapter we look at the specifications and uses of the six enterprise models. Each model offers something that the others don't, although, of course, the higher-numbered models are considerably more expensive than the lower-numbered models.

You need to choose the model that is right for your network architecture based on your answers to the following questions. Where a model is specified, you can assume that all higher-numbered models support the desired feature, except for RAID-1, which is unique to the IP400 series. Now ask yourself these questions:

- **Do I need direct WAN connectivity?** If you do, you need at least an IP330.

- **Do I need VPN capability?** If you do, you need at least an IP71. (The IP71 is part of Nokia's SOHO suite of appliances, which have varying user interfaces and are not discussed here.)

- **Do I need Gigabit Ethernet capability?** If you do, you need at least an IP530.

- **Do I need hot-swappable or redundant components?** If you do, you need at least an IP650.

- **Do I need more than five Ethernet ports?** If you do, you need at least an IP410.

- **Do I have more than 50 network devices that need firewall protection?** If you do, you need at least an IP120.

- **Do I need VPN hardware acceleration?** If you do, you need at least an IP330.

- **Do I want SSH remote access capability?** If you do, you need at least an IP71.

- **Do I want hardware RAID-1 (mirroring) capability?** If you do, you need an IP440 or an IP410.

Enterprise Models

Nokia's Enterprise models all come bundled with full versions of Check Point's FireWall-1/VPN-1 software, as well as full versions of ISS's intrusion detection software, RealSecure. In addition, they all offer dynamic routing protocols and other routing configuration features (including VRRP for failover configurations), so firewall network integration does not have to include a separate router in most cases. Apart from the IP120, all in this series are upgradeable to varying degrees, since they are essentially PCs with off-the-shelf components and Nokia's IPSO operating system. Remember that although firewall and IDS software comes bundled with the Nokia, you still need to purchase a license from the vendor or a reseller prior to using the product. Both Check Point and ISS offer time-limited evaluation licenses for those who want to test implementations prior to purchase.

IP120

The IP120 strikes a good balance among features, performance, and cost for the small to medium-sized office. It is the first in the IP series of appliances to run on the IPSO operating system, and it is the first to support the full version of Check Point's FireWall-1. With 128MB of RAM, it is also able to handle full Check Point Next Generation (NG) installations. It is also the first appliance to support dynamic routing protocols through the IPSO routing daemon (ipsrd; see Chapter 9, "Advanced Routing Configuration") and has all the "standard" remote access protocols implemented, including File Transfer Protocol (FTP), Secure Shell (SSH), and Hypertext Transfer Protocol/Secure Hypertext Transfer Protocol (HTTP/HTTPS). As stated earlier, the IP120 is not upgradeable as the other models are; it has the small form factor of a SOHO appliance but with more features, including the following:

- Three on-board 10/100 Ethernet ports
- Two serial ports (AUX and console)
- 128MB RAM
- A National GX1, 300MHz CPU
- Static routing capability
- Dynamic routing, including RIP ng, OSPF, IGMP, VRRP, and optionally IGRP and DVMRP (the latter two require purchase of a license)

- BOOTP/DHCP relay capability

- IPv6 support

- SNMP v3 support

- Telnet, FTP, HTTP/HTTPS, and SSH servers

- Full version of Check Point FireWall-1, including full remote and site-to-site VPN capabilities

- Full version of ISS RealSecure

IP330

The IP330 is the first in the IP series that adds wide area network (WAN) support to its list of features. Supported protocols include Point-to-Point Protocol (PPP), Frame Relay, High-Level Data Link Control (HDLC), asynchronous transfer mode (ATM), Integrated Services Digital Network (ISDN), V.35/X.21, T1/E1, HSSI, and Fiber Distributed Data Interface (FDDI). A two-port Ethernet card can be added, giving the IP330 a maximum of five Ethernet interfaces. An analog modem can be added for remote, out-of-band management, and a virtual private network (VPN) hardware accelerator card is available. An internal analog modem is standard through the built-in RJ-11 port.

The IP330 has a small footprint and is rack-mountable in standard 19-inch racks, where it will only take up one unit of space. Along with the IP330's support for VRRP, this makes it ideal for stacked, failover implementations in small or medium-sized businesses where space is at a premium. (See Chapter 10, "High Availability," for more details.) Let's take a look at the specifications for the IP330:

- Three on-board 10/100 Ethernet ports

- 256MB RAM

- K6-2, 400MHz CPU

- Console port, RJ-11 port

- Static routing

- Dynamic routing, including RIP ng, OSPF, IGMP, VRRP, and optionally IGRP, BGPv4, and DVMRP (the latter three require purchase of a license)

- BOOTP/DHCP relay capability

- IPv6 support

- SNMP v3 support

- Telnet, FTP, HTTP/HTTPS, and SSH servers

- Full version of Check Point FireWall-1, including full remote and site-to-site VPN capabilities

- Full version of ISS RealSecure

- WAN support

- One compact PCI slot for add-ons

- 1U rack-mountable

IP400 Series

The IP400 series consists of three models: the IP440, the IP410, and the IP400. None of the appliances in the IP400 series is currently available for purchase from Nokia, although they were quite popular at one time and many 400 series deployments are still in use. Nokia will continue to support the existing IP400 series user base for the foreseeable future. The IP400 and the IP410 differ only in the processor they are built around—a high-end Pentium II or a low-end Pentium II, respectively. The latest IP440 models shipped with a Pentium III processor.

Both models come with a CD-ROM drive and a diskette drive. They are distinguishable from all of the other Nokia IP models in that they have no boot manager (see the sidebar "What Is a Boot Manager?"), meaning that certain upgrades must be done using a boot diskette. (See Chapter 5, in the section "Managing IPSO Images," for details.)

No Ethernet interfaces come standard with the IP400 series; typically, at least one four-port Ethernet Quad Card is purchased, although the four PCI slots allow up to 16 Ethernet interfaces, if you choose to use that many. WAN options are the same as for the IP330: PPP, Frame Relay, HDLC, ATM, ISDN, V.35/X.21, T1/E1, HSSI, and FDDI protocols are supported.

Configuring & Implementing...

What Is a Boot Manager?

A *boot manager*, sometimes called a *boot loader*, is a small program that runs just after system startup but before the operating system kernel is loaded into memory. Its main function is to load the kernel from disk into memory, which then handles normal system startup and initialization. Nokia's boot manger has gone through several changes over the years and has been present on the system hard drive, a specially formatted diskette drive, or (most recently) in flash memory, the latter to ease upgrades and provide some measure of resiliency in the event of a hard disk crash. The boot manager will, if left unattended, simply bootstrap the system with the default kernel image, but the process can be interrupted and given options from a rudimentary command shell. This functionality is typically useful, for example, to boot into "single-user" or nonnetworked mode, for system maintenance. See Chapter 8 for in-depth coverage of booting and IPSO boot manager options.

An analog modem can be added for remote, out-of-band management, and a VPN hardware accelerator card is available. The IP400 series also provides for optional hardware RAID configuration, but only RAID Level 1 (disk mirroring) is available. Here are the specifications for the IP400 series:

- Console and auxiliary serial ports

- 256MB RAM standard, upgradeable to 768MB RAM

- PIII, 600MHz CPU

- Static routing

- Dynamic routing, including RIP ng, OSPF, IGMP, VRRP, and optionally IGRP, BGPv4, and DVMRP (the latter three require purchase of a license)

- BOOTP/DHCP relay capability

- IPv6 support

- SNMP v3 support

- Telnet, FTP, HTTP/HTTPS, and SSH servers

- Full version of Check Point FireWall-1, including full remote and site-to-site VPN capabilities

- Full version of ISS RealSecure

- WAN support

- Four PCI slots

- 3U rack-mountable

- CD-ROM and diskette drives

- Hardware RAID-1 available

IP530

The IP530 is the first in the IP series of appliances to support Gigabit Ethernet. As in the IP400 series, a maximum of 16 Ethernet interfaces are possible with the four on-board interfaces and the three PCI expansion slots. One internal PMC slot can be used for VPN hardware acceleration, leaving the PCI slots free for network interfaces if needed. WAN options are the same as for the IP330 and IP400 series: PPP, Frame Relay, HDLC, ATM, ISDN, V.35/X.21, T1/E1, HSSI, and FDDI protocols are supported. Two Type II PCMCIA slots have been added for analog modem support.

The IP530 is meant to be a "high-density" port device, meaning that it is useful in situations in which many network interfaces are required. The on-board Ethernet ports offer slightly more throughput than network interface devices added through the PCI bus (and consequently, the IP530 has a slightly higher interface throughput than the IP650); when coupled with Gigabit Ethernet support, this model is useful for large businesses with high throughput requirements but that do not need the carrier-class features of the 600 or 700 series. The specifications for the IP350 series are as follows:

- Four on-board 10/100 Ethernet ports

- Console and auxiliary serial ports

- 256MB RAM standard, upgradeable to 768MB RAM

- PIII, 700MHz CPU

- Static routing

- Dynamic routing, including RIP ng, OSPF, IGMP, VRRP, and optionally IGRP, BGPv4, and DVMRP (the latter three require purchase of a license)

- BOOTP/DHCP relay capability

- IPv6 support

- SNMP v3 support

- Telnet, FTP, HTTP/HTTPS, and SSH servers

- Full version of Check Point FireWall-1, including full remote and site-to-site VPN capabilities

- Full version of ISS RealSecure

- WAN support

- Three compact PCI slots (Gigabit Ethernet available)

- Two Type II PCMCIA slots

- 2U rack-mountable

IP650

The IP650 is one of Nokia's high-end firewall appliances, and is the first in the IP-series to offer carrier-class features such as hot-swappable PCI slots, fan trays, and power supplies. The IP650 does not have any on-board Ethernet ports, but has five PCI slots, and so can have a maximum of 20 Ethernet interfaces. Gigabit Ethernet is supported, as well.

You can use an on-board Peripheral Component Interconnect (PCI) mezzanine card, or PMC, slot (see the sidebar "What Is a PMC slot?") for a VPN accelerator card, freeing PCI slots for network interfaces. WAN support is similar to previous models, with PPP, Frame Relay, HDLC, ATM, ISDN, V.35/X.21, T1/E1, HSSI, and FDDI protocols supported. Two Type II PCMCIA slots have been added for analog modem support.

Configuring & Implementing…

What Is a PMC Slot?

PMC is short for *PCI mezzanine card*, and the *PMC slots* that Nokia refers to in its documentation are simply PCI slots that allow an expansion card to be plugged in so that it is *parallel* rather than perpendicular to the motherboard. Because any PCI card you plug into a PMC slot is parallel to the board, it takes up less vertical space. For that reason, these slots are used frequently in high-density devices and smaller rack-mount devices in which space is at a premium. Nokia uses them in their 600 and 700 series devices.

According to Nokia, the IP530 has a slightly greater network interface throughput than the IP650, merely because the IP530 was designed with on-board Ethernet ports that do not need to access the PCI bus. This makes the IP650 suitable for large businesses that are more concerned about reliability than throughput. Organizations that want both will be satisfied with the 700 series, described in the following section. Here are the specifications for the IP650:

- Console and auxiliary serial ports

- 256MB RAM standard, upgradeable to 1GB RAM

- PIII, 700MHz CPU

- Static routing

- Dynamic routing, including RIP ng, OSPF, IGMP, VRRP, and optionally IGRP, BGPv4, and DVMRP (the latter three require purchase of a license)

- BOOTP/DHCP relay capability

- IPv6 support

- SNMP v3 support

- Telnet, FTP, HTTP/HTTPS, and SSH servers

- Full version of Check Point FireWall-1, including full remote and site-to-site VPN capabilities

- Full version of ISS RealSecure

- WAN support

- Five hot-swappable PCI slots (Gigabit Ethernet available)

- Hot-swappable fan trays

- Hot-swappable, redundant power supply optional

- Two Type II PCMCIA slots

- 2U rack-mountable

IP700

The IP700 series consists of the IP710 and the IP740. Both offer the IP650's carrier-class features such as hot-swappable PCI slots, fan trays, and power supplies.

The IP700 series has four on-board 10/100 Ethernet interfaces and four PCI slots, and so can have a maximum of 20 Ethernet interfaces. Gigabit Ethernet is supported as well. The main difference between the 700 models and the previous ones is firewall throughput; Nokia claims that speeds of over 2GB per second are possible with the IP740. (See Table 1.1 for more information.)

An on-board PMC slot can be used for a VPN accelerator card, freeing PCI slots for network interfaces. WAN support is similar to previous models, with PPP, Frame Relay, HDLC, ATM, ISDN, V.35/X.21, T1/E1, HSSI, and FDDI protocols supported. Two Type II PCMCIA slots have been added for analog modem support.

The IP700 series is designed for the largest businesses that demand both performance and reliability. Let's take a look at the IP700 series specifications:

- Four on-board 10/100 Ethernet ports

- Console and auxiliary serial ports

- 512MB RAM standard, upgradeable to 1GB RAM

- PIII, 866MHz CPU

- Static routing

- Dynamic routing, including RIP ng, OSPF, IGMP, VRRP, and optionally IGRP, BGPv4, and DVMRP (the latter three require purchase of a license)

- BOOTP/DHCP relay capability

- IPv6 support

- SNMP v3 support

- Telnet, FTP, HTTP/HTTPS, and SSH servers

- Full version of Check Point FireWall-1, including full remote and site-to-site VPN capabilities

- Full version of ISS RealSecure

- WAN support

- Four hot-swappable PCI slots (Gigabit Ethernet available)

- Hot-swappable fan trays

- Hot-swappable, redundant power supply optional

- Two Type II PCMCIA slots

- 2U rack-mountable

Designing & Planning...

Nokia Network Interface Throughput

Table 1.1 shows the published maximum network interface throughput rates for all Nokia devices discussed in this chapter. (See www.allasso.fr/base/docs/FireWallPerformanceBrief3.pdf for more information.)

Table 1.1 Nokia Device Maximum Network Interface Throughput Rates

Model	FW-1	SHA-1/3DES VPN-1	SHA-1/3DES VPN-1 with Nokia Accelerator Card
IP120	102Mbps	2Mbps	N/A
IP330	139Mbps	7Mbps	20Mbps
IP440	176Mbps	16Mbps	80Mbps
IP530	507Mbps	18Mbps	115Mbps
IP650	244Mbps (348Mbps with Gigabit Ethernet)	18Mbps	84Mbps
IP740	2Gbps (2025Mbps)	22Mbps	137Mbps

Continued

How did Nokia achieve such high throughput rates? Part of the reason is that Nokia worked with Check Point to enhance the throughput of its devices with *Firewall Flows*, an OS kernel modification that increases packet throughput rates by placing a copy of the firewall connection table at the device driver hardware interrupt layer of the networking stack. This solution allows packet accept/reject decisions to be made at the earliest possible moment, thus increasing packet throughput by as much as 400 percent. Flows is designed to give the best boost to performance during long-lived TCP/UDP connections with many small packets and is not used at all with encrypted or Internet Control Message Protocol (ICMP) traffic. Despite this fact, it can still be quite beneficial on average. Nokia refers to the normal path taken by packets in a flows-disabled Check Point firewall as *Slowpath*, and uses the term *Flowpath* to refer to the path such packets take in a flows-enabled firewall. The Flows modification is available in all the models discussed in this book and is supported in IPSO version 3.3 and later. See Chapter 8 for more details.

Administration Made Easy

You will need to configure your Nokia when you unpack and initially install it, and you should maintain that configuration throughout the life of the device, perhaps with updates and modifications. When you think about it, administering a production firewall or other network-critical device can be quite time consuming. You have to worry about security hotfixes, OS upgrades, software patches, and routing configuration changes—and that's just for starters. We're not mentioning the day-to-day problems that can arise and interfere with your plans. You will find that Nokia has made this process quite easy, relatively speaking.

The initial configuration of the NSP is even easier than it was in the past. Previously, you had to set up a console connection to the device for first-time boot, at which time you entered device hostname and interface information, allowing a network connection to be established so that you could complete the configuration. Starting with IPSO 3.5 FCS 6, the Nokia device has a built-in Dynamic Host Configuration Protocol (DHCP) client and will configure a network interface on its own when booted for the first time, assuming you have a DHCP server available. (Actually, any time the device boots and finds a missing or invalid global configuration file, it will initiate the first-time boot sequence. See Chapter 4 for details.) Once you have an interface configured, Nokia's Web-based administrative interface, the Voyager, can be used for just about anything you need to do as an administrator, including point–and–click operating system and firewall software upgrades (see Figure 1.1).

Figure 1.1 Interface Configuration Through the Voyager Web Interface

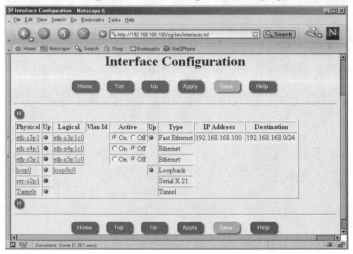

For administrators who don't like to maintain one device at a time, Nokia has a product called Horizon Manager that enables remote, centralized upgrades and maintenance of multiple devices simultaneously. Some of the things you can do with Horizon Manager include OS upgrades, hotfix applications, system backups, firewall configuration, and remote command execution.

If you only have a console connection to your Nokia device or you're someone who likes to live at a command prompt, you won't be disappointed. Voyager can be used over a console connection from the IPSO shell with the text-mode browser Lynx (see Figure 1.2).

A command-line tool called *Iclid* can be used to show and monitor various configuration settings. Iclid has a syntax quite similar to that of Cisco's IOS command shell and offers the nice feature of tabbed command completion and command history display present in most modern UNIX shells. (See Figure 1.3 and refer to Chapter 7 for more details.)

Because IPSO is based on UNIX and boots into a standard C-shell (csh), UNIX power users will feel quite at home here (see Figure 1.4). Beware, though, that changes made through standard command-line utilities such as *ifconfig* or *route* or edits to system configuration files will not normally persist across system reboots or even across changes made with Voyager. However, there are ways to use the standard tools to make permanent changes (see Chapter 8 for more details).

Figure 1.2 Package Management Through the Lynx Interface

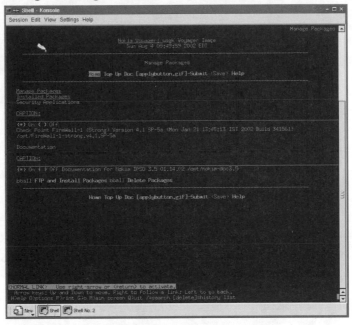

Figure 1.3 Displaying VRRP Status Using Iclid

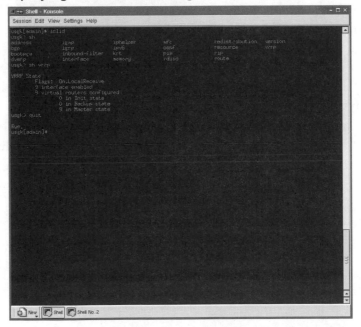

Figure 1.4 Output of Common Shell Commands

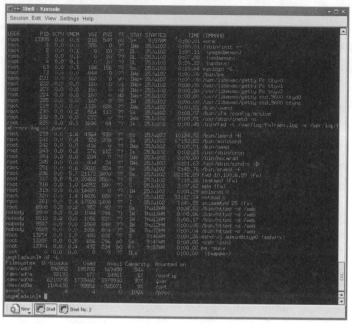

Finally, Nokia has gone to some effort to harden the IPSO operating system and provide a solid and secure basis from which to run a firewall, IDS sensor, or router. IPSO itself is based on FreeBSD UNIX and has been pared down in size to about 30MB. The root partition is mounted read-only; unnecessary network services have been turned off; no compiler, development tools or libraries are present (with the notable exception of GDB, the GNU debugger, which is useful for crash analysis); and the hard drive is partitioned for you in a sane and sensible fashion. There are very few UNIX manual pages, and, as you might expect from a 30MB OS, all but the most essential system binaries are gone. (We discuss the IPSO operating system in detail in Chapter 2.) If you must have things like Perl, Bash, or MRTG, see Appendix B for some popular software that Nokia has ported to IPSO.

Summary

The Nokia Security Platform consists of six enterprise models, from the IP120 to the IP740. All offer a wide range of features and hardware specifications, and it is easy to find something that fits the network architecture of both the small office and the largest ISP's or Telco's. The primary feature points that distinguish one model from another include direct WAN connectivity (IP330 and up), 16 or more network interfaces (IP400 series and up), Gigabit Ethernet (IP530 and up), and hot-swappable or redundant components (IP650 and up). All the devices are based on the Nokia IPSO operating system, and all of them can be almost entirely configured through Nokia's intuitive Voyager Web interface. These appliances' ability to function as full-fledged routers, with WAN support and support for many of the most common dynamic routing protocols, means that they can function as a drop-in replacement for the commonly seen "border router-firewall" configuration. The rack-mountable appliances are becoming very popular for use in high-availability VPN deployments, where they are configured in pairs with VRRP and Check Point's gateway clustering.

Nokia has implemented a feature called Firewall Flows, which works with Firewall-1 and can dramatically improve firewall throughput for most types of traffic.

Administration of the IP series devices can be easily accomplished several ways: using the Voyager tool through a graphical browser, using the Voyager tool through the text-mode browser Lynx, and through command-line utilities such as Iclid or even the standard UNIX shell. Nokia has hardened the IPSO operating system, which is based on UNIX; as a result, these devices are ready to run out of the box (after network configuration, of course). Nokia also has a product called Horizon Manager that enables remote, centralized administration of multiple devices.

Solutions Fast Track

Introducing the Nokia IP Series Appliances

☑ All the Nokia enterprise models include full versions of Check Point's FireWall-1 and ISS's RealSecure, and all have at least 128MB of RAM.

☑ All the enterprise models offer remote access via Secure Shell (SSH), Telnet, and FTP, and all offer serial console access for out-of-band or direct connectivity.

☑ All the enterprise models offer dynamic routing support, although BGP, DVMRP, and IGRP require the purchase of a license from Nokia for their use.

☑ The IP330 and higher models support direct WAN connectivity.

☑ The IP330 and higher models are rack-mountable.

☑ The IP400 and higher models support more than five Ethernet interfaces.

☑ The IP530 and higher models offer Gigabit Ethernet support.

☑ The IP600 and IP700 series appliances offer redundant and hot-swappable hardware components.

Administration Made Easy

☑ All the Nokia appliances discussed in this chapter can be administered through any standard Web browser using the Voyager interface.

☑ All the Nokia appliances discussed in this chapter can be administered through the text-mode Web browser Lynx from a command prompt.

☑ The command-line tool Iclid can be used to monitor or show various system parameters in real time.

☑ You can use standard UNIX shell commands to display or change system configuration settings; however, changes you make in this way won't persist across reboots or across changes made with Voyager.

☑ The IPSO operating system is based on FreeBSD UNIX and is hardened by default.

☑ Firewall Flows is a feature unique to Nokia that can increase Firewall-1 packet throughput by as much as 400 percent.

Frequently Asked Questions

The following Frequently Asked Questions, answered by the authors of this book, are designed to both measure your understanding of the concepts presented in this chapter and to assist you with real-life implementation of these concepts. To have your questions about this chapter answered by the author, browse to **www.syngress.com/solutions** and click on the **"Ask the Author"** form.

Q: I noticed that firewall and IDS software comes bundled with the Nokia Enterprise models. Can I use this software right out of the box?

A: No, you still need to purchase a license from the vendor or a reseller prior to using them.

Q: Are the enterprise models limited in the number of firewalled hosts they can protect?

A: In general, no, but it depends on the Check Point license you purchase with the device. Unlimited licenses are available.

Q: Does Nokia offer 24-hour hardware replacement as a support option?

A: Yes. See http://support.nokia.com.

Q: Can I write shell scripts, as I can on my other UNIX firewalls?

A: Yes. The UNIX C shell is the standard command-line shell in IPSO. See Chapter 8 for details.

Q: Can I use HTTPS with the Voyager interface?

A: Yes. In fact, you can make this the *only* way to access the Voyager Web interface. See Chapter 4 for details.

Q: Is the Flows function enabled by default?

A: Yes.

## Chapter 2

Overview of the Nokia IPSO Operating System

Solutions in this chapter:

- **History and Overview**
- **Access and Security Features**
- **Users and Groups**
- **Directory Structure**
- **Configuring IPSO**

☑ **Summary**

☑ **Solutions Fast Track**

☑ **Frequently Asked Questions**

Introduction

Nokia designed the IP series appliances with several goals in mind:

- To provide a stable and high-speed routing platform for integration into enterprise networks

- To provide a modern, stateful network firewall

- To provide a secure platform "out of the box" so that administrators can rightfully spend their time looking after their networks and not have to worry about "hardening" their firewall's platform operating system

These design goals were combined to produce the Nokia IP-series appliance. In the following sections, we discuss the history of the IPSO operating system and the Voyager interface, tell you what they are based on, and describe how Nokia has improved them over the years. We also discuss the basic layout of the IPSO file system and discuss some of its features. Appendix A can be used as a reference for readers who have minimal or no UNIX background.

The version of IPSO that we cover in this book and introduce in this chapter is 3.6. This version has some new features compared with earlier releases that we discuss in detail in later chapters—things such as VLAN-aware routing, initial configuration using DHCP, clustering, and CLISH, the command-line shell. This chapter concentrates on IPSO's security features and how the operating system is logically laid out.

History and Overview

The problem of a fast and efficient routing appliance was already solved when, in December 1997, Nokia bought Ipsilon Networks, a California-based company that developed and sold high-speed switching products. Ipsilon had also developed a Web-based management tool for its products that the company termed the *Network Voyager*. Nokia took the Ipsilon products as a base and integrated its own operating system and Check Point's FireWall-1 product into an appliance designed for high-speed packet forwarding and modern, stateful firewalling. The operating system Nokia engineers developed to run on the appliance was termed *IPSO*.

IPSO Is UNIX

The UNIX operating system had its origins at Bell Labs in 1969; over the years it evolved into many variants, one of which was termed *4.4BSD*, developed at the

University of California at Berkeley (*BSD* meaning *Berkeley Software Distribution*). A portion of the core operating system source code base for 4.4BSD was made freely available and formed the basis for many modern UNIX or UNIX-like operating systems, among them FreeBSD. (See www.freebsd.org for more information on FreeBSD, which is still an ongoing and very active OS project.) The networking code present in the BSD-style UNIX variants has been developed continuously in an open fashion over the last 30 years and is some of the most stable and widely used in the world.

FreeBSD version 2.2.6 was released in March 1998 and provided a solid basis for Nokia's engineers to develop the IPSO operating system. Although since then IPSO has diverged from the original FreeBSD code base, it still remains a stable and efficient BSD-based networking platform at its core. Nokia has managed to trim down the original operating system, removing unnecessary binaries, hardening the OS configuration, and improving the core routing and networking functionality. Modern versions of IPSO weigh in at just under 35MB compressed and about 120MB uncompressed.

Commercial Software Available for IPSO

IPSO comes bundled with some additional software available for you to use, although most of it requires a license before you use it in production. Check Point's FireWall-1 is the primary reason that most people use Nokia appliances; IPSO 3.6 supports Check Point NG FP-2 as well as versions 4.1 SP-5a and 4.1 SP-6. There is also a version of ISS's RealSecure intrusion detection package (version 6.5 is the latest available), as well as SystemWatch, a system monitoring and alerting tool.

Nokia's Horizon Manager is also available as an enterprisewide monitoring and device management solution. It allows you to do things like remotely upgrade IPSO on many devices at once, from a centralized management console. If you don't have any of these software packages with your Nokia appliance, they are all available for download from Nokia's support site, along with documentation.

Access and Security Features

Firewalls, by their very nature, are placed in networks so that at least one interface is exposed to what you as an administrator consider *the big, bad world*. After all, that's why you have a firewall in the first place: to restrict the flow of traffic between trusted and not-so-trusted networks. Usually, the untrusted side of your firewall is the Internet, although this is not always the case. In any event, a network device that lives in such a position must be installed and configured with care. The usual method goes something like this:

1. You install an operating system on your hardware of choice. You might or might not have many chances to specially configure the operating system during the install; most installations are automated and provide little choice along the way. You might have to add or remove hardware before the installation, and you might have to find and configure device drivers for your hardware during the installation.

2. You remove packages, networking options, and graphical user environments (unless, of course, your operating system *is* a GUI).

3. You remove unnecessary network services, system binaries, games, and the like.

4. You configure remaining network services so that they are restricted or configured more securely.

5. You configure network interfaces and test routing and connectivity.

6. You install and configure your firewall software. This software could be built into the operating system, but usually it is not.

7. You install the testing and monitoring tools that you use every day but that didn't come with your operating system.

The process of removing unnecessary packages and network services from an operating system and reconfiguring what is left to be more secure is known as *OS hardening*, and it can be quite an art form. Done improperly, it will at best be ineffective and at worst could cause your firewall to be more vulnerable to attack than when you started. Even when done properly, the hardening process can be quite time consuming. Nokia realized that saving time here and shipping a device that was hardened *ahead of time* would appeal to most time-starved administrators, and that is what the company did. In fact, Nokia took the opposite approach: It started with an empty system and added binaries, libraries, and network services as they were necessary. We discuss the details of Nokia's hardening in the following sections, and we talk about remote network access and the IPSO file system structure. By the time you are done reading this chapter, you should have a good understanding of IPSO and how it is put together.

Designing & Planning...

Nokia Manual Pages

The hardening and trimming process that took place when IPSO was being designed caused system documentation in the form of UNIX manual pages to be mostly left out. Here are the few manual pages that remain, arranged according to the manual section they are in:

- **Manual Section 1** clish, ftp, id, mail, netstat, scp, slogin, ssh-add, ssh-agent, ssh-keygen, ssh, tcpdump, telnet.
- **Manual Section 8** camcontrol, mtrace, pccardd, ping, sshd, tftpd, traceroute.

If you do need documentation for a command that is not on this list, you can get it at the freebsd.org Web site, where there is a searchable archive of all the FreeBSD man pages for the current and all prior releases. We are interested in version 2.2.6, since that is the release IPSO was based on: www.freebsd.org/cgi/man.cgi?manpath=FreeBSD +2.2.6-RELEASE.

Remote Access

The Nokia IP devices have many of the standard remote and local access network protocols available for you to use. Each is discussed in the following sections. All the available protocols operate in what is called the *client/server* model, in which a network *client* initiates a TCP connection to a network *server* that is listening for such connections. In all cases, enabling any of the listed protocols means having the server active and listening for incoming connections.

The Client/Server Model and Listening Sockets

TCP, the *Transmission Control Protocol*, forms the basis for many client/server-based communication protocols for which reliability is paramount. A TCP connection can be in any one of a dozen or so states, depending on whether the connection is being initiated, is in progress, or is in the process of being closed.

Four pieces of data are used to uniquely identify each connection: a source IP address, a destination IP address, a source port number, and a destination port number. Ports can be in the range 1 through 65535; which port is assigned to which application is mostly standardized, at least for certain port ranges. (You can see port assignments in the file /etc/services.)

For example, suppose an SSH server with IP address 192.168.8.1 is listening for incoming connections on TCP port 22 (the default for SSH). A client makes a connection from 192.168.8.15 and gets assigned a random high port (ports greater than 1024) by the SSH client—in this case, 33090. If a new connection is established from the same client host, it will be assigned a new port number and will be considered separate from the previous connection, even though it is both from and to the same host. The combination of an address and port number is sometimes called a *socket*, or a *listening socket* when you are talking about a network server. You can see the status of any current network servers and connections with the command *netstat −an*:

```
Active Internet connections (including servers)
Proto Recv-Q Send-Q  Local Address    Foreign Address    (state)
tcp    0      0        *.22              *.*                LISTEN
tcp    0      0    192.168.8.15.33090  192.168.8.1.22    ESTABLISHED
tcp    0      0    192.168.8.15.33667  192.168.8.1.22    ESTABLISHED
```

The first line tells you that an SSH server is listening for incoming connections on TCP port 22 on this host (or rather, *something* is listening for connections on TCP port 22). This is a useful debugging tool, especially when you want to know if a server is functioning properly and is, in fact, listening for incoming connections. If you are using your Nokia box as a firewall, you should see something like this in the netstat output:

```
tcp    0      0    *.256              *.*                LISTEN
tcp    0      0    *.259              *.*                LISTEN
tcp    0      0    *.261              *.*                LISTEN
tcp    0      0    *.262              *.*                LISTEN
tcp    0      0    *.264              *.*                LISTEN
tcp    0      0    *.265              *.*                LISTEN
```

These are some of the control ports that Check Point's FireWall-1 listens on by default. Most of the services mentioned here (with the exception of SSH) have runtime configuration settings in the file /var/etc/inetd.conf. In most

UNIX systems, this file contains lists of network servers and how they should be run; in IPSO, this file will only have an entry for the Telnet service by default, because all other services are disabled. If you disable the Telnet service in Voyager, this file will then be empty.

Telnet

Telnet is a clear-text, TCP-based remote login and command protocol. Nokia enables it by default in all its enterprise devices, although I recommend that you disable Telnet before put your firewall into production. Secure Shell (SSH) is a secure replacement for Telnet (and FTP) that has many more features and should be used instead. Many administrators still use Telnet on a daily basis because they are not aware that SSH clients are available for almost all UNIX and Windows platforms. If you must use Telnet, restrict it to a lab environment, but in any case be aware of the security implications of using a clear-text remote login protocol. As an added measure of security, you can configure Telnet so that the one-time password scheme *S/Key* is mandatory.

FTP

FTP, or *File Transfer Protocol*, is, as its name suggests, a way to transfer files to or from a remote server. Like Telnet, FTP is a clear-text protocol and should be used only when necessary. Unlike Telnet, the FTP server is disabled by default on new Nokia installations. FTP is commonly used as a server that allows anonymous uploads or downloads, where passwords are typically just e-mail addresses. The Nokia FTP server is not configured to accept anonymous logins and by default only allows the admin user to log in. As with Telnet, be aware of who might be *listening* to your network traffic as you initiate an FTP session to your Nokia firewall as user admin, since your password will be visible on the wire. S/Key logins can also be made mandatory for incoming FTP connections.

SSH

As stated, Secure Shell is a secure replacement for Telnet and FTP. Starting with IPSO version 3.4, Nokia began shipping OpenSSH with their operating system. OpenSSH is a free and open-source implementation of the SSH protocol available anonymously from ftp://ftp.openbsd.org. The version of OpenSSH used by Nokia, 2.1.1p4, is disabled by default in all IPSO versions that support it. Free SSH clients exist for many operating systems, including Windows, and most UNIX operating systems now ship with the OpenSSH client and server by default, so there is little reason *not* to use SSH. OpenSSH has some useful features, including local and remote port forwarding, X11 tunneling, strong encryption by default, and *scp,* or *secure copy*.

NOTE

In June 2002, CERT released an advisory detailing security flaws in the OpenSSH implementation for versions 2.3.1p1 through 3.3. (See www.cert.org/advisories/CA-2002-18.html.) This is a rather well known and widely publicized advisory, so it bears mentioning that the version of OpenSSH Nokia uses (2.1.1p4) is *not* vulnerable as described in the advisory. Nokia addresses this advisory in its knowledge base resolution number 13610, which you can read from https://support.nokia.com/ knowledge/frmResolutionView.jsp?ResolutionId=13610, if you have a support contract with Nokia.

HTTP/HTTPS

The Voyager Web-based configuration interface is enabled by default on all IPSO releases and is configured to be accessible over standard HTTP on that protocol's default port 80. Nokia uses the open-source Web server Apache, at version 1.3.6 in all IPSO releases after 3.3. It is possible (and highly recommended) to reconfigure Voyager to be only accessible via HTTPS, and you can also manually change the port number that Apache listens on. (See Chapter 4 for details.)

SECURITY ALERT

In June 2002, CERT released an advisory regarding a flaw in the way the Apache Web server handles data encoded in chunks. (See www.cert.org/advisories/CA-2002-17.html.) This advisory did apply to the version used by Nokia, which, as of August 2002, is still working on a fix. Nokia knowledge base resolution number 13458 (available at https://support.nokia.com/knowledge/frmResolutionView .jsp?ResolutionId=13458) addresses the vulnerability and gives some suggestions on how to mitigate the risk of a remote compromise. The advisory basically states that the risk associated with the Apache vulnerability is dependent on how your firewall's security policy is configured. Some suggestions are given to help reduce this risk:

- Require SSL encryption for all Voyager connections.
- Change the Voyager SSL port number from its default 443 to a TCP high port (above 1024).
- Allow Voyager access only from trusted sources in your security policy.
- Configure User or Client authentication to restrict access to Voyager.

Console Access

Finally, if you cannot or will not allow remote access to your Nokia device, all the models come with at least one serial port configured for local console access. Nokia provides DB-9 serial cables that are designed to work with their products; one cable is shipped with each device. If you need a replacement, standard null modem cables work as well. The console port is configured to work with any standard serial client, such as Hyperterm or Minicom, at 9600/8/N/1. You can also plug a modem into your Nokia device's console port, allowing for out-of-band access over phone lines in emergencies.

Other Security Features

Nokia made some other design decisions with IPSO that were directly related to security. Here is a list of the most visible features:

- The root partition is mounted read-only.
- Sendmail is used to send mail only, through a relay server. No incoming mail is accepted.
- A DNS server is not installed.
- Berkeley *r* commands (*rlogin, rsh, rcp, rexec*) are not present.
- There is no X-Windows server or libraries.
- No exportable file systems (such as NFS) or Remote Procedure Call (RPC) services are installed.
- No remote information services (finger, talk, who) are installed.
- Chargen, echo, and daytime are disabled by default.
- There is no printing subsystem or server.

- No mail or news servers (POP, IMAP) are installed.

- Device access can be restricted to the serial console *only*.

- There are no extra CGI programs other than those used by Voyager under admin access.

- IPSO's Dynamic routing protocols all have strong authentication capabilities via keyed MD5.

- The IPSO shadow password scheme uses MD5.

- IP access lists and rate shaping can be configured independently of Check Point's FireWall-1 and can limit denial-of-service attacks.

Users and Groups

The IPSO operating system has only one user enabled by default at system installation time: the *admin* user. This user has a user ID (UID) of 0, like standard UNIX root accounts, and so has all the privileges of the root user. (Incidentally, the root account is present in IPSO; it is just disabled.) You set a password for the admin user during the initial system configuration and should thereafter use the admin user to login and do system maintenance, including logging into the Voyager GUI.

Another user is created for you during installation: the *monitor* user. This account is meant to be used by administrators to whom you want to give read-only access to your Nokia system. The password for the monitor user account is disabled by default, so it must be enabled by the admin user prior to its first use.

You can see several other users present in the system password file /etc/master.passwd. These are *bin*, *nobody*, and *daemon*. These users are not meant (or able) to be used as login accounts; rather, they are used by system processes that want to run at a reduced privilege level (as opposed to processes that run with the permissions of UID 0). For example, the Apache Web server *httpd* runs as though it were started by user *nobody*. You can see which processes run with the privileges of which user account by typing *ps –aux* at the command prompt. Here is what part of that output looks like:

```
usgk[admin]# ps aux

USER      PID  %CPU %MEM   VSZ   RSS TT STAT STARTED      TIME  COMMAND

...

root      296  0.0  5.8 21492  3496 ?? Ss   25Jul02 226:02.77  fwd 10.100.6.99 (fw)

root      317  0.0  6.4 20708  3840 ?? S    25Jul02  19:49.42  isakmpd (fw)

root      318  0.0  1.0 15152   616 ?? S    25Jul02   6:34.05  mdq (fw)

root      361  0.0  2.7 19800  1612 ?? S    25Jul02   4:50.94  in.asmtpd 25 (fw)

root     8908  0.0  0.2   952    88 ?? Ss    1Aug02   0:48.02  /bin/httpd -d /web

nobody  22071  0.0  0.0  1068     8 ?? IW    9Aug02   0:01.16  /bin/httpd -d /web

nobody  22356  0.0  0.0  1080     8 ?? IW    9Aug02   0:00.72  /bin/httpd -d /web

nobody   1432  0.0  0.0   952     8 ?? IW   Fri09AM   0:00.00  /bin/httpd -d /web
```

You can see that all the Apache processes *(/bin/httpd -d /web)* run as user *nobody*. This is an important security feature. If someone were to gain remote access to your Nokia firewall by exploiting the Apache Web server running on it, once in they would not have root (or admin) privileges. In fact, they would have to run a local exploit of some kind to gain root privileges after breaking into your system. The fact that Nokia has hardened IPSO by mounting the root partition read-only and removing development tools and libraries makes finding or building a local root exploit in that case very difficult.

Other nonprivileged or administrative users can be created in IPSO versions 3.2 or later, although Nokia recommends against this practice, stating that a single-user system is more secure than a multiuser one. As part of Nokia's OS hardening process, any changes made by a user are recorded in the system logfile or *syslog*. This includes things like logging in, mounting or unmounting file systems, password changes, and changes to the system security policy. Each new user you create (even new privileged users) has his or her own home directory, to further enable accountability.

You shouldn't need to change the Nokia group file (/var/etc/group) unless you add an unprivileged user account to your NSP. If you want that account to be able to *su* to admin once it is logged in, you need to add the account to the *wheel* group. Chapter 5 discusses user and group management in more detail.

Directory Structure

The directory structure in the IPSO operating system is similar to that of many other UNIX operating systems—so if you have UNIX experience, you will feel right at home. (Refer to Appendix A if you need a UNIX refresher or introduction.) There are some differences in the way Nokia laid out its file system, however (see Figure 2.1). One of the major differences is that the root partition, where the kernel image and system binaries are stored, is mounted read-only by default. This means that you will not normally be able to alter or create new files on this partition. The admin user can remount the root partition read/write, however, with the following command:

```
mount -uw /
```

When you are done making modifications, remount the root partition read-only again with the following:

```
mount -o ro /
```

This was done to protect the root partition contents from accidental or malicious damage; it is harder for you as an administrator to make a mistake that prevents the system from booting if you must consciously make the root partition read/write. This step should be unnecessary, however, because you can always place your own scripts and programs in /opt, and nothing you could change in the root partition would be persistent across a reboot, anyway. The only time you might need to remount the root partition is when you are upgrading from an old version of IPSO and you are required to upgrade the boot manager. In that case, the new boot manager image file must be placed in /etc.

The rest of the system partitions are mounted read/write; this includes /var, /opt, and /config. Table 2.1 shows the disk partitions created in a default IPSO 3.6 installation, along with their purposes and specifications. This layout is drawn from the system file /etc/fstab.

Figure 2.1 Basic Layout of the IPSO File System

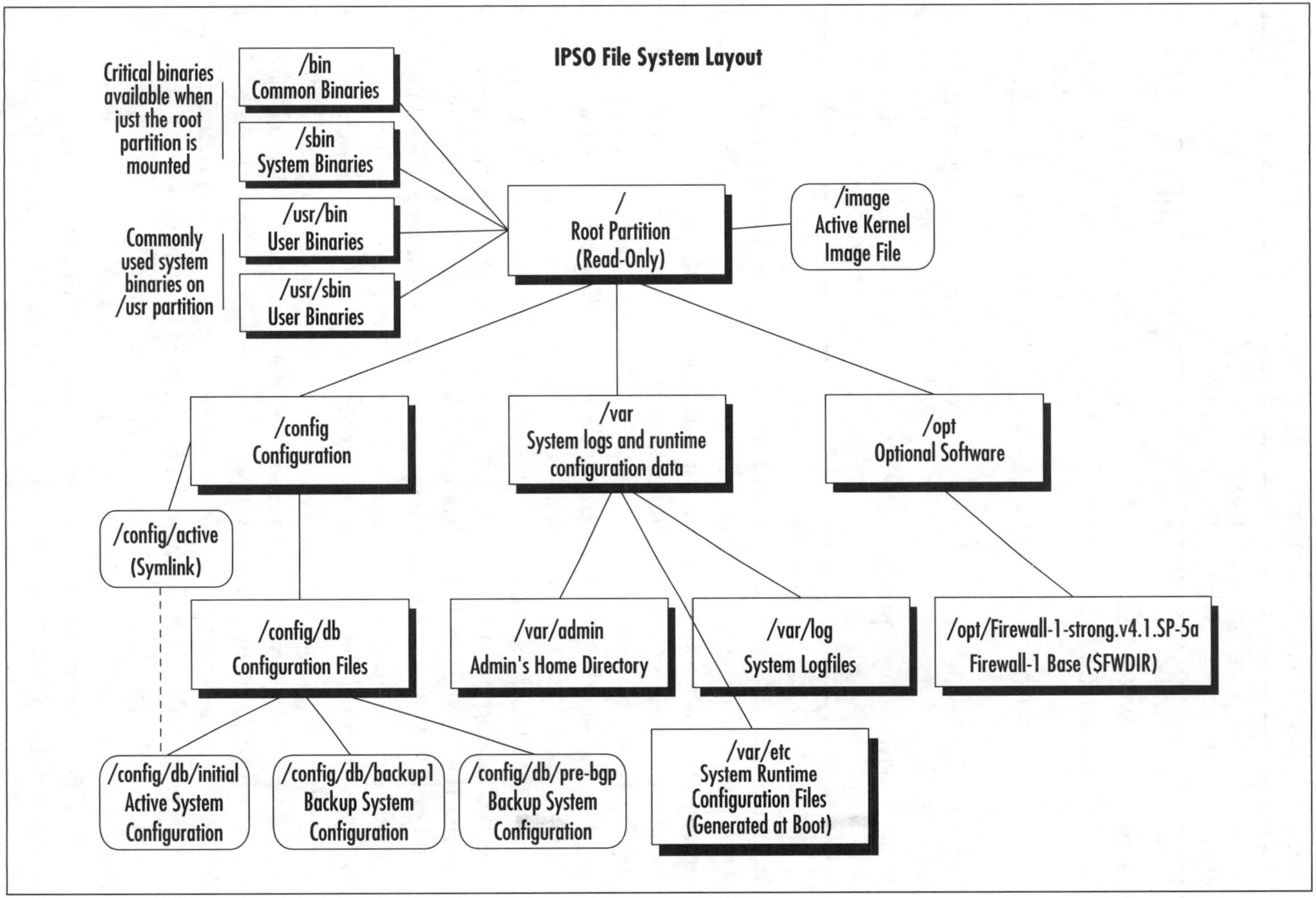

IPSO File System Layout

/image
Active Kernel
Image File

/
Root Partition
(Read-Only)

/bin
Common Binaries

/sbin
System Binaries

/usr/bin
User Binaries

/usr/sbin
User Binaries

Critical binaries
available when
just the root
partition is
mounted

Commonly
used system
binaries on
/usr partition

/config
Configuration

/config/active
(Symlink)

/config/db
Configuration Files

/config/db/initial
Active System
Configuration

/config/db/backup1
Backup System
Configuration

/config/db/pre-bgp
Backup System
Configuration

/opt
Optional Software

/opt/Firewall-1-strong.v4.1.SP-5a
Firewall-1 Base (SFWDIR)

/var
System logs and runtime
configuration data

/var/log
System Logfiles

/var/admin
Admin's Home Directory

/var/etc
System Runtime
Configuration Files
(Generated at Boot)

Table 2.1 IPSO File System Details

Name	Device	Type	Read/Write?	Fsck?	Usage
/config	/dev/wd0a	ufs	Yes	Yes	Global system configuration
Swap	/dev/wd0b	Swap	N/A	No	System swap space
/var	/dev/wd0d	ufs	Yes	Yes	System logs and "variable" process runtime data
/opt	/dev/wd0c	ufs	Yes	Yes	Optional or user added software
/	/dev/wd0e	ufs	No	Yes, first	Root partition; holds kernel image and key system binaries
/proc	Proc	procfs	Yes	No	Kernel configuration and runtime process data

Ufs, the type of file system, is a standard on most BSD UNIX versions, including IPSO. */proc* holds runtime kernel and process data, although is generally not viewed or altered by users in favor of the *ipsctl* interface. Some system binaries draw data from the /proc file system as they run.

The name in the Device column is the system name given to the raw device that represents that particular disk partition. On your system, these names might be different from the ones listed in the table, depending on which model appliance you have. Device names for things like Ethernet cards and disk drives will be related to the device manufacturer or device class that they belong to; in this case, the *wd* portion of the disk partition's name indicates a Western Digital (or similar) IDE hard drive. IDE drives have four *slices,* which are really what most people call a *DOS partition.* (Confusing, yes. Thank the influence of MS-DOS.) Each slice can contain a file system, which itself can have any number of *partitions.* Nokia formats its disks with the entire drive occupying one slice, so you won't see a slice specifier in a device name as you do on Solaris or FreeBSD. The number 0 in *wd0* means that this is the first disk (disks are numbered starting at 0, so on an IP440 with two hard drives, they would be called *wd0* and *wd1*), and the final letter indicates the partition you are referring to in a given slice. The partition is simply a logical piece of a disk slice that refers to a part of the file system installed on that slice, so, for example, the *b* partition on the first hard drive is written *wd0b* and refers to the system swap space.

The Fsck column of the table deserves some explanation. During a proper system shutdown (with the *shutdown* or *halt* commands), each partition or file system is marked to show that it was cleanly unmounted and so will not be checked for errors during system startup. If for some reason the system is not shut down cleanly (due to a power failure, for example), each file system will not have been properly unmounted and so will need to be checked for errors. The program that does the checking is called *fsck* (for *file system check*) and is run during the Nokia device's startup sequence, before each partition is mounted. Most of the time, fsck will run and fix any errors it finds automatically, although every once in a while it needs manual attention. The root partition is always checked for errors first, because it must be mounted before system startup can continue.

Special Directories and Disk Space

Several subdirectories in the IPSO file system are worth mentioning. Table 2.2 outlines these directories and their purposes. An arrow (->) in the table means that the directory to the left of the arrow is a symbolic link to the directory on the right side of the arrow. *$FWDIR* refers to the environment variable that holds the absolute path to the FireWall-1 base directory, if the firewall is enabled.

Table 2.2 IPSO Special-Purpose Directories

Directory	Purpose
/web	Voyager Web pages and CGI scripts
/tmp->/var/tmp2	Temporary file space
/var/crash	Holds crash dump files after a system crash
/var/monitor	Monitor user's home directory
/var/admin	Admin user's home directory
/etc->/var/etc	System configuration files
/var/log	System log files
$FWDIR/log ->/var/fw/log	Firewall log files

You also might wonder how much disk space you have and how it is allocated per partition. IPSO is partitioned for you, and although the sizes of the partitions vary by model number, in general you will find that the /var and /opt partitions have the most space available. The other partitions are really meant to be static in size once IPSO has been configured. As a reference, the IP440 I am using as a test platform as I write this chapter gives me the following when I run *df −k* (sizes in kilobytes):

```
usgk[admin]# df -k
```

Filesystem	1K-blocks	Used	Avail	Capacity	Mounted on
/dev/wd0f	396952	195736	169460	54%	/
/dev/wd0a	38193	177	34961	1%	/config
/dev/wd0d	6210208	1737167	3976225	30%	/var
/dev/wd0e	1106438	112807	905116	11%	/opt
procfs	4	4	0	100%	/proc

Keep in mind that newer models have bigger hard drives. You can see that /var has the most free space, which makes sense when you consider that /var holds firewall and system logs as well as temporary file space. Nokia actually uses a set of formulas to determine disk partition sizes. Here are the formulas for any IPSO of version 3.4 or higher (from Nokia knowledge base resolution #1285):

```
/config:              32MB
swap:                 1/4 the size of disk with a maximum of 1GB
leftover space:       (size of disk - config - swap)
/:                    (leftover space / 2) / 7
/opt:                 (leftover space / 7)
/var:                 (leftover space - (opt + root))
```

Dealing With Floppy and CD-ROM Drives

Sometimes you will have to deal with floppy or CD-ROM drives because the IP400 series has both. IPSO has support for mounting MS-DOS formatted floppy disks, but you first need to create a mount point for the floppy. Do this with **mkdir /var/floppy**, then run the *mount* command:

```
mount_msdos /dev/fd0 /var/floppy
```

Once the floppy has been mounted, you can *cd* into /var/floppy and access the files on it with the usual commands (*cp*, *mv*, and *ls*), just like a normal file system directory. To unmount the floppy once it has been mounted, just type:

```
umount /var/floppy
```

For CD-ROMs, once a CD has been put in the drive, you can use the following command to mount it:

```
mount -t cd9660 -o ro /dev/wcd0c /cdrom
```

You must unmount the CD-ROM before you can eject it. To unmount the CD-ROM, use the following command:

```
umount /cdrom
```

Make sure that you move out of the floppy or CD-ROM mount point directories prior to unmounting either of those devices or you will get an error indicating failure after running the *unmount* command.

Configuring IPSO

The /config partition is where Nokia stores the global configuration file /config/active. This file is simply a flat text file that contains configuration directives in a special format. (It is actually a *symbolic link* to /config/db/initial, which is the real configuration file.) It must be present and valid (in other words, not corrupted) at boot time for your Nokia device to configure itself from it; otherwise, the device will go into "first-time boot mode" and attempt to configure itself via DHCP or wait for you to configure it via the serial console port. Here is what you might see in a small part of the /config/active file:

```
interface:eth-s2p4c0:ipaddr:192.168.0.2:mask 24
monitor:monitord:group:ifthroughput:pthroughput:binding:ipsctl:interface:
    *:stats:ipackets t
ipsrd:vrrp:interface:eth-s2p2c0:virtualrouter:40:monitor:monif:eth-s1p3c0:
    priority 10
ipsrd:vrrp:interface:eth-s1p4c0:virtualrouter:30:monitor:monif:eth-s2p2c0 t
process:sshd:path /usr/sbin
ipsrd:vrrp:interface:eth-s2p4c0:virtualrouter:60:monitor:monif:eth-s2p2c0:
    priority 10
passwd:daemon:uid 1
ipsrd:vrrp:interface:eth-s3p1c0:virtualrouter:80:advertiseinterval 1
```

Since this file is read at every system boot, and since IPSO reconfigures itself according to the contents of this file, altering this file in some way is the only way to change things such as interface IP addresses or to add a static route. Prior to IPSO 3.6, Voyager was meant to be the only interface that would allow you to update the system configuration permanently. Nokia introduced CLISH, the command-line shell, in IPSO 3.6, and now any configuration can be done using this command shell, along with Voyager. You can also make backups of past configurations (before a major configuration change, for example); you will see the old configurations in /config/db, along with the active file. Having global system configuration localized to one file is a security feature in that it makes it easy to restrict access to system configuration and is much simpler than using many separate files.

Apart from daily system configuration and maintenance issues, a common task for an administrator to perform is to run a custom startup script. If you ever need to run a script or executable file at system startup, you can add your commands to the /var/etc/rc.local file. IPSO will execute the rc.local script after all other startup and initialization has taken place. This method could be used, for example, to start some custom monitoring scripts you have written.

Summary

All of Nokia's IP series enterprise appliances are based on the IPSO operating system, which was developed from a branch of the FreeBSD operating system, itself based on 4.4BSD UNIX. This basis makes for a very stable networking and routing platform. Given that most Nokia appliances are sold to be used as firewalls, Nokia took some effort to harden IPSO and make it a more secure platform for firewall use. Some of the things Nokia did include shutting off unnecessary services, restricting system configuration and user accounts, logging system access, and removing development tools and libraries.

Your Nokia appliance can be accessed remotely via Telnet, FTP, HTTP/HTTPS, or SSH and locally via serial console port. Only Telnet is enabled by default, but enabling or configuring network access is easy using the Voyager interface. It is possible to change the port that the Apache Web server listens on, and you can restrict Voyager connections to HTTPS only.

The IPSO admin user is the equivalent of the UNIX root user in terms of privilege and is the only user enabled by default in a new IPSO installation. A monitor user can be enabled to allow read-only access to the NSP, and it is possible to add other privileged and unprivileged users after installation. New, unprivileged users must be added to the wheel group in order to be able to *su* to the admin account.

The IPSO file system is logically just like any other UNIX file system, but it features some changes that increase security. The IPSO root partition is mounted read-only, and changes to system settings and mount points are all logged via the syslog facility.

IPSO can be configured using Voyager or the CLISH command-line shell interface. Changes made through normal means (by editing text files) will not persist across reboots. All the system configuration files are rewritten at boot by the global configuration file, /config/active. This is the file that Voyager or CLISH modifies when it is used to make permanent changes. Having a centralized configuration file increases security and simplicity.

Solutions Fast Track

History and Overview

☑ IPSO is based on FreeBSD UNIX, version 2.2.6.

☑ The IPSO operating system has been prehardened and trimmed down to provide a more secure platform for firewalls or routers.

☑ The IPSO operating system's networking core is based on many years of accumulated stability, originating in 4.4BSD UNIX.

Access and Security Features

☑ Nokia enterprise devices can be accessed remotely via Telnet, FTP, SSH, HTTP, and HTTPS.

☑ It is possible to restrict Voyager to SSL-only connections on the port of your choice.

☑ All Nokia devices come with at least one serial port configured for local console access.

Users and Groups

☑ The IPSO *admin* account will be the only user account enabled after first-time installation. This account has root privileges.

☑ Once it is enabled, the IPSO monitor account can be used to access Voyager in read-only mode.

☑ Some of IPSO's system processes run with reduced permissions, lessening the damage that could be caused in the event of a remote compromise.

☑ It is possible to add more user accounts to IPSO.

Directory Structure

☑ The IPSO root partition is mounted read-only as a security measure.

☑ /image is the currently active kernel image.

☑ The /opt partition contains optional software packages, such as Check Point FireWall-1.

Configuring IPSO

- ☑ /config/active is a symbolic link to the current active configuration file.

- ☑ You cannot make permanent changes to IPSO by editing system configuration files; you must use Voyager or CLISH.

- ☑ /var/etc/rc.local can be used to execute your own customized startup scripts.

Frequently Asked Questions

The following Frequently Asked Questions, answered by the authors of this book, are designed to both measure your understanding of the concepts presented in this chapter and to assist you with real-life implementation of these concepts. To have your questions about this chapter answered by the author, browse to **www.syngress.com/solutions** and click on the **"Ask the Author"** form.

Q: I see that all the system configuration files mention things like "generated by syslog_xlate." Can I use the program syslog_xlate or others like it to edit configuration files and make the changes stick?

A: Yes, although this is an undocumented procedure. This procedure used to be one of the ways to make command-line changes within IPSO, but it is no longer needed now that CLISH is part of IPSO 3.6.

Q: Can I run FreeBSD binaries on my IPSO system?

A: No. The FreeBSD binary format is incompatible with IPSO's format.

Q: Can I upgrade my hard drive to a model with more space?

A: No. Although you can replace the hard drive in your NSP with another from Nokia, upgrading it is not supported, because of the partitioning scheme used by Nokia. You can send system logs to a remote log server, however, if disk space becomes an issue.

Q: Where is Perl? I can't administer a system without Perl.

A: Nokia provides Perl as an unsupported, additional package that can be downloaded from its support site. See Appendix B for installation instructions.

## Chapter 3

Initial Configuration

Solutions in this chapter:

- **Preparing to Boot for the First Time**
- **First-Time Boot Configuration**
- **Continuing the Configuration**

- ☑ **Summary**
- ☑ **Solutions Fast Track**
- ☑ **Frequently Asked Questions**

Introduction

Initial configuration of your Nokia appliance is relatively straightforward and can be accomplished in a very short period of time. Nokia designed its appliances so that if you power them on without an active configuration, they step you through a very simple, console-based menu of options designed to get you up and running with Voyager access in a matter of minutes. From there, the Web-based Voyager interface makes it simple for you to continue the configuration or import a saved configuration from a previous install.

In this chapter, we show you how to prepare for the initial configuration by setting up the required cabling and local network connections, then entering some basic information over a console connection such as hostname and IP address. You will then test your Voyager configuration interface in preparation for complete base router configuration in Chapter 4. Automatic configuration via DHCP is a new feature in IPSO 3.5 and 3.6; in this chapter, we discuss initial configuration using DHCP as well.

Preparing to Boot for the First Time

You need to configure your local workstation for serial and possibly Ethernet connectivity to your Nokia device. This means choosing the proper cabling for your network layout and knowing prior to configuration the following information:

- The IP address of the workstation or laptop you will be using to connect to your Nokia appliance. This should be a nonroutable address. We use 192.168.1.2 for our example configuration.

- IP address, netmask, default route, speed, and duplex settings for the first Ethernet interface on the appliance. We use 192.168.1.1/24, with a default route of 192.168.1.2, at 10Mbps half-duplex.

- The unqualified hostname you will be assigning your Nokia device. We use *gatekeeper*.

- The password for the admin user.

Local Workstation

To prepare for the initial configuration of your Nokia appliance, you need a workstation, laptop, or VT100-capable terminal that you can either directly connect to the Nokia via a console cable or perhaps indirectly (through a hub or switch) through a standard Ethernet connection. If you choose the DHCP method of autoconfiguration, you need only the latter. Until IPSO 3.5, a direct console connection was the only way to configure a Nokia appliance out of the box. The DHCP client on the NSP makes this process somewhat easier now.

In addition to proper cabling and network connections, you need a serial terminal emulator of some sort, such as Hyperterm (Windows) or Minicom (Linux or other UNIX platforms). Note that it is possible to do the entire Nokia base configuration through a VT100 terminal directly connected to the console port; you just won't be able to use Voyager through a graphical Web browser. In that case, you can continue the initial configuration via lynx.

Physical Connections

Nokia supplies a DB-9 serial cable with all its devices. This cable allows for console connections from properly configured clients. If you don't have one of the Nokia cables, you can always use a standard null-modem cable for the serial connection. The local end of the serial cable plugs into one of your workstation's serial ports, while the remote end plugs into your Nokia's console port. The console port is always labeled *Console* and is usually on the front of the device for ease of use in rack-mounted installations. Your terminal emulator's settings should match those shown here:

- **Bits/second (BPS)** 9600.
- **Data bits** 8.
- **Parity** None.
- **Stop bits** 1.
- **Flow control** None.
- **Terminal emulation** Auto or VT100.

If you want to continue the configuration using Voyager and a graphical browser, you need an Ethernet cable. You can directly connect a crossover cable from your workstation to the first Ethernet port (eth1) on your Nokia device, or you can indirectly connect a straight-through cable from your workstation to a hub or switch and from there to the appliance over another straight-through cable. Note that your Nokia's eth1 port will be the leftmost or topmost on-board Ethernet port, depending on the model (see Figure 3.1).

Figure 3.1 Initial Ethernet Connection

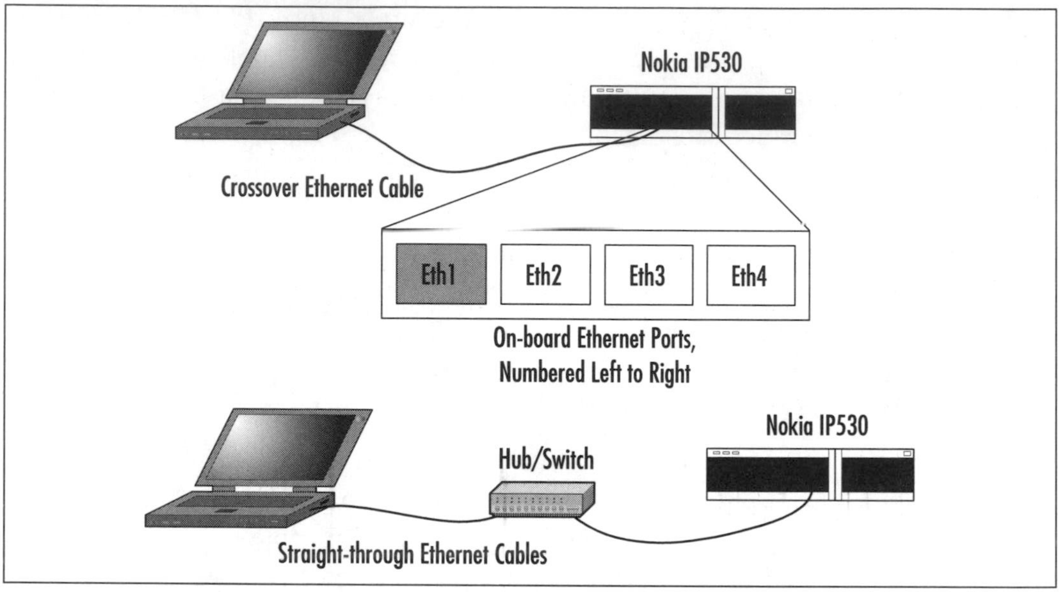

First-Time Boot Configuration

Here we step you through a first-time boot, explaining the procedure for both console and DHCP configuration.

Console Configuration

Configuring your Nokia appliance for first-time use is just a matter of answering a few questions at a console prompt, then choosing how to finish the setup.

Setting the Hostname

The first time you power on your Nokia, you should be presented with a "Hostname?" prompt after a delay while the device bootstraps itself. Simply type the hostname you have selected for your device, and confirm it when asked to do so. Hostnames should be unqualified (without the domain part) and can consist of the letters *a–z* or *A–Z*, the numbers *0–9*, and the characters dash (-) and period (.). Make sure that you enter the correct hostname here—especially if you will be installing Check Point NG later. Check Point NG relies on certificates for its Secure Internal Communication (SIC); these certificates are generated during firewall configuration based on your device's hostname. Changing your hostname after your firewall has been configured means reinitializing SIC, which could be fairly time-consuming.

Entering the Administrative Password

You are next prompted for the admin user's login password. This password must be at least six characters long and can contain the same characters that are legal for the system hostname. You will be prompted for the password twice, just to make sure you typed it correctly. It should go without saying that for security purposes, you must make sure that your password is not a "dictionary word."

Selecting the Browser Type

Here you decide how you want to finish the configuration: with Voyager over a graphical Web-browser and Ethernet connection or via the console with lynx, a text-based browser. Normally, you will want to choose option 1, Web-based Voyager, because the graphical user interface (GUI) interface to Voyager is much more user-friendly, especially if you've never used lynx before. Here is what the prompt will look like:

```
You can configure your system in two ways.


1) Configure an interface and use our
Web-based Voyager via remote browser


2) VT100-based Lynx browser.


Please enter a choice [1-2, q]:
```

If you choose option 2, you will be asked if you want to start lynx now. Enter **y** and log in as user **admin** with the password you entered previously. After logging into lynx, you should see the Voyager opening screen, minus the graphics (see Figure 3.2). We talk more about the specifics of configuring with lynx in the section "Continuing the Configuration" that follows.

Figure 3.2 The Lynx Opening Screen

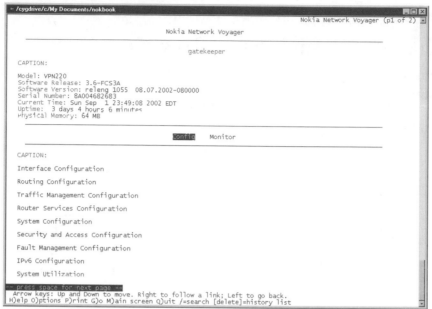

Configuring & Implementing...

Configuring Alternative Interfaces

Although most of the examples you will see in Nokia's literature refer to configuring an Ethernet interface for initial use, you can configure any interface supported by your Nokia appliance, including ATM, T1, FDDI, Frame Relay, or analog modem. The questions you are asked in each case will be different from the standard Ethernet configuration questions, for obvious reasons. For example, if you wanted to configure a serial T1 line, you would be asked the following questions. You should be able to get answers to these questions from your ISP if you don't know them:

1. Local and remote IP addresses; in this case, the default route will be set to the remote address automatically

2. The T1 encoding (AMI or B8ZS)

3. The T1 framing (D4 or ESF)

4. Whether or not to enable ANSI FDL messages

5. The DS0 time slots (fractional T1 only)

Continued

6. The DS0 time slots (64Kbps or 56Kbps)

7. The serial data link (Cisco HDLC, PPP, or Frame Relay)

8. Specific serial datalink properties, depending on which one you chose

For an analog modem, you will be asked the following, after choosing the serial port to which the modem is connected (which will have a physical name that looks like ser-s2p1):

1. Whether or not to enable logins on the modem

2. Whether or not to enable automatic dial-back for incoming calls

3. A phone number for the modem to dial back if you answered **y** to the second question

The best way to prepare for a configuration like this would be to write down all the specialized connection information for your particular protocol ahead of time, knowing that the Nokia device needs a complete picture of the interface it is setting up for you.

Configuring the Internal Interface

If you choose to use a remote browser by selecting option 1 mentioned previously, you are asked a series of questions regarding the configuration of an internal interface. The first prompt displays a list of physical interfaces on your Nokia device and asks you to choose the one you want to configure. (We are assuming that you only have Ethernet interfaces installed on your Nokia appliance; if you have serial or ATM interface hardware, for example, it is possible to configure those interfaces for first-time use. See the sidebar "Configuring Alternative Interfaces" for some examples.) Here is the list of interfaces from which you choose:

```
Select an interface from the following for
configuration:

1) eth-s1p1
2) eth-s1p2
3) eth-s1p3
4) eth-s1p4
```

```
5) quit this menu
```

```
Enter choice [1-5]:
```

Press **1** for eth–s1p1, the Ethernet interface in slot one, port one—the left-most or uppermost on–board interface, depending on the model you are using. Next, you are asked the IP address of the interface, which is in standard dotted-quad notation, with a CIDR mask. Enter **192.168.1.1/24**. You are then asked to enter a default route. Note that this is not strictly necessary if you are directly connecting to your Nokia via a crossover cable, but if you do enter a default route here, you will probably have to change it later to your network's actual default gateway. You are then asked to enter the interface speed, which can be 100Mbps or 10Mbps, and the interface duplex, which can be full or half. Choose **10Mbps half–duplex**.

Finally, you are asked if you want to change any of the settings you entered:

```
Confirm the setup summary (type Y), or return to Step 4 (type N) to make
different selections.
```

Type **y** if you are sure the settings you entered are correct. If you choose **n**, you will go back to the interface selection menu and be forced to enter all the information over again.

DHCP Configuration

When you power on your Nokia for the first time, you know that it will present a "Hostname?" prompt to anyone who might be watching at a serial console. What you might not know is that if the hostname prompt sits idle for more than 30 seconds, your appliance will activate a DHCP client and attempt to configure its internal interface automatically. This is a new feature in IPSO 3.5 and later. You must configure your DHCP server to make this work, however. The Nokia device won't simply assign itself an IP address from your existing DHCP lease pool, for example. This is a security feature. The following sections discuss the details of setting up your DHCP server.

Configuring the DHCP Server

Certain requirements must be met by your DHCP server's configuration in order to get the DHCP client on your Nokia device to acquire an address. The minimum requirements are:

- It must provide a hostname.

- It must provide a static IP address.

- It must provide a mapping to the serial number on your appliance. (The MAC address of the internal interface is OK here as well, but is impractical for first-time installations because you won't know the MAC address until you actually get into Voyager and view it.)

- The minimum IP address lease time required is one year.

You can find the serial number of your appliance on the back of the device; it should be 11 digits long. Here is a partial server configuration that will work if integrated into your main DHCP configuration file:

```
subnet 192.168.1.0 netmask 255.255.255.0 {

# Default gateway
option routers 192.168.1.2;
option subnet-mask 255.255.255.0;

# Eastern standard time
option time-offset -5;
default-lease-time -1;
max-lease-time -1;

host nokiabox {
    # Serial number of your Nokia goes here
    option dhcp-client-identifier "8A345678911";
    fixed-address 192.168.1.1;
    option host-name "gatekeeper";
    }
}
```

The deliberate nature of these settings ensures that you won't mistakenly assign a DHCP address to a Nokia box that gets powered on without an active configuration file.

Configuring the Nokia Client

Continuing the setup from here is simply a matter of plugging an Ethernet cable that has connectivity to your network's DHCP server into the Nokia's first Ethernet port and powering the device on. It could take several minutes for the DHCP configuration to complete. Assuming that the workstation from which you will be doing the configuration is also on the same network, you could find it useful to ping, from your workstation, the fixed IP address that will be assigned to the appliance. When you get a reply, merely point your Web browser to the fixed address and log in to the Voyager interface as user **admin**. The password will be set to **password** if you used DHCP to set up the Nokia client; make sure to change it once you get Voyager up and running. You are now ready to continue the configuration.

NOTE

Your Nokia appliance needs to be on the same logical network as your DHCP server when it is powered on. DHCP broadcast traffic will not traverse a router to another network without the help of a DHCP relay agent.

Continuing the Configuration

If you chose **Web-based Voyager** when prompted for the browser type to use during the system setup, you can test the Voyager connection to your appliance, then refer to Chapter 4, where system configuration is discussed in detail. If you chose to configure your Nokia through lynx, this section will get you up and running by configuring your internal interface. Once you get the feel for using lynx, you can use Chapter 4 as a reference to continue the configuration.

Lynx is an open-source, text-based browser that is installed by default on all Nokia IP series devices. Lynx takes a little getting used to, but you can use it very quickly once you learn a few key bindings. Here are the most useful key bindings for moving around in lynx:

- **Tab or Down Arrow** Move forward from link to link on the page.
- **Up Arrow** Move backward from link to link on the page.

- **Enter or Right Arrow** Select the currently highlighted link; check or uncheck an HTML form check box.

- **Left Arrow** Move back one page.

- **?** Help screen.

- **q** Quit.

As you can see, most of what you need to do can be accomplished with only the Arrow keys. Entering text into an HTML text box is as simple as moving to the underlined text entry field and typing directly into it, then using one the Up or Down Arrow key to move out of it. Press **q** and **y** when prompted to quit your lynx session.

Lynx can also be used as a filter to convert HTML documents into text. Here is an example, working on the HTML help documents in /Web/htdocs/ voyagerhelpfiles:

```
usgk[admin]# ls
config_20129.html        interface_21378.html    interfaces_21377.html
    main_21353.html
dyno_20125.html          interfaces_21354.html   main_20010.html
    main_21376.html
dyno_20131.html          interfaces_21355.html   main_20011.html
    services_20012.html
image_20128.html         interfaces_21356.html   main_20124.html
    summary_20126.html


usgk[admin]# lynx -dump main_20010.html | more
Gives the following formatted text output:


                  Nokia Voyager: usgk Voyager Image


                       Help for Configuration


   Configuration
   Use this page to access the various configuration options for usgk


   Interfaces: Use this page to view a configuration summary for all of
   the interfaces on the system. You can also activate or deactivate any
```

```
of the interfaces or follow links to the configuration pages for each
interface.
...
```

You can get more information on lynx at www.trill-home.com/lynx/lynx_help/Lynx_users_guide.html.

Here are the steps involved in configuring an Ethernet interface using lynx, from the opening screen:

1. Highlight **Config** and press **Enter**.

2. Highlight **Interfaces** and press **Enter**.

3. Highlight the logical interface name that you want to configure and press **Enter**.

4. Activate the interface by selecting the **Active** check box and pressing **Enter**.

5. Enter an IP address, netmask, and new logical name if desired.

6. Choose **Apply** and **Save** to save your changes.

Here are the same steps, in detail: From the opening screen in Figure 3.2, simply press **Enter** with the text highlight over **Config** and use the Down Arrow key or the Tab key until the highlight is on **Interfaces**. Then press **Enter**. You should see something like Figure 3.3.

Figure 3.3 Global Interface Configuration in Lynx

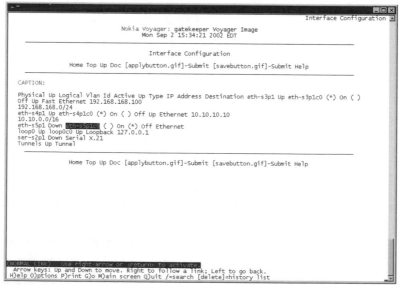

As you can see, this particular Nokia device has three Ethernet interfaces and one serial interface as well as a loopback interface. Each interface has a physical name (eth-s5p1) and a logical name (eth-s5p1c0). The logical name can be changed to whatever you like, to help identify the purpose of the interface. Tabbing down until one of the logical interfaces is highlighted and pressing **Enter** shows you the logical interface configuration, where we can edit the interface name, IP address, and several other parameters (see Figure 3.4). We can change the Active selector from off to on by highlighting **on** and pressing **Enter**. The asterisk should move from the off position to the on position. Editing the text for the IP address, mask, and logical name is simply a matter of moving with the **Tab** or **Down Arrow** key until the cursor is in the desired text field, typing the data, and moving out of the text field. Remember to select **[applybutton.gif]-Submit** to apply your changes and **[savebutton.gif]-Submit** to save your changes, so that they will persist across the next reboot. Lynx shows you the name of the image file that represents the Apply button with applybutton.gif, since it can't actually display the image.

Figure 3.4 Logical Interface Configuration in Lynx

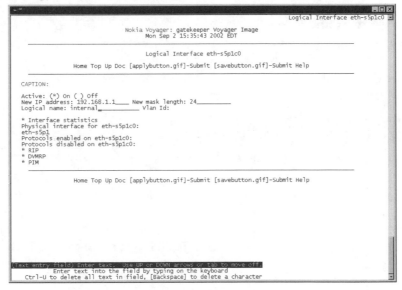

Make sure that you are comfortable moving around and making changes with lynx before moving on to Chapter 4, because that chapter is written with the graphical Voyager interface in mind.

Configuring & Implementing...

Dealing With Terminal Problems

You could find yourself connected to your Nokia firewall at a serial console or pseudo-terminal with *strange things* happening. Your display could become distorted by console errors and warnings displayed right in the middle of your lynx or vi editing session, or you might accidentally *cat* the contents of a binary file and find yourself staring at mysterious symbols and characters, unable to read the screen at all. More frequently, your Backspace key might not work properly. Here are some things you can do to fix these problems, along with some other tips:

- **Console errors ruining your lynx or vi display** Press **Control + L** to redraw the screen.

- **Backspace key doesn't work** Type **stty erase**, then press **Backspace**, which should look like **stty erase ^?** on the screen, before you press **Enter**.

- **Your entire screen is garbage** Try blindly typing **stty sane** and pressing **Enter**. If that doesn't work, try typing **echo**, then pressing **Control + v,** then pressing **Esc,** then typing **c**. On a readable display this should look like **echo ^[c** on the screen before you press **Enter**.

The default terminal type for logins to your Nokia is vt100. This type is suitable for dumb console connections, but it's usually inadequate for logins (to the console port or remotely) from an X-Windows workstation. Use xterm instead.

If you need to change the terminal type after you have already logged in, simply type **setenv TERM xterm** or, more generally, **setenv TERM <terminal type>** from the default C-shell (csh) prompt. From a Bourne-style shell (Bash, ksh, sh), use **TERM=xterm; export TERM**. You can see your currently selected terminal type by typing **echo $TERM**.

Summary

Preparing for your Nokia's initial configuration means selecting the proper cabling and knowing ahead of time what hostname, IP address, and admin password you will use for your device. At a minimum, you need Nokia's serial cable or a standard null-modem cable and possibly an Ethernet cable. Entering your hostname properly is very important when you know you will be configuring Check Point NG. Turning your Nokia appliance on for the first time and getting it configured is just a matter of answering a few simple questions over a direct console connection. You can also use a specially configured DHCP server to accomplish the task.

During this initial phase, you will configure one of the Nokia's network interfaces, then use this interface to complete the installation. It is possible to configure a Nokia device entirely through a console connection, using only lynx, a text-based Web browser. You will be able to choose the method of configuration you would like to use during the initial console question-and-answer session.

Once these initial pieces of information have been entered or set, you can continue the configuration with the Web-based Voyager GUI or with the lynx browser. Using lynx is mostly a matter of knowing five or six straightforward key bindings, and lynx can be quicker to use than the GUI interface. Continuing the configuration using the graphical Voyager is covered in Chapter 4.

Solutions Fast Track

Preparing to Boot for the First Time

☑ You can use the Nokia-supplied console cable or a standard null-modem cable to connect to your NSP's console port.

☑ The workstation from which you are configuring your appliance must have a vt100 serial console emulator, and it should be set to 9600/8/N/1. You can also connect from an actual vt100 capable terminal.

☑ If you want to use the Voyager GUI after the initial setup is complete, you will need to connect from your workstation to whatever Ethernet port you previously configured.

First-Time Boot Configuration

☑ When the Nokia device is booted for the first time, you will be prompted for a hostname and admin password, and then you will be asked to choose how you want to continue the configuration.

☑ You can choose to use the Voyager GUI interface or the text-based lynx interface.

☑ If you choose to use lynx, all the interface and subsequent device configuration will be done over the console connection.

☑ If you choose to use the Voyager GUI interface, you will be guided through a series of questions that will configure and enable your Nokia's internal interface.

☑ You can configure your Nokia using a specially configured DHCP server. In that case, the default admin password is *password*, and the hostname and internal IP address are set for you.

Continuing the Configuration

☑ You can accomplish most of the configuration using lynx with the four Arrow keys and the Tab and Enter keys.

☑ You can start the Voyager GUI configuration by opening a Web browser and directing it to the Nokia device's internal IP address.

Frequently Asked Questions

The following Frequently Asked Questions, answered by the authors of this book, are designed to both measure your understanding of the concepts presented in this chapter and to assist you with real-life implementation of these concepts. To have your questions about this chapter answered by the author, browse to **www.syngress.com/solutions** and click on the **"Ask the Author"** form.

Q: Is there a way to start the first-time boot configuration process on a Nokia device that has already been configured?

A: Yes. Delete **/config/active** and reboot.

Q: Why does my IP300 series appliance boot directly into CMOS setup?

A: Some terminal emulators send out a signal, which could be interpreted as a tab to the Nokia device, which prompts it to load the CMOS setup during the boot process. This is a known problem with Win2k SP2 running HyperTerminal.

Q: Why can't I access my Nokia on its internal interface after going through the initial configuration? I can't ping or access it via Web browser.

A: Check your cabling first. Ensure that you have a link light on the Nokia and on your workstation. If a hub or switch is involved, remove that and plug in a crossover cable. If you still have a problem, you might have made a mistake on either the IP address or the netmask. You need to use lynx to make any changes, if that is the case.

Q: My IP600 series appliance cannot get past loading the boot manager at system startup. How can I solve this problem?

A: Call your reseller. In some instances, the I/O card has been corrupted in this model and must be replaced.

Q: I upgraded my Nokia device and tried to reconfigure it from scratch by deleting /config/active. Now it is stuck in an endless reboot cycle—it never gets to a console prompt. What could be wrong?

A: If you upgraded from IPSO version 3.2.1 or before without first upgrading your boot manager, this situation can happen. The solution is to manually boot from your old IPSO's kernel, then upgrade the boot manager. See Nokia knowledge base resolution #5017 for details.

## Chapter 4

Introducing the Voyager Web Interface

Solutions in this chapter:

- Basic System Configuration, Out of the Box
- Configuring the System for Security
- Understanding Configuration Options

☑ Summary

☑ Solutions Fast Track

☑ Frequently Asked Questions

Introduction

Administrators tasked with installing a firewall for the first time typically have to be very knowledgeable when it comes to configuring the underlying operating system to function efficiently as a firewalled router. The administrator must know how to configure interface IP addresses and speed/duplex settings, how to configure hostnames and DNS properly, and how to configure static or dynamic routing, among many other things.

We have seen that the IPSO operating system that is at the core of the Nokia appliances is UNIX-based, but we don't need to have in-depth knowledge of UNIX to go through a first-time or even repeat configuration. The Nokia Voyager allows us to configure all of the previously mentioned features and much, much more through a simple, Web-based interface. The vast majority of changes we make do not require a system reboot but take effect immediately (another helpful side-effect of IPSO's UNIX base).

In this chapter, we walk you through a very thorough initial configuration of your Nokia appliance, all done from within Voyager. The emphasis is on security, so when we talk about network access and services, we show you how to, for example, disable Telnet access and enable SSL for secure Web access through Voyager. We give you an alternative to FTP or show you how to make use of FTP more secure, if it must be used. We also go over each of the Voyager configuration options so that when you are done you will have a very good idea of just what can be accomplished with this powerful interface. Later, Chapter 6 will guide you through enabling and configuring the Check Point Firewall bundled with your Nokia Security Appliance. Administrators looking for guidance on dynamic routing can then refer to Chapter 9.

Basic System Configuration, Out of the Box

Once the initial system is configured, your Nokia runs a minimal installation of Apache Web server, and the server runs on the standard port 80 by default. IPSO 3.3 through IPSO 3.6 FCS3 (the latest as of this writing) use Apache/1.3.6. You can view the Apache version on your Nokia by running the command */bin/httpd −v*. This server is running for the purpose of serving out the Web pages necessary for you to configure your Nokia Security Platform (NSP) using the Nokia Voyager Web interface.

You always have the option of running the Voyager interface using the lynx text browser through a console connection, but once you have assigned an IP address to your Nokia, you will be able to connect with any Web browser on the network to configure the system. Although lynx is a useful tool, many administrators prefer the nicer Voyager GUI available through a graphical Web browser.

Configuring & Implementing…

Apply and Save, Save, Save!

No, this isn't an advertisement—it's a reminder that you must remember to save your configuration changes using the Save icon within your Voyager GUI if you want to save any changes you make to the system. At every configuration screen in the Voyager interface, you have icons at the top and bottom of each page that give you the options to go Home, Up, Top, Apply, or Save. After every change that you Apply to the system, the change takes effect immediately, but you must select **Save** to write your changes to the /config/active file if you want changes you make to be preserved through a reboot of the system.

Front Screen

When you went through the initial configuration as described in Chapter 3, you set up your internal interface with the Nokia. Now you can begin configuring your appliance by typing in the IP address of this interface in a Web browser such as http://10.10.10.10 or using a DNS-resolvable name instead of an IP address, if available. Next enter the admin username and password when prompted for authentication. This step brings you to the front screen of the Voyager interface, which should resemble the image in Figure 4.1.

You should notice that some very important system information is listed on this initial screen, such as the Nokia's model, software release, and version, as well as the serial number, which you'll need when you call in a support or maintenance request. The information on this front screen is the same regardless of the Nokia model you possess. To continue from this initial screen, you have two buttons at the bottom of the screen. By selecting **Config**, you will enter the main configuration screen (see Figure 4.2), which gives you all the possible options for configuring your NSP. In versions previous to IPSO 3.6, this screen looks slightly different, but most of the options are the same. From the initial screen, select **Monitor** to enter a read-only area, which allows you to view system status and other interesting information about the system.

Figure 4.1 The Voyager Front Screen Display

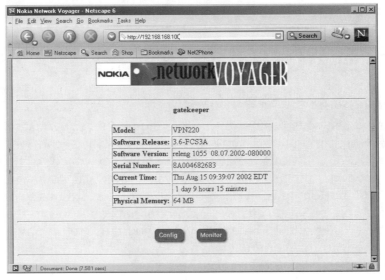

Figure 4.2 The Main Configuration Screen

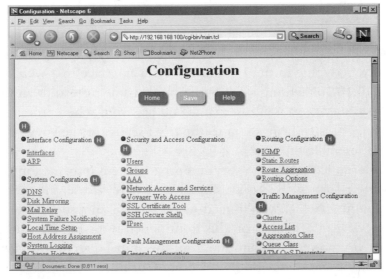

> **NOTE**
>
> If you have a "monitor" user configured, this user can click either button for read-only access to all system settings.

Navigating Voyager

When you are moving around within the Voyager interface, it is important that you do *not* use your browser's Back button to return to a previous screen. If you do this, you could end up getting cached pages that display incorrect information, which can cause confusion and possible misconfiguration. Instead, use the buttons that are provided for navigation across the top and bottom of each screen. These buttons and each of their functions are as follows:

- **Home** Takes you to the front screen.
- **Top** Takes you to the main Configuration screen or main Monitor screen, depending on which you are working under.
- **Up** Takes you to the previous page.
- **Apply** Applies changes entered on that page.
- **Save** Saves all changes that have been applied to the system, since either the last save or the last reboot.
- **Help** Displays help documentation relevant to the page you are on when you select it.

You will also see several small Help buttons available throughout the various screens. You can identify these by the blue, circular icon with a white *H* displayed in the center. Each one gives you detailed help information for each section in which the button is displayed. This help feature pops up in a separate browser window, so you don't lose your current place within the Voyager interface.

If you installed the documentation package available for your version of IPSO, a Doc button is available along with the other navigation buttons on each page. This documentation provides even more help for each section of the configuration. In IPSO 3.6, there is even a *CLI Reference Guide* to assist you in using the new CLISH tool. In the documentation, select the **Content** button at any time to see a list of topics you can choose from.

Configuring Basic Interface Information

When configuring interfaces, you should know what IP address and netmask you will assign each interface in advance. For the examples that follow in this chapter, let's assume that you have a simple Nokia firewall with three interfaces: external (Internet facing, routable IP), internal (nonroutable IP), and SSN (nonroutable IP). Assume an upstream router owned by the ISP that provides the Internet circuit as your default gateway.

In this section, we walk you through the process of configuring an Ethernet interface on your NSP. You will learn how to add or delete an IP address to an interface, manually set the speed and duplex, and check the status of your interfaces.

IP Addresses

When setting up the internal and secure server network (SSN or DMZ) interfaces, you should choose a network subnet within the Internet Assigned Numbers Authority (IANA) reserved IP address space, which are outlined in RFC 1918.

Adding an IP Address to an Interface

Follow these steps to configure an interface on your Nokia platform:

1. Bring up the Voyager Web interface via http in your Web browser.

2. Click **Config**.

3. Click **Interfaces**, the first link in the first column under the main Configuration screen. You will see the Interface Configuration page displayed as in Figure 4.3. This table shows you all your available interfaces along with their current status and configuration options.

4. Select the logical interface that you want to assign an IP address. In our example, we'll select **eth-s4p1c0**, the second Ethernet interface listed in our table in Figure 4.3.

5. Click the toggle button to **On** to make the interface active, and type in the new IP address and mask length in your browser. All netmasks configured through Voyager will be in aggregate or bit mask format. For example, 255.255.0.0 is a 16-bit mask, so to set that mask on an interface, you would type **16** for the mask length. There is a good netmask cheat sheet at http://noc.mwci.net/info/netmask.shtml, which might

help you convert a netmask in dotted quad notation and the aggregate, and vice versa. Or, if you have *Check Point Next Generation Security Administration* by Syngress Publishing, Inc. (ISBN 1-928994-74-1), you'll find a cheat sheet in Appendix A.

Figure 4.3 The Interface Configuration Screen

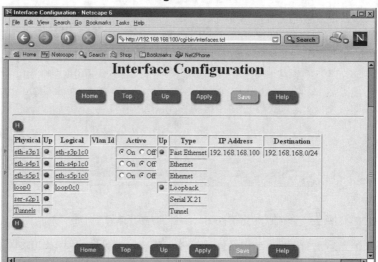

6. Optionally, you can change the logical name of the interface from the default eth-s4p1c0 to a name that might make it easier to identify, such as either **internal** or **external**. The default name of the interface might not be easy to read, but it helps you identify the interface you are configuring on the Nokia. For example, eth-s4p1c0 is the Ethernet interface in slot 4, port 1. These numbers vary depending on how many interfaces you have installed and which you are configuring. See Figure 4.4 for an example interface configuration before you go on to the next step.

7. Click **Apply**. Once you apply your changes, they take effect immediately.

8. Click **Save**. You must save your configuration if you want your settings to be retained after a reboot. If you forget to save your changes, you need to start all over again after you reboot the system.

9. Click **Up** to return to the previous interface configuration screen. You should see your new interface entered into the table that we first saw in Figure 4.3.

Figure 4.4 Configuring IP Addresses

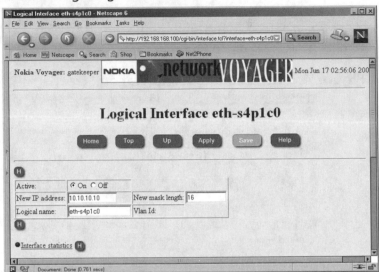

Deleting an IP Address from an Interface

Once you have set the new IP address on an interface and apply the changes, you will see the Logical Interface page displayed, as in Figure 4.5. Notice that next to the IP address, you have a check box labeled *delete.* To remove this IP address from eth-s4p1, follow these three easy steps:

Figure 4.5 An Applied Interface Address

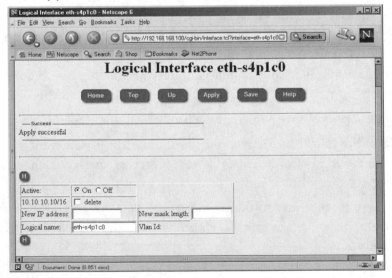

1. Click the **delete** check box.
2. Click **Apply**.
3. Click **Save**.

Configuring & Implementing…

Voyager's /config/active File

The /config/active file contains all the system configuration information. Actually, /config/active is a symbolic link that points to the file /config/db/initial. If you attempt to make a change on the command line (for example, with ifconfig), these changes will be lost when the system is restarted. The safest way to make persistent modifications on your Nokia is to use either the Voyager Web interface or the Command Line Interface Shell (CLISH), which is a new tool in IPSO 3.6. To use CLISH, simply type **clish** at the command prompt, and you will be presented with a *Nokia>* prompt.

You'll need to use one of these tools when you edit config files in /etc as well (for example, /etc/hosts), since these files are wiped out at each boot by the /config/active settings. If you keep a backup of this file, you could restore a system configuration this way, but any package-specific configuration would not be contained here (such as Check Point FireWall-1 rules, objects, licenses, and so on). For more on backup and restore, read Chapter 5.

Notice how anytime you need to save a change, the Save button "lights up" in Voyager. Once this button is selected, all changes applied to the system until this time will be written to the /config/active file, and the button will be grayed out again. This button is a good indicator of whether you have made any changes that need to be saved.

Lastly, if you want to erase all settings on a Nokia system and start from scratch, you can remove the file /config/active, and when you reboot your Nokia, it will begin to go through the initial configuration process all over again, prompting you to enter a hostname and so on. You need to have a direct console connection to perform this task.

Speed and Duplex

Most of the Ethernet interfaces that ship with the Nokia models are 10/100MB interfaces, unless you request a Gigabit Ethernet interface in your system. If you want to see the speed and duplex at which your interface is autonegotiating, or if you want to force these settings manually, you can do so under the Physical Interface configuration screen.

From the Interface Configuration screen, click the link under the physical interface column that you want to configure. For our example, let's select **eth-s3p1**. From here you have the option to disable the interface by toggling the Active On/Off button, as seen in Figure 4.6. The Physical Status table also informs you of the type, media, maximum transfer unit (MTU), and MAC address for this particular interface.

Figure 4.6 Physical Interface Configuration

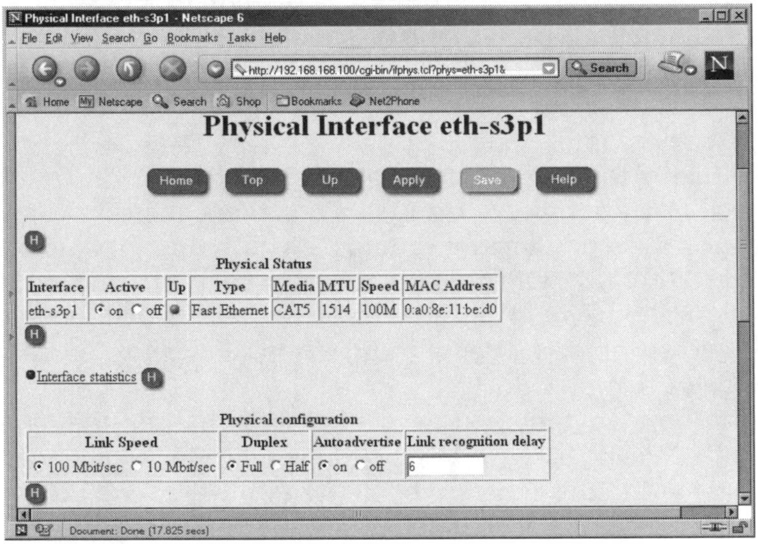

Confirming Interface Status

Now that you have your interfaces configured, how do you know if they have a link? There are a few ways that you can view your interface status within Voyager or from the command line. If you have just finished interface configuration, you can see the status displayed as either Up or Down with a green ball icon or a red ball icon, respectively, as shown in Figure 4.7. You can access this page in Voyager from the main configuration screen by clicking the Interfaces link.

Figure 4.7 Interface Status Icons

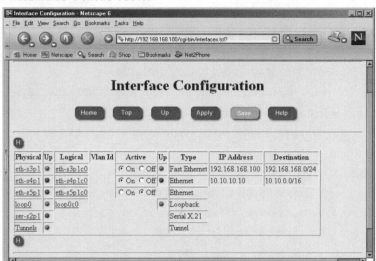

In the Interface Configuration screen, you have two columns per interface that describe whether the interface is up or not. The first Up column relates to the physical interface. If there is a link, this icon is green; otherwise, it will be red. The second column refers to the logical state. This icon is red if the link is down, and it is green if the link is up. If you disable the interface by changing the active state to Off, no icon is displayed.

Another way you can view interface status is via the Monitor link. If you are within Voyager Configuration already, click the **Home** link first, then click **Monitor** from the front screen. From here, you can click **Interface** under the Static Monitor heading. You should now see a page similar to the one in Figure 4.8. If you scroll down a little, you will see the interface information, which is the same information you would see if you were on the command line, typing in **ifconfig –a**. Compare the following output with Figure 4.9:

```
gatekeeper[admin]# ifconfig -a
ser-s2p1:   flags=4126<UP,POINTOPOINT,MULTICAST,PRESENT> encaps none
eth-s3p1c0:   lname eth-s3p1c0 flags=e7<UP,PHYS_AVAIL,LINK_AVAIL,BROADCAST,
    MULTICAST,AUTOLINK>
        inet mtu 1500 192.168.168.100/24 broadcast 192.168.168.255
        phys eth-s3p1 flags=4133<UP,LINK,BROADCAST,MULTICAST,PRESENT>
        ether 0:a0:8e:11:be:d0 speed 100M full duplex
eth-s4p1c0:   lname eth-s4p1c0 flags=e7<UP,PHYS_AVAIL,LINK_AVAIL,BROADCAST,
```

```
        MULTICAST,AUTOLINK>
                inet mtu 1500 10.10.10.10/16 broadcast 10.10.255.255
                phys eth-s4p1 flags=4133<UP,LINK,BROADCAST,MULTICAST,PRESENT>
                ether 0:a0:8e:11:be:d4 speed 10M half duplex
eth-s5p1c0:   flags=e0<BROADCAST,MULTICAST,AUTOLINK>
                phys eth-s5p1 flags=4132<UP,BROADCAST,MULTICAST,PRESENT>
                ether 0:a0:8e:11:be:d8 speed 10M half duplex
loop0c0:   flags=57<UP,PHYS_AVAIL,LINK_AVAIL,LOOPBACK,MULTICAST>
                inet6 mtu 63000 ::1 --> ::1
                inet mtu 63000 127.0.0.1 --> 127.0.0.1
                phys loop0 flags=10b<UP,LINK,LOOPBACK,PRESENT>
soverf0:   flags=2923<UP,LINK,MULTICAST,PRESENT,IPV6ONLY>
stof0:   flags=2903<UP,LINK,PRESENT,IPV6ONLY>
tun0:   flags=107<UP,LINK,POINTOPOINT,PRESENT>
```

Figure 4.8 Monitoring Interfaces

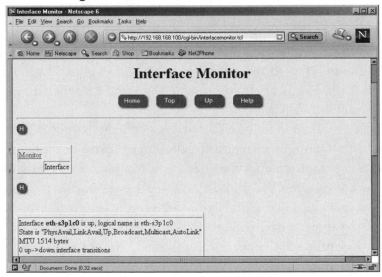

Figure 4.9 Monitoring Interfaces

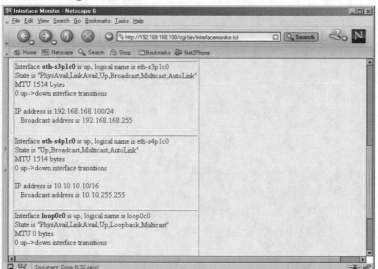

Adding a Default Gateway

If your Nokia firewall will be routing traffic to several networks, such as the Internet, you'll want to configure a default gateway. The default gateway is typically the next-hop router closest to the Internet, which you point to by entering a default route into the routing table. You specifically tell the device that this gateway is the default, and if a packet does not match any other entry in the routing table, it will get sent to this gateway. Typically, you want only one default gateway in the routing table. If you are doing load balancing or failover routing, you might have more than one, but often these will be dynamic routes and not static routes.

To configure a default gateway on your NSP, follow these instructions:

1. Bring up the Voyager Web interface using **http** in your Web browser.

2. Click **Config**.

3. Click **Static Routes** under the Routing Configuration heading.

4. Under the Static route, Default: Gateway column, select **On**. Leave the next-hop type as **normal**. You may also fill in a description if you desire (see Figure 4.10). Your other options in the next-hop type are **reject**, which drops all packets, sending an unreachable Internet control message back to the originator, or **blackhole**, which drops all packets quietly without notifying the sender.

Figure 4.10 Adding a Default Gateway

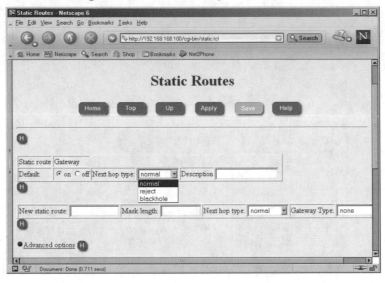

5. Click **Apply**.

6. For Gateway Type, select **address**, as shown in Figure 4.11.

Figure 4.11 Adding the Default Gateway

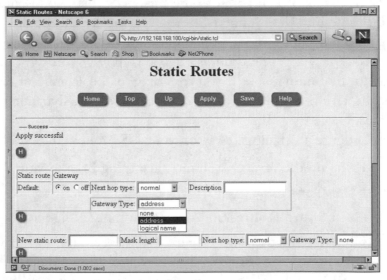

7. Click **Apply** again.

8. Fill in the IP address of the gateway.

9. Click **Apply** one last time. At this point, the route is added into the system, and it will be functional, but don't forget the next step!

10. Click **Save**.

Now you have successfully added a default gateway to your Nokia. If you log in to the console of your Nokia and run a *netstat –rn* command, you should see an entry similar to the following. However, your default route might not be displayed if that interface is not physically up:

```
gatekeeper[admin]# netstat -rn | grep default
default             10.10.1.1          CU          0          0      eth-s4p1c0
default                                RCU         1          0
```

As you can see in Figure 4.12, you have the option of setting a priority on your default route entry. This priority determines the route that will be used if there are multiple routes that are otherwise equivalent; lower-priority routes take precedence. You can enter a number between 1 and 8; however, you should know that the only time a lower-priority route will *not* be used is if that interface is down. So, it would not make sense to configure two routes with different priorities on the same interface. If the priorities are the same, the gateways will be treated with equal cost as multipath routes. If you are looking to set up dynamic gateway failover on the same interface, you might want to consider one of the dynamic routing protocols that are discussed in detail in Chapter 9.

Figure 4.12 The Default Gateway

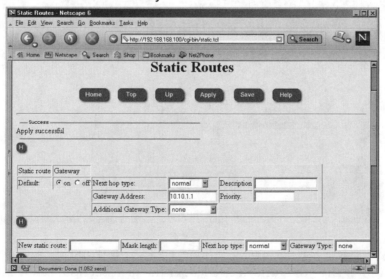

Setting the System Time, Date, and Time Zone

It's important that you set the correct time and date in your NSP so that your system and/or firewall logs will record the correct time that events have occurred and so any scheduled cron jobs will run at the time specified.

Time and Date

To manually configure the time and date, click the **Local Time Setup** option under the System Configuration heading in the main Configuration screen. Alternatively, you can configure Network Time Protocol (NTP), which allows you to synchronize your NSP time with the time from a NTP server, either on your network or on the Internet. The option to enable NTP is found under the Router Services heading from the main Configuration screen.

Let's start by setting the correct time zone for your region. The Nokia appliance will be configured for Greenwich mean time (GMT) out of the box. Many organizations with a global presence use GMT, which is the universal time standard. Others prefer to use a local time zone, such as Eastern standard time (EST) for those in the vicinity of New York in the United States. To select your time zone, choose a city from the list on the Time screen, displayed in Figure 4.13.

Figure 4.13 The Time Screen

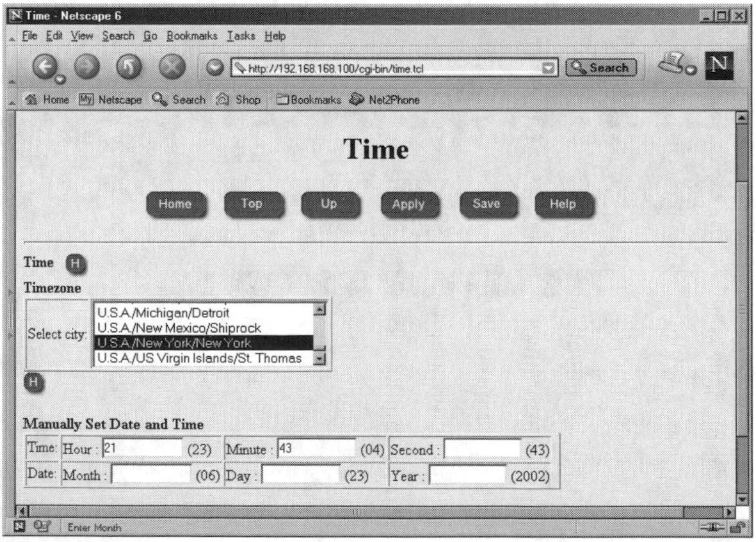

Once you select the correct time zone, click **Apply** and then click **Save**. Then you can change the time, if needed, in the next section, labeled Manually

Set Date and Time. Simply enter the hour, minute, and/or second. If you leave any of these fields blank, it will not change the value. The current value is listed in parentheses next to each text entry box. Follow the same syntax when you change the date. Enter the month, day and/or year. The current value is displayed in parentheses next to each text box.

Configuring the Network Time Protocol

If you decide to set up NTP, for security purposes it is probably best to synchronize to a server residing within your network. The Nokia can also be run as an NTP server. When you turn on NTP, it could take a while for the clock to update, so be patient. Bring up the NTP configuration screen, shown in Figure 4.14, by clicking **NTP** under the Router Services heading from the main Configuration screen.

Figure 4.14 The NTP Configuration Screen

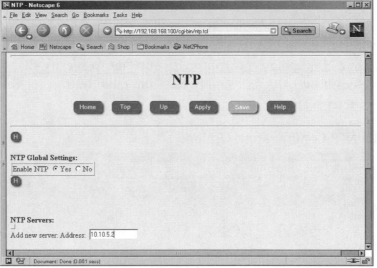

Understanding NTP

NTP is a time protocol that allows administrators to synchronize local clocks over the Internet in a distributed client/server model. This protocol uses UDP 123 for communication, and you might need to allow UDP 123 through if you are trying to synchronize time through a firewall. NTP has been around since the mid-1980s and has had a few revisions since its inception. The current version of NTP is v3, but you can utilize any of the previous versions on your NSP for flexibility. Version 3 code has been improved to remove minor bugs found in previous versions, but the main advantage is that it has been enhanced for maximum stability and reliability over high-speed, gigabit networks. This means that even at lower speeds, the algorithms used will be more accurate.

Once NTP is enabled, it can begin to gather time data from other servers and calculate the offset needed to correct the local clock based on the remote server's time. It's also possible for the server to communicate with others that are considered peers and compare all their clocks so that they can have the most accurate timekeeping between them. A great deal of hard work and effort have been put into keeping the time as accurate as possible in this protocol, and several other factors are taken into consideration, such as the time lag in receiving the data and errors that could affect the transmission, depending on how far from the time source your server is located. If you would like to know more about NTP, version 3 of the protocol is detailed in RFC 1305.

Configuring NTP

Once NTP is enabled, several settings are available in the Voyager configuration screens. As you can see in Figure 4.15, you can configure multiple NTP servers with which your Nokia can synchronize. If you want to specify that one server should be preferred over the rest, simply click the radio button to **Yes** for that server in the Prefer section.

Figure 4.15 NTP Configuration Options

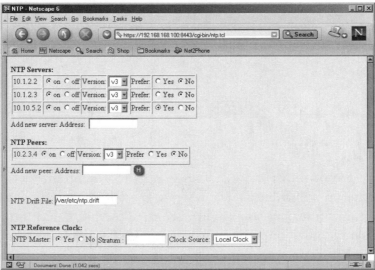

Another option is to set up NTP peers, which are other servers with which you want to compare your local time settings. Your local time is not used in the calculation with the NTP servers that were listed previously, but when you include peers in the configuration, your time is compared with the peer times to calculate a time that is most accurate between them.

Finally, if you want other servers to retrieve their time from you, click **Yes** at the bottom of the screen labeled *NTP Reference Clock: NTP Master*. You can enter a number from 0 to 8 in the Stratum field, which specifies the level of your NTP server in the hierarchy. Nokia recommends that you leave this at the default, 0. Your local clock will be the source of the data provided in the master state.

Configuring Domain Name System and Host Entries

Along with assigning IP addresses to all the hosts on your network, administrators will also configure DNS and host table entries on most every PC. You might not want to set up name servers on a firewall, however, since you most likely will not be running user-facing applications directly on the box. There are some advantages to running a DNS resolver on a firewall, but there can be some major detriments to it as well. Configuring host entries, however, will be a necessary step on your Nokia firewall if you want to install a FireWall-1 license (see the "FireWall-1 Licensing" sidebar).

Since it is suggested to install your firewall while it is not plugged into any untrusted networks, it will be best to start with DNS disabled on the firewall. If you have DNS enabled and the system cannot reach its name servers, the system could become sluggish and system performance will be affected. It is important that once you do configure DNS, you configure it properly. If a primary name server goes down, all traffic, including your VPN connections, will be affected.

The firewall should be able to resolve its own external IP address to the name of the host computer. The Nokia platform needs to have the hostname associated with its external IP address for FireWall-1 licensing purposes as well; this is done through the Host Address Assignment link found under the System Configuration heading in the Voyager GUI. You must use this interface to configure host entries instead of editing a Hosts file. Here you should also add IP addresses for devices that your firewall might communicate with frequently, such as a management server and/or enforcement module.

Another DNS record that you should create is a PTR record for your firewall's external IP address or any other address(es) that you will be using for

Network Address Translation (NAT). Some Web sites and FTP servers require that you have a reverse resolvable IP address before they will grant you or your users access to download their files. If you have obtained a block of IP addresses from your ISP, chances are that the ISP controls the PTR records for your addresses. Sometimes they provide you with a Web site where you can administer these yourself. Other times you need to find the right person who can make the changes for you. If you have your own ASN, you can set up your own in-addr.arpa domain and create your own PTR records.

If you will be running the FireWall-1 HTTP Security Server on your Nokia, you will want to enable DNS. otherwise, the firewall will display "Unknown WWW Server" in users' Web browsers.

Designing & Planning...

FireWall-1 Licensing

You will not be able to apply your FireWall-1 license until you have configured the host address assignment for the Nokia's external interface. When you run through the initial configuration, you usually specify an internal IP address, which is set up in the host table for you. However, most FireWall-1 licenses are issued on external addresses, and you must configure this setting within Voyager before the license addition is successful.

DNS

Domain Name Service (DNS) is used to resolve domain names to IP addresses, and vice versa. Behind the scenes, your PC uses DNS whenever you're using your Web browser or sending e-mail, among other things. Your Nokia device will not function as a domain name server, since the system was built as a high-performance security platform and running DNS servers on such a system doesn't make much sense. However, your device will operate as a DNS client. Most UNIX systems use an /etc/resolv.conf file to store their DNS settings, and the Nokia is no exception. However, you configure the NSP resolv.conf file via the Voyager GUI.

To configure DNS, click **DNS** under the System Configuration heading from the main Configuration screen. Doing so brings you to the main DNS Configuration screen, similar to the one displayed in Figure 4.16.

Figure 4.16 The DNS Configuration Screen

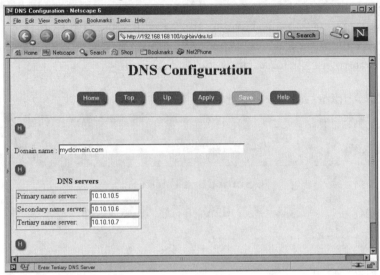

To enable DNS lookups, simply enter one or more name servers in the fields provided, click **Apply** and then **Save**. To disable DNS, delete the IP addresses listed, and then click **Apply** and **Save**. For obvious reasons, you should always use IP addresses rather than names for your name servers here. You can verify that your changes have been applied by looking at the /etc/resolv.conf file on the system:

```
gatekeeper[admin]# cat /etc/resolv.conf
#   This file was AUTOMATICALLY GENERATED
#   Generated by /bin/resolv_xlate on Sun Jun 23 22:51:24 2002
#
#   DO NOT EDIT
#
search mydomain.com
nameserver 10.10.10.5
nameserver 10.10.10.6
nameserver 10.10.10.7
```

The Hosts Table

As mentioned earlier, it is necessary to configure at least one static host entry on your Nokia in Voyager. To enter this configuration screen, displayed in Figure 4.17, click **Host Address Assignment** under the System Configuration heading from the main Voyager Configuration screen. Once you are in the Static Host Entries configuration page, you should have an entry for the local host on IP address 127.0.0.1, also called the *loopback address*. You should never remove this host entry, because the system uses it for various local operations.

Figure 4.17 Adding a New Hostname

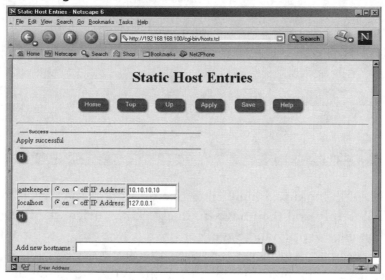

To add a new hostname, enter either the fully qualified domain name (FQDN) or a simple hostname in the field for "Add new hostname." We are using the name *gatekeeper*, which was the name assigned to this Nokia during initial system configuration. Next click **Apply**, and then type in the IP address associated with the gatekeeper. This should be the IP address that you will use if licensing the FireWall-1 product on your Nokia as well, and it is typically the firewall's external IP address. Click **Apply** again and then **Save** to complete the host address assignment.

Configuring a Mail Relay

The Nokia Security Platform will not run a mail server, but you can configure it to deliver mail by setting up a mail relay within the system configuration in

Voyager. This might be useful if you want to receive important system messages from syslog, configure mail alerts within your FireWall-1 Security Policy, or write some custom script that send mail.

When you configure your mail relay, you have the option of specifying a remote user on the mail relay server. This optional field allows you to choose a specific username on the remote system that will receive all mail that is meant for "admin" or "monitor" users on the Nokia system. The default username is *root*:

1. To enable a mail relay in Voyager, start by clicking **Mail Relay** under the System Configuration heading from the main Configuration screen.

2. In the empty box next to Mail Server:, enter the IP address of the mail server you will be using. This machine should be running an SMTP server and configured as a mail relay. See Figure 4.18.

Figure 4.18 Mail Relay Configuration

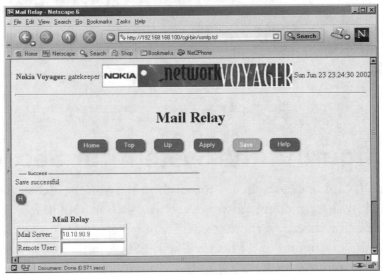

3. Click **Apply**.

4. Click **Save**.

Configuring System Event Notification

If you click **System Failure Notification**, located on the main Configuration screen under the System Configuration heading, you will be able to turn this function on or off. If this function is enabled, an e-mail will be generated to whomever you specify. Note that the mail relay must be configured for this to function. The notification e-mail will contain information such as the system hostname, software version, the location of certain crash files, and a dump trace to help identify the problem. See Figure 4.19 for a sample notification configuration. Don't forget to click **Apply** and **Save** your changes.

Figure 4.19 System Failure Notification Configuration

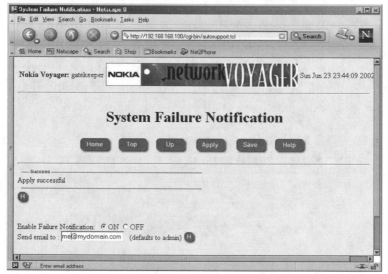

Configuring the System for Security

By default, Nokia takes a secure approach to network access by disabling most services. However, a couple insecure services such as Telnet and HTTP are enabled for functional purposes to help you get started. This section walks you through the configuration of Secure Shell (SSH) and disabling Telnet as well as changing from clear-text HTTP to SSL-encrypted Voyager access.

SSH is an encrypted Telnet provided in IPSO 3.4 and above as part of the operating system, so you aren't required to install any additional packages to use it, as in previous versions. Nokia's implementation of SSH is OpenSSH version 2.1.1. All you need to do in order to get started with SSH is enable the server daemon, and then you are on your way to a more secure system. You need an SSH client to establish a connection to the Nokia to use it; several such clients are freely available for download. Some of the most common clients are Putty, TTSSH, OpenSSH, SecureCRT, and F-Secure. For a comprehensive list of both free and commercial clients for various operating systems, visit www.freessh.org.

Enabling SSH Access

Configuring SSH is a quick and easy three-step process:

1. To configure SSH access, go to the main Configuration page and click **Secure Shell (SSH)** under the Security and Access Configuration heading.

2. Click **Yes** to enable the SSH daemon.

3. Finally, click **Apply** and **Save**.

See Figure 4.20. The default options on this screen are safe to accept. If you want to tighten access further, it is recommended that you do it in stages. Perhaps after you know that the default configuration works, you might want to disable admin login and set up a new user who can log in and *su* to the admin account.

Figure 4.20 The Main SSH Configuration Screen

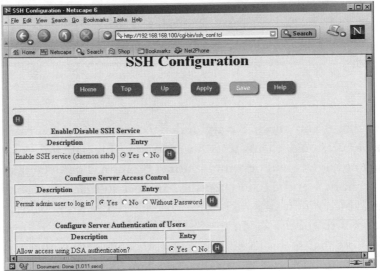

> **NOTE**
>
> The command *su* allows a user who is already logged in to become superuser or any other user on the system. On Nokia systems, the admin user is equivalent to root on most other UNIX systems. In order to use *su*, the user must be a member of the wheel group.

SSH Versions 1 and 2

You have the option of allowing SSH versions 1, 2, or both in the configuration settings. SSH version 2 is generally believed to be more secure than 1 and should be your first choice. See Figure 4.21 for additional options.

Figure 4.21 Additional SSH Options

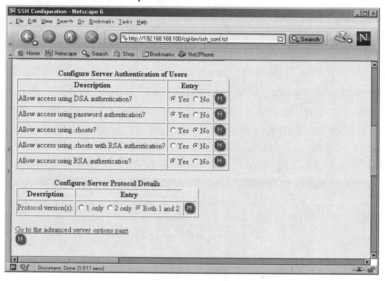

Be aware that if you check **1 only** under Configure Server Protocol Details, you will enable version 1 clients to connect to your firewall, but not version 2 clients, which are newer and becoming more common. The default setting is to allow both versions 1 and 2 SSH clients to connect so that you don't have to worry about which client you are using. A useful trick with newer (version 2-capable) clients is to specify **–1** on the SSH command line when connecting to an unknown host that seems to be rejecting your connection attempts. This forces the client to downgrade itself to version 1, perhaps allowing the connection. Similarly, **–2** forces the client to use protocol version 2. For the cautious, choose to allow only version 2, because it is considered to be more secure and the common free SSH clients now support protocol version 2.

Host Keys

A public/private host key pair is generated the first time you set up SSH and is displayed on this screen after you enable the SSH daemon. The host key is used to identify the host to the client during the connection. On the first connection attempt, the client receives the host's key and is asked whether to accept the key and save it or to reject it. SSH clients maintain a list of all known hosts in a file on the local system. If on a subsequent connection attempt the host key does not match the key obtained originally, the client will be warned that a possible man-in-the-middle attack could be occurring, giving them the option to terminate the connection and verify the new key. By default, the host key on IPSO is set to 1024 bits.

Authorized Keys

You can configure SSH to be more or less secure by choosing from a few different types of authentication schemes. Probably the most secure method is the use of RSA and/or DSA (SSH v2 only) authentication. This method uses the public key infrastructure (PKI) to verify the user's authenticity. In order for this system to work, you must generate a unique public/private key pair and configure the client with this information. Then, you publish the public key to the Nokia by entering it into the SSH Configuration page within Voyager. This information is stored in the $HOME/.ssh/authorized_keys file on the system. Only the user with the associated private key (and the passphrase to unlock that private key) will be able to log in. Using authorized keys provides the ultimate security between client and server.

In order to configure authorized keys in Voyager, first log in to Voyager and click **Config**, then follow this procedure:

1. Click **SSH (Secure Shell)** under the Security and Access Configuration heading from the main Configuration screen.

2. Ensure that the SSH daemon is already enabled, and then scroll down to the bottom of the page, and click the link to **Go to the authorized keys page**.

3. From here, you can enter the client's RSA public key for version 1, which would be obtained from the SSH client, typically in a file called identity.pub. You can also enter the DSA key in OpenSSH format (typically in a file called id_dsa.pub on the ssh client) or in SSHv2 format (the key file could look something like id_KEYTYPE_KEYLEN_X.pub.

Starting the Daemon

Once you enable SSH in the Voyager configuration, the daemon is started automatically. You can verify whether the daemon is running or not by logging into the system locally and typing **ps –auxw | grep ssh**. If the daemon is running, you will see output similar to the following:

```
gatekeeper[admin]# ps -auxw | grep ssh
root       669  0.0  1.1   276  652  d0  S+    6:09PM   0:00.02 grep ssh
root       650  0.0  2.5   404 1476  ??  Is    6:06PM   0:00.62 /usr/sbin/
    sshd-x -D
```

If you try to kill the sshd process, the process monitor (pm) restarts sshd automatically. Available sshd options are listed in Table 4.1.

Table 4.1 SSHD Server Options

switch	option	Description
-f	Filename	Define the server configuration file. The default file is /var/etc/sshd_config.
-d	N/A	Turn on debugging.
-i	N/A	Run the server from inetd.
-q	N/A	Run in quiet mode, no logging.
-p	Port #	TCP port the server will listen on. The default port is 22.
-k	Number of seconds	How often to regenerate the server key. The default time interval is 3600 seconds.
-g	Number of seconds	Authentication grace period. The default is 300 seconds.
-b	Bits	RSA key size. The default RSA server key is 768 bits.
-h	Filename	The file where the SSH host key is stored. The default file is /var/etc/ssh_host_key.
-4	N/A	Use IPv4 only.
-6	N/A	Use IPv6 only.
-D	N/A	Don't fork and detach on startup.

Disabling Telnet Access

If you followed the procedure to enable SSH access, and you have an SSH client installed and tested on your workstation, you should go back into Voyager and disable Telnet access. You will no longer need Telnet as long as you have SSH to access the system. Since you won't be using it, it is not wise to leave it open on the system as one more method for an attacker to attempt to gain access to the box. Figure 4.22 illustrates the default values of the network access services in IPSO 3.6.

Figure 4.22 Default Network Access Settings

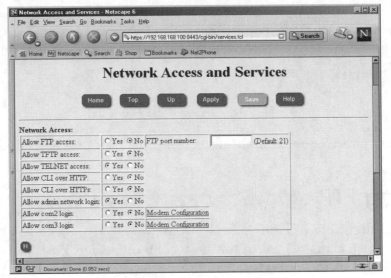

To disable Telnet through Voyager, click the **Network Access and Services** link from the main Configuration screen under the heading Security and Access Configuration. From there, click the radio button for **No** in the table directly across from "Allow TELNET access." Finally, click **Apply**, then click **Save** to disable Telnet and commit the changes.

An Alternative to FTP

By default, FTP is disabled in your Nokia, as you saw in Figure 4.22, and the majority of boxes out there will not need this service running. Therefore, it would be prudent to leave FTP disabled within Voyager, and you can enable it only when necessary. FTP has been known to have had several security vulnerabilities and transfers all data, including usernames and passwords in the clear. If you need to transfer files to or from your system, use Secure Copy (SCP) instead. This tool allows you to do encrypted file transfers to or from your NSP (if you have SSH enabled), which is much more secure than the standard FTP protocol.

The only time that you might need to enable FTP on a Nokia is when you are performing remote file transfers of packages or IPSO images during system maintenance and you happen to have those packages on a local Nokia system already. You can use FTP on your local Nokia to retrieve the packages or images from all the other systems on your network when you use the automated tools within Voyager. Through the Voyager GUI, FTP and HTTP are your only options. This might be fine if your box is local and protected by a firewall, but you might want to simply SCP the files to each Nokia manually before you begin maintenance on them. For example, if you want to get the ipso.tgz file onto your Nokia using SCP, you could use a command like the one that follows:

```
gatekeeper[admin]# scp admin@192.168.200.8:ipso.tgz .
admin@192.168.200.8's password:
ipso.tgz          100% |****************************|
```

For more information on updating IPSO or installed packages, please see Chapter 5.

Securing FTP

If you still want to use FTP on your Nokia, we can give you a couple of recommendations for making the use of this protocol more secure. First, you can require S/Key one-time passwords in IPSO 3.5 or later for Telnet and FTP authentication. You can also restrict FTP to local networks only by use of access lists or via your firewall policy. By implementing both of these actions together, you can use FTP in a secure fashion.

To configure the S/Key passwords, you first need to obtain a one-time password (OTP) generator. Most UNIX systems come with a generator on the command line called *key*, this is also available on IPSO. If this tool is not available to you, you need to find one to download. A Windows client called winkey32.exe, is available from Nokia Support in Resolution #1255. S/Key did not function properly in IPSO versions prior to 3.5, so if you want to use S/Key authentication, you first need to update IPSO to 3.5 or later. See Chapter 5 for instructions on updating your IPSO image. Select S/Key passwords as follows:

1. Log in to Voyager and click **Config**.

2. Select the link **Users** under the Security and Access Configuration heading.

3. Scroll down to the bottom. There you will see a section on configuring S/Key for each user. Select either **Allowed** or **Required** for each user. The default setting here is for S/Key to be disabled.

4. Click **Apply**.

5. Three new boxes will appear. Fill in the current user password in the first box, and enter an S/Key secret password in the next two boxes that is between four and eight alphanumeric characters long. See Figure 4.23.

Figure 4.23 S/Key Configuration

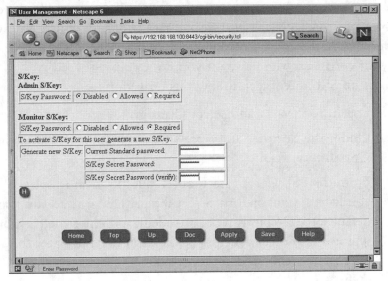

6. Click **Apply**. The sequence number (starting at 99 and decreasing each time S/Key is used) and the seed will be displayed. This information will also be displayed when you attempt to log in to the system. You will use this information as input to the S/Key OTP generator along with the original password you supplied to the system in order to begin using the S/Key authentication method.

7. Click **Save**.

Configuring Secure Socket Layer

Secure Socket Layer (SSL) allows you to view the Voyager Web interface through an encrypted tunnel. You can then use HTTPS instead of plain-text HTTP in the location window of your Web browser. Just as with ssh/scp, utilizing encryption for your connections to Voyager adds an extra layer of security to your session.

Creating the Self-Signed Certificate

The first step in configuring SSL is to create an SSL certificate for the Web server to use for authenticity. You can choose to generate a certificate request to send to a trusted third–party certificate authority (CA) for them to sign, which will cost you some money, or you can sign your own certificate, assuming that you trust yourself, and forgo the extra fee. I would recommend generating a self-signed certificate through the Voyager interface. It is just as secure to use a self-signed certificate. The only difference is that your Web browser will ask you to verify that you want to accept the certificate that is not signed by a known CA. There is no difference in the quality of the encrypted connection, and you can begin using your certificate right away if you do it yourself.

To set up SSL in Voyager, follow this procedure:

1. Log in to Voyager and select **Config**.

2. Under the Security and Access Configuration heading, click **SSL Certificate Tool**.

3. From the SSL Certificate Tool (Request) screen (displayed in Figure 4.24), you have several options. Select the private key size you want to use (the default of 1024 bits is recommended), and enter the passphrase that you will use to protect your private key. You need to enter this same passphrase on a later screen, so don't forget it.

Figure 4.24 The SSL Certificate Tool

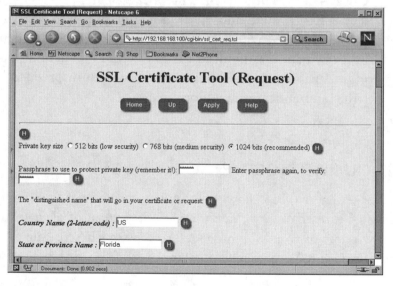

4. Next you need to configure the distinguished name (DN) that identifies this certificate as unique and belonging to this machine. The values that are required are in bold, and they are Country Name (2-letter code), State or Providence Name, Organization Name, and Common Name (FQDN). Lastly, you must specify if you want to create a self-signed X.509 certificate or generate a signing request. Select the radio button for **A self-signed X.509 certificate** (see Figure 4.25).

Figure 4.25 The SSL Certificate Tool, Continued

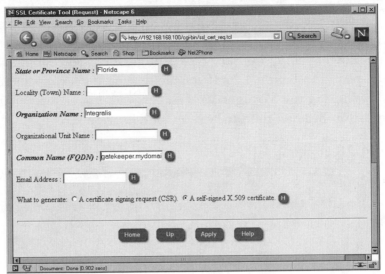

5. Click **Apply**, and the new X.509 certificate, private key, and fingerprint will be displayed.

6. Next, scroll down and click **the Voyager SSL Certificate page** link at the bottom of the result page. This choice brings you to a new window where you need to cut and paste the certificate and private key from the result page. You might want to open this page in a separate window to complete the next step.

7. Copy the new X.509 certificate into the Voyager SSL Certificate screen, including the entire BEGIN and END line. This information should go in the first big text input area labeled *New Server Certificate*.

8. Now copy the new private key, including the entire BEGIN and END line, into the next text area labeled *Associated private key*.

9. Enter the passphrase that you used in Step 3.

10. Click **Apply** and **Save**.

11. Click **Up**. This brings you to the Voyager Web Access screen, which is discussed next. See Figure 4.26.

Enabling HTTPS for Voyager

Now that you have generated a self-signed certificate, as discussed in the previous section, you can enable encryption for secure Voyager access and configuration. If you are following along from the SSL configuration, you should already be at the screen displayed in Figure 4.26. If you are starting here, you can also get to this screen by clicking the **Voyager Web Access** link under the Security and Access Configuration heading from the main Configuration screen.

Figure 4.26 Enabling HTTPS

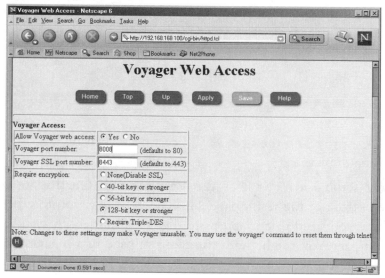

To set up secure Voyager Access via SSL, enable it as follows:

1. Change the SSL port number to some high port > 1024. The default port is 443, but since this is a well-known port for HTTPS connections, it would be wise to pick another port that is not as common.

2. Next, select the minimum grade of encryption that you want to allow. By default, SSL is disabled and no encryption is required. Select **Require Triple-DES**, which gives you up to a 168-bit key if you have a Web browser that can support a key that size.

3. Click **Apply**.

4. If you try to click **Save** now, your connection will be refused. You must reconnect to Voyager using HTTPS and the port you choose for the connection—for example: *https://192.168.168.100:8443/cgi-bin/httpd.tcl*.

5. You will now be prompted to accept the self-signed certificate, which you generated previously. Choose to remember the certificate permanently and click **Continue**. See Figure 4.27.

Figure 4.27 Accepting the Certificate

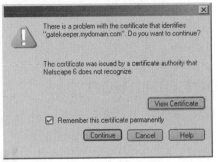

6. If you receive a domain name mismatch error next because you are connecting to an IP address but the certificate was generated with an FQDN, click **OK** to continue.

7. Enter your authentication information again to access Voyager.

8. Click **Save**.

Configuring & Implementing...

Emergency Voyager Access

When you enable SSL/HTTPS in the configuration for Voyager Web Access, you disable the unencrypted HTTP access that you had up to that point. If you cannot connect via HTTPS for some reason and you need to get remote Voyager access, you have these options to reset Voyager from the console or remote command line:

1. Restart Voyager with no encryption listening on port 80 with the *voyager -e 0 80* command.

2. Run *clish* and set the encryption level back to 0 on Voyager with the following options: *Nokia> set voyager ssl-level 0*

3. Run *lynx* to configure the system with a text-based Voyager interface locally, set the encryption level to **none**, and **Apply** the change.

Understanding Configuration Options

In this section, you are provided with an overview of all the configuration menu options found in Voyager. You should feel comfortable using this section of the chapter as a quick reference guide to each configuration link available under the main Configuration screen in Voyager. We'll be describing the highlights of each option so that you are aware of all the things you can do remotely through the Voyager Web interface.

Interface Configuration

Voyager provides a simple Web-based interface that you can access remotely to configure interface parameters and ARP settings:

- **Interfaces** Configuring physical and logical interfaces, including IP addresses, speed and duplex settings, and the like.

- **ARP** Address Resolution Protocol settings, adding static ARP entries, clearing the ARP table.

System Configuration

A wide variety of tools are available under the System Configuration heading. Each item under this section allows you to perform common system administration tasks, such as upgrading the IPSO images and scheduling jobs through crontab. Here is a description of each item:

- **DNS** Domain Name System—configure as a client only.

- **Disk Mirroring** Add or delete disk mirrors. This option is available for IP-500 and IP-700 series only. This is different from the RAID-1 available in the IP400 series, which was mentioned previously.

- **Mail Relay** Enter an IP address of a mail server that will accept mail from the Nokia for final delivery.

- **System Failure Notification** Enable or disable notification of system failures. Mail Relay must be configured for this option to function.

- **Local Time Setup** Manually set the date, time, and time zone of the system.

- **Host Address Assignment** Configure the Hosts table on the Nokia (/etc/hosts).

- **System Logging** Configure a remote syslog server or accept syslog from other devices.

- **Change Hostname** Change the hostname of the Nokia. If you have installed Check Point NG, *do not* change the hostname. The Secure Internal Communications certificate depends on the hostname.

- **Manage Configuration Sets** Save the current Voyager settings (/config/active) and toggle back and forth between various Voyager configurations.

- **Backup and Restore** Make a one-time backup or schedule a backup of the system. You may also use this screen to restore from a previous backup. You can even set it up to FTP the backup file off the server when complete.

- **Job Scheduler** Add scheduled cron jobs to the system.

- **Manage IPSO Images** Toggle between installed IPSO images and delete images.

- **Install New IPSO Image (Upgrade)** Download the IPSO image from a remote HTTP or FTP server and upgrade from an existing image.

- **Manage Installed Packages** Toggle packages (such as Check Point FireWall-1) off and on, FTP new packages, install new packages, and delete packages.

Several of these functions are discussed in more detail in Chapter 5.

SNMP

Enable or disable Simple Network Management Protocol (SNMP), set community strings, and configure a server to receive traps. The default settings should be usable, but you can enable or disable many different trap options here.

IPv6

Configure the Nokia system to use IPv6 IP addressing instead of the more common IPv4. There are many options to select from under this topic, such as logical interfaces, IPv6 over IPv4, static routes, host address assignment, and network access and services, to name a few. Recent press releases state that Check Point NG FP3 will support IPv6. Note that prior to IPSO 3.6 the Apache server running on IPSO did not support IPv6 connections, meaning that you could not use Voyager over IPv6 on earlier versions of IPSO.

Reboot, Shut Down System

This screen allows you to do a system halt or reboot through Voyager and displays the currently selected image that will be used on the next boot.

Security and Access Configuration

The items located under the Security and Access Configuration heading allow you to perform access administration to your Nokia system by providing you with an interface for manipulating users and services available on the platform. Many of these are discussed in more detail throughout the book:

- **Users** Change passwords, add new users, and configure S/Key authentication.

- **Groups** Set up groups for file permissions and assign users to these groups.

- **AAA** Configure authentication, authorization, and accounting.

- **Network Access and Services** Enable or disable network protocols such as Telnet usually found in inetd.conf.

- **Voyager Web Access** Enable or disable Voyager Web access, configure the ports used to access Voyager, and determine if SSL encryption is required.

- **SSL Certificate Tool** Generate a request for a certificate or create your own self-signed X.509 certificate for SSL access.

- **SSH (Secure Shell)** Enable or disable SSH, make various configuration changes, and determine which version server you will run (1 or 2).

- **IPSec** IP Security; configure security associations (SA) to other IPSec-compliant devices in order to generate a VPN. This option supports native IPSec (without FireWall-1).

- **Check Point FireWall-1** Enable or disable Check Point FireWall-1 4.1 to start at boot time. Also configure FloodGate-1 v4.1 and ifwd. If you are running NG, this page only allows you to configure ifwd, since these options have moved to the cpconfig utility instead.

Fault Management Configuration

This section allows you to set certain alarm parameters for your NSP. You can have an active role in viewing and filtering alarms such as disk space, interface link, and temperature alarms.

- **General Configurations** Enable or disable Fault Management and configure general parameters such as log file size and the like.

- **Current Alarm List** View active alarms and cancel them.

- **Alarm Log** Display all past alarms, even if you cancelled them in the Current Alarm List.

- **Alarm Filtering** List all alarm types; allows you to suppress alarms.

Routing Configuration

You have a robust set of tools for routing configuration in the NSP. There are several network protocols to choose from, such as BGP, OSPF, and RIP:

- **BGP** Border Gateway Protocol. Configure your Nokia to participate in BGP exterior routing.

- **OSPF** Open Shortest Path First network protocol. Enable or disable OSPF on each interface.

- **RIP** Routing Information Protocol. Enable or disable RIP on each interface.

- **IGRP** Interior Gateway Routing Protocol. Enable or disable IGRP on each interface.

- **IGMP** Internet Group Management Protocol. Used in IP multicast routing, this protocol maintains the multicast group database.

- **PIM** Protocol-Independent Multicast. Enable or disable PIM on each interface.

- **DVMRP** Distance Vector Multicast Routing Protocol. Enable or disable DVMRP on each interface.

- **Static Routes** Add, edit, or delete routes and configure your default gateway.

- **Route Aggregation** Create new aggregates by lumping together similar routes into a more general route for route redistribution and advertisement.

- **Inbound Route Filters** Configure inbound route filters, set protocol rank, and determine which routes learned should be accepted.

- **Route Redistribution** Allows you to redistribute routes between static routes, aggregate routes, interface routes, BGP, OSPF, RIP, and IGRP.

- **Routing Options** Configure various routing options such as the next-hop selection algorithm and protocol rank and restart the routing subsystem.

If you want to delve into more depth on these protocols and how to configure them on your system, read Chapter 9.

Traffic Management

Use the tools provided in Voyager under the Traffic Management heading to customize your Nokia for your network environment. You can make the Nokia firewall a member of a cluster, configure your Nokia to behave like a firewall with access lists, or set up quality of service (QoS) for bandwidth management:

- **Cluster** Enable and configure firewall gateway clustering. This is a new feature in IPSO 3.6 and should prove to be a very popular high-availability option. See Chapter 10 for more information.

- **Access List** Configure access control lists (ACLs) on your Nokia.

- **Aggregation Class** Set up a maximum bandwidth rate, which you can use in the ACL config.

- **Queue Class** Create new queue classes, which are service definitions for setting precedence for certain types of traffic.

- **ATM QoS Descriptor** Create or delete an ATM QoS descriptor, which determines the traffic bandwidth parameters of an ATM.

- **Dial-On-Demand Routing** Allows you to use ACLs to determine if a packet should bring up an ISDN line.

- **DSCP-VLAN Priority** Enable or disable DSCP-to-VLAN or VLAN-to-DSCP priority mappings.

- **COPS** Configure the Nokia to utilize Common Open Policy Service (COPS). COPS is used in a client/server model where the server is a policy server or policy decision point (PDP) and the client is a policy enforcement point (PEP). The PEP will get control decisions from the PDP for things such as QoS policies, IPSec, or admission control. This protocol is described in RFC 2748.

Router Services

You don't pass broadcast traffic through a gateway without running some sort of relay. This section tells you how to configure a bootp relay on the gateway per interface and set up a relay for any UDP broadcast traffic. You may also advertise your NSP as a default gateway, configure failover routing, and set up NTP to synchronize system time:

- **BOOTP Relay** Enable or disable a bootp/DHCP relay on each interface.

- **IP Broadcast Helper** Enable or disable forwarding on any UDP broadcast traffic you determine on each interface.

- **Router Discovery** Enable the Nokia as an ICMP router discovery server so that it advertises itself as a default gateway.

- **VRRP** Virtual Router Redundancy Protocol allows you to share virtual IP and MAC addresses for failover routing. This is a popular failover mechanism with Check Point FireWall-1.

- **NTP** Network Time Protocol. You can run NTP as a client or a server.

Asset Management Summary

Asset Management Summary simply displays a summary of hardware information.

Licenses

You must apply licenses if you want to use certain routing protocols, such as DVMRP or IGRP. This is where those licenses are applied.

Show Configuration Summary

Shows a summary of network configuration, such as interface status, IP addresses, routing protocols, ARP, and routes.

Copyright Information

Displays all copyright information.

Summary

After you run through the initial configuration of your NSP, you will want to begin basic system configuration so that your NSP is usable. The remote administration GUI provided with the Nokia device is the network Voyager configuration tool. You connect to Voyager through a Web browser via HTTP, and the first thing you'll want to do is to set up the network properties for your gateway. Start by configuring the interfaces with IP addresses, link speed, and duplex settings in the Interface Configuration screen. Then you might want to set up the default gateway on the system from the Static Routes configuration screen.

A few other basic system settings include the system date, time, and time zone, which can be configured from the Local Time Setup link under the System Configuration heading from the main config screen, or you can synchronize with an NTP server via the NTP link. Do you want to be able to resolve Internet addresses from your Nokia? Then you need to configure name servers in the **DNS** configuration page. You also need to click the Host Address Assignment link to set up a host entry for the firewall's external IP address. This is particularly important if your Nokia will be running Check Point FireWall-1 software. You should configure your system to notify you if something is wrong. To accomplish this task, enter a mail server IP address under the Mail Relay link and enable the System Event Notification option.

Next, you will be concerned with securing the Nokia platform. Luckily, Nokia ships its products with security in mind. Most network protocols are already disabled, and the ones that are open by default have encryption alternatives, such as HTTPS instead of HTTP, SSH instead of Telnet, and SCP instead of FTP. The configuration parameters necessary to perform these substitutions were explained step by step in this chapter, allowing you to make your system as secure as possible from the start.

The last thing addressed in this chapter was the large number of configuration options available to you through Voyager's main Configuration screen. You have various tools under Interface Configuration, System Configuration, SNMP, IPv6, Reboot, Shutdown System, Security and Access Configuration, Fault Management Configuration, Routing Configuration, Traffic Management, Router Services, Asset Management, Licenses, Show Configuration Summary, and Copyright Information at your disposal in one location within Voyager.

Solutions Fast Track

Basic System Configuration, Out of the Box

☑ Access Voyager with HTTP from your Web browser—for example, http://10.10.10.1.

☑ Remember to click **Save** to commit any changes to the Voyager configuration. If you forget to save, you will lose configuration on the next reboot.

☑ Do not use your browser's Back button to move around in Voyager. Instead, use the navigation icons provided at the top and bottom of the screen. Failure to do this could result in misconfigurations.

☑ Associate your gateway's hostname with its external IP address in the Host Address Assignment configuration page.

Configuring the System for Security

☑ Secure Shell (SSH) is included in IPSO 3.5 and later. SSH provides an encrypted alternative to Telnet, and it's very easy to configure. Find an SSH client from www.freessh.org.

☑ Once SSH is enabled, remember to disable Telnet. Once you have a secure remote access login, there is no need to leave Telnet open to possible attack.

☑ Use SCP instead of FTP, and disable FTP within Voyager.

☑ You can generate a self-signed certificate in Voyager to be used in the SSL configuration. This way you can enable encryption to the Web interface quickly without losing any functionality or security.

Understanding Configuration Options

☑ Configuration tools available in Voyager are grouped under headings that describe the administrative tasks under which each can be identified. This makes it easier for you to find the tool you are looking for.

☑ Clusters are new in IPSO 3.6, and they provide a high–availability solution to Check Point FireWall-1 subscribers.

☑ Disk mirroring is new in IPSO 3.6 and is available to IP500 and IP700 series only.

☑ VRRP is a popular routing failover mechanism for Check Point FireWall-1, which allows two or more Nokias to share virtual IP addresses and MAC addresses.

Frequently Asked Questions

The following Frequently Asked Questions, answered by the authors of this book, are designed to both measure your understanding of the concepts presented in this chapter and to assist you with real-life implementation of these concepts. To have your questions about this chapter answered by the author, browse to **www.syngress.com/solutions** and click on the **"Ask the Author"** form.

Q: Why does my initial Telnet connection hang for a long time before I receive the login prompt?

A: This will usually occur when DNS is configured. The system tries to perform reverse resolution on the IP address of your Telnet client, and if the machine cannot resolve the address, it hangs for a while until it gives up. The quickest solution to this problem is to either disable DNS or set up the hostname and IP address of the client in the Host Address Assignment configuration screen.

Q: Why am I getting the error message "FW_IPADDR: cannot get my IPADDR" when I try to apply my FireWall-1 license?

A: You must assign a hostname to the IP address on which the firewall is licensed. Generally, this is the host name of the Nokia and the external IP address. To do this, click **Host Address Assignment** under the System Configuration heading from the main Configuration screen.

Q: I tried to generate a certificate with the Certificate Tool in Voyager, but whenever I copy the cert and private key into the next window, I receive an error and don't get a confirmation that it was successful. What am I doing wrong?

A: Make sure that you are copying the entire BEGIN and END lines into the text window, including the dashed lines, and that there are no additional spaces at the end of the pasted text. If that doesn't help, try using a different Web browser.

Q: What are all the entries I see in my system logs and console "[LOG_INFO] sshd–x[163]: Generating 768 bit RSA key"?

A: Every 15 minutes, the SSH daemon regenerates its server keys (not to be confused with host keys). You can safely ignore these messages.

Q: Can I use SFTP with Nokia's OpenSSH server?

A: No. The version of OpenSSH that Nokia uses does not support SFTP, but it does support SCP. If you are trying to use SCP and are getting failed connections, try the command *scp1* instead.

## Chapter 5

Basic System Administration

Solutions in this chapter:

- **Rebooting the System**
- **Managing Packages**
- **Managing IPSO Images**
- **Managing Users and Groups**
- **Configuring Static Routes**
- **System Backup and Restore**
- **System Logging**
- **Scheduling Tasks Using cron**

☑ **Summary**

☑ **Solutions Fast Track**

☑ **Frequently Asked Questions**

Introduction

Once you have configured your Nokia so that it is up and functioning within your network environment, you might wonder how to accomplish the routine, day-to-day tasks that are part of a network administrator's job. Things such as package management and upgrades, performing system backups, and even replacing your IPSO operating system are often necessary to do at regular intervals.

Voyager was designed with the administrator in mind, and almost all the day-to-day tasks that you could think of can be handled through its interface. With each release of IPSO, Nokia adds more functionality to Voyager. For example, IPSO 3.5 and later allows you to schedule periodic tasks through cron with Voyager, something that could previously be done only from the command shell.

Most tasks you will need to do are discussed in this chapter; for those of you wondering about more advanced administrative tasks or if you are a die-hard shell zealot, Chapter 8 covers some of them, including using the command line for configuration changes.

Rebooting the System

It is very important that you shut down your Nokia system cleanly so that any unsaved data is copied to the disk and the file systems are unmounted safely. In order to reboot your Nokia system from the command line, type **reboot** and press **Enter**. From Voyager, follow these steps:

1. Log into Voyager.

2. Click **Config**.

3. Scroll down to the bottom of the main Configuration screen and select **Reboot, Shut Down System**.

4. Click either **Reboot** or **Halt**. Reboot will shut down the system and restart it again, and Halt will shut down the system for a power off. See Figure 5.1.

NOTE

If you are used to typing **sync; sync; reboot** to restart a UNIX system, you can certainly do that as well. However, the *reboot* command does flush the file system cache to disk, so it is no longer necessary to use the *sync* command.

Figure 5.1 System Reboot

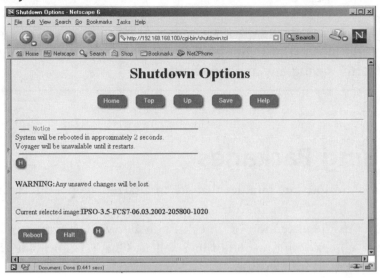

If you do not shut down your system cleanly for whatever reason, perhaps due to a power outage or if you simply hit the power switch or there was a system crash, your Nokia will probably boot up fine on its own, but there could be a time when the system does not come up without some intervention. When the file systems are not cleanly unmounted, UNIX systems will perform an fsck (file system check) during the boot process to check blocks and sizes, pathnames, connectivity, reference counts, and cylinder groups for file system integrity. If there is an error that the system cannot fix during the automatic fsck process, it will stop booting and wait for you to press Enter on your keyboard. The following is the message you will see on the console:

```
Automatic file system check failed. Enter pathname of shell or RETURN for sh:
```

Follow these steps to run fsck manually:

1. Press **Enter**. You will then see an sh prompt (#). The system is in maintenance mode, so you have limited access to it at this stage.

2. Change directories to /sbin by typing #**cd /sbin**.

3. Run **fsck −y**. This command runs manually. Answer **yes** to any questions you are prompted with during the process. When the check is complete, you will return to the shell prompt.

4. Type **reboot** to restart the boot process, and the system should come up on its own this time.

> **NOTE**
>
> You can use the commands *reboot* or *halt* from within the CLISH tool as well. If you type **reboot save** or **halt save**, the system will shut down cleanly after saving any applied changes.

Managing Packages

Nokia *packages* are software bundles that are in a tarred, gzipped format ready to be installed on an IPSO system. You can get packages compatible with IPSO from Nokia, with the exception of Check Point FireWall-1, which must be obtained from Check Point or one of its resellers. Chapter 6 provides FireWall-1 specific configuration information.

All Nokia packages are stored in the /opt file system. This is also the directory for administrators to put optional software.

Installing New Packages

When you download a new package to your NSP, you should not uncompress nor extract the package files in any way prior to starting the installation. The IPSO tools provided expect to find most packages with a .tgz extension and will extract the files necessary as part of the package installation procedure.

Voyager

First let's walk through the process of installing a new package using the Voyager Web interface. (If you want to use the command line instead, skip to the next section.) When installing packages through Voyager, you must specify an FTP server that you can use to download the package:

1. Log into Voyager and click **Config**.

2. Select **Manage Installed Packages** from under the System Configuration section.

3. Click the link to **FTP and Install Packages** from the Manage Packages configuration page.

4. Fill in the required fields for the FTP session. This information includes the FTP server name or IP address, the directory where the packages are

stored on that server, and a login name/password. You may leave the username and password fields blank if you want to use anonymous FTP. See
the example illustrated in Figure 5.2. If you want to use the login directory, you might need to enter a single period (.) in the FTP dir box.

Figure 5.2 FTP Packages

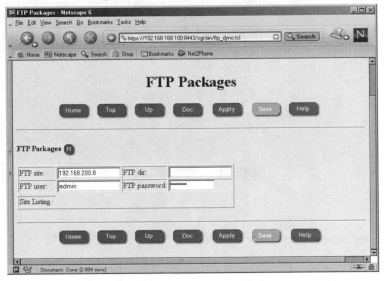

5. Click **Apply**. The page will update once a connection has been made to
   the FTP server. A list of packages available on that server will be displayed in the Site Listing box.

6. Choose the packages that you want to download by highlighting them
   in the Site Listing box. See Figure 5.3.

7. Click **Apply** again. This time, the Nokia device will begin to download
   the files. The page will update every 15 seconds during the download so
   you know that it is in progress. You will also see a message on the top of
   the screen similar to the following:

```
Last FTP Attempt: /opt/packages/RSNS_NokiaRelease_6_5_2001_353a.tgz
Status: Downloading
Status Can Be Refreshed By Either Waiting 15 Seconds or Clicking
Apply
```

8. When the download is complete, you will see the message "Status:
   Download Successful" at the top of the page. Scroll down to the box
   now displayed that is labeled *Select a package to unpack*. You should see the

package(s) that you retrieved in the previous step. Highlight the package you want to install.

Figure 5.3 Selecting a Package for Download

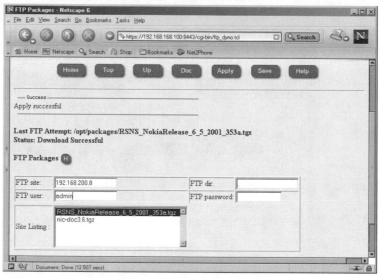

9. Click **Apply**. Doing so will extract the package and list some package details on the screen, as shown in Figure 5.4.

Figure 5.4 Unpacked Package Details

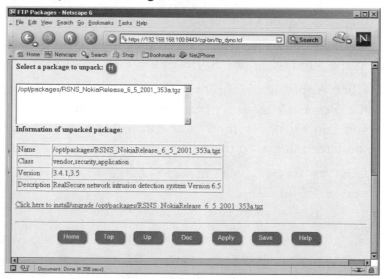

10. Select the link **Click here to install/upgrade**, which ends with the package name. In this example, the package used is /opt/packages/ RSNS_NokiaRelease_6_5_2001_353a.tgz. You will see a page similar to the one shown in Figure 5.5.

Figure 5.5 Installing the New Package in Voyager

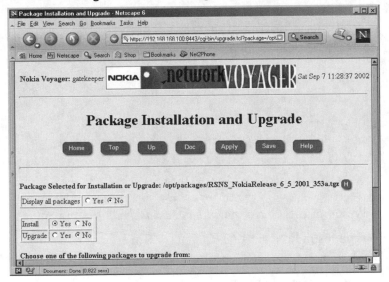

11. Toggle the radio button to **Yes** to install a new package. If you want to upgrade the package from one already installed instead, choose **Yes** under the Upgrade option and from the list provided, select the software package that you want to upgrade.

12. Click **Apply**. The package is now installed and active. You can now view this package on the Manage Packages configuration screen along with all the other installed packages.

13. Click **Save**.

WARNING

If you are installing NG for the first time, you must install Check Point FireWall-1 NG FP2 using the bundled wrapper file named CP_FP2_IPSO.tgz instead of trying to install the individual packages. The wrapper will install NG FP1 and then update to FP2 automatically. If you are already running NG FP1, you shouldn't have any problem upgrading to FP2 using the separate packages. See Chapter 6 for more details.

The Command Line

The command-line tool that is used to install new images is *newpkg*. Follow these steps to install a package using the newpkg utility. To use this procedure, you should already have the package downloaded to the system in the /var/admin directory. Available command-line options for this tool are described in Table 5.1. Do the following:

1. From a command prompt on the Nokia device, type **newpkg –i**. The following options will be displayed:

```
Load new package from:
1. Install from CD-ROM.
2. Install from anonymous FTP server.
3. Install from FTP server with user and password.
4. Install from local filesystem.
5. Exit new package installation.
```

2. Type **4** at the *Choose an installation method (1-5):* prompt and press **Enter**.

3. Type a single period (.) and press **Enter** at the *Enter pathname to the packages [or 'exit' to exit]:* prompt. You will see the following output:

```
Loading Package List


Processing package nic-doc3.6.tgz ...
Package Description: Documentation for Nokia IPSO 3.6 07/08/02


Would you like to :


1. Install this as a new package
2. Skip this package
3. Exit new package installation


Choose (1-3):
```

4. Type **1** and press **Enter** to install the new package. You will then see the following output:

```
Installing nic-doc3.6.tgz
nic_doc36 does not exist previously. Proceeding with Installation.
```

```
Done installing nic_doc36

End of new package installation
cleaning up ..done
Use Voyager to activate packages
```

Table 5.1 newpkg Command-Line Arguments

Switch for newpkg	Description
-i	Installs the package but does not activate it. Prompts you for media type, new packages, and old packages that you want to install or upgrade.
-s <server>	Specifies the FTP server IP address.
-l <username>	Enter the FTP username. (You don't need to enter a username if you will be using anonymous FTP.)
-p <password>	Enter the FTP user's password.
-m <CDROM | AFTP | FTP | LOCAL>	Choose your media type. Your options are CDROM, AFTP, FTP or LOCAL.
-d	Prints debug messages.
-v	Verbose mode for FTP.
-n <new package>	Enter the full pathname to the new package you are installing.
-o <old package>	Enter the full pathname to the package from which you are upgrading.
-S	Sets the newpkg to install the package silently. If you enable silent mode, you must specify the following arguments: -o, -m, -n, and possibly –s and -l, –p if the media type is not LOCAL.
-h	Prints the usage for newpkg (help).

Enabling and Disabling Packages

Once you have installed packages, you might need to go into Voyager to enable them. Likewise, you can easily disable packages from the same screen:

1. Log into Voyager and click **Config**.

2. Click **Manage Installed Packages** from the System Configuration heading. See Figure 5.6.

Figure 5.6 Enabling and Disabling Packages

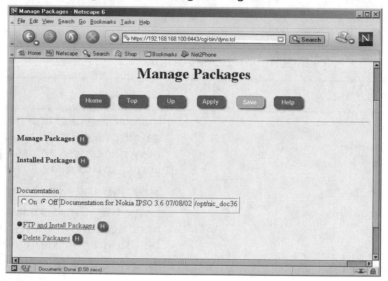

3. All the installed packages are listed with the option of being turned *Off* or *On*. Their current state is displayed. To enable a package that is disabled, toggle to the **On** position. Enabling a package will start any relevant processes so you can start using the software immediately.

4. To disable a package that is currently enabled, toggle the button to the **Off** position. You may enable or disable one or more packages at one time from this screen. Disabling a package will kill any running processes related to that package but will not uninstall it, so you may enable it again later.

5. Click **Apply** and then click **Save**.

After enabling a package, you will receive notification at the top of the Manage Packages configuration screen that the package has been registered and that the Voyager environment has been changed due to the new package. Any necessary environment variables have been updated within the login environment as well, but you might need to end your session and start a new one for these settings to take effect on the command line. This is because these settings are updated in the users' .cshrc or .profile and are run once at the beginning of each login session. You may also source these files to initiate the new variables into your current environment. To do this, simply type **source .cshrc** from the /var/admin directory.

Designing & Planning...

Simple Software Backout Procedure

Using the Manage Installed Packages tool in Voyager, you have an easy method of toggling packages off and on, giving you the ability to disable one version of installed software and enable another. This tool is ideal for administrators since it provides a very quick and simple way to back out of new package upgrades, if necessary.

For example, consider that you are running Check Point FireWall-1 4.1 SP-5 and you are planning an upgrade to FireWall-1 NG. As part of your upgrade procedure, it is always prudent to have a contingency plan in case the upgrade is not successful for any reason. With your Nokia system, you can simply toggle the new Check Point NG package to **Off** and toggle the Check Point 4.1 SP-5 package to **On**. Click **Apply** and then click **Save**, and the system will switch to running whatever package you have enabled at that time. The entire configuration will be saved in the old package. If you want to try NG again at a later time, just reverse the procedure.

Removing Packages

To remove previously installed packages, follow these instructions after logging into Voyager:

1. Click **Config**.

2. Click **Manage Installed Packages** from the System Configuration heading.

3. Click the link to **Delete Packages**.

4. Select the packages you want to delete by selecting the radio button for **Delete** instead of Keep. You may choose any packages from the list that are not currently active, so you won't be able to accidentally remove a package you are using. See Figure 5.7.

5. Click **Apply** and then click **Save**.

Figure 5.7 Deleting Packages

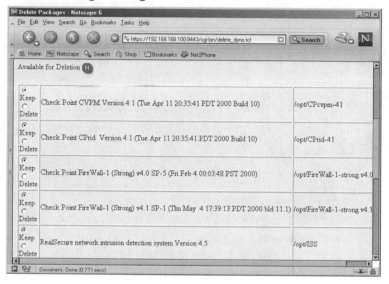

Managing IPSO Images

You may manage Nokia's IPSO images similarly to the way you manage packages. An IPSO image is the base operating system of your Nokia Security Platform. These images are located in the /image directory on your hard drive, and they contain a system kernel and system binaries. You should have at least one image on the system when you receive it, and you can add new images at any time.

Configuring & Implementing...

IPSO Release Notes

Please read all IPSO release notes before upgrading your system. You must take into account special considerations, depending on your Nokia model, and sometimes you cannot apply the latest image without first applying an older image. For example, IPSO 3.6 can be installed on the following model numbers:

■ IP110 and IP120

Continued

- IP330
- IP440
- IP530
- IP650
- IP710 and IP740

Do not attempt to install 3.6 on any other models or you might leave the system in an unusable state, and the only way to make it usable again is to RMA the unit for Nokia to reimage the box. IPSO 3.6 can be upgraded on these models only if you are running one of the following previous versions of IPSO. Note that IPSO 3.5.1 is *not* supported:

- 3.3 or 3.3.1
- 3.4, 3.4.1 or 3.4.2
- 3.5

If you are running IPSO 3.2.1 or earlier and you want to upgrade to IPSO 3.4.x or later, you must do a manual boot manager upgrade. For that reason, we recommend that if you are on IPSO 3.2.1 or earlier, you first upgrade to IPSO 3.3 and then to 3.4.x or later. Nokia incorporated the boot manager update automatically into IPSO 3.3 and later. So if you are on IPSO 3.3 or later and the boot manager needs to be updated during a new image install, it will happen automatically, or you can force a boot manager upgrade using the *newimage –b* option.

Upgrading to a New IPSO

If you want to use the Voyager interface to upgrade the IPSO image, you need to have the image file ipso.tgz available on an FTP or HTTP server that is accessible from your NSP. Upgrade IPSO image through Voyager:

1. Log into Voyager and click **Config**.

2. Scroll down to the System Configuration heading and select **Install New IPSO Image (Upgrade)**.

3. Fill in the URL to the image and select **Test Boot New Image**. Fill in any of the other relevant information as shown in Figure 5.8:

   - Enter HTTP Realm (for HTTP URLs only). This is the name of the realm that you are authenticating to in a Web browser.

- Enter User Name (if applicable). If you are using HTTP or FTP, you might need to enter a username.

- Enter Password (if applicable). If you enter a username, enter the password here.

Figure 5.8 Updating Images Through Voyager

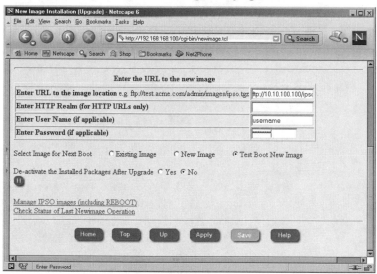

4. Click **Apply**. You will receive the following message:

```
"File download and image installation could take long time
(depending

upon  the network speed).
Click Apply if you want to continue".
```

This message is accurate; when writing this section, it took approximately 30 minutes for the installation to complete through Voyager.

5. Click **Apply** to begin the download and upgrade process.

NOTE

If you do not have a name server configured on your Nokia appliance, you need to enter the server's IP address instead of DNS resolvable name in Step 3. You will know this is the case if you receive the following error messages: "Error: Invalid URL or server error" and "fetch: 'www.nokia.com': cannot resolve: Resolver Error."

6. Next you will see a screen that says, "New image installation has started…" and then you will be brought back to the New Image Installation (Upgrade) Status page, which displays the status of the download and installation. This page will continue to refresh. Be patient. If the download is not progressing for some reason, you will be notified. If you want to check the progress of the download, just log into the NSP and run the **ls -al** command on /var/tmp. The ipso.tgz file will be there and the file size should continue to grow.

7. When the update is complete, you will see the message "Please reboot immediately," as shown in Figure 5.9. Reboot the system cleanly. Refer to the section "Rebooting the System" that appears earlier in this chapter if you need help with rebooting.

Figure 5.9 Voyager IPSO Upgrade Complete

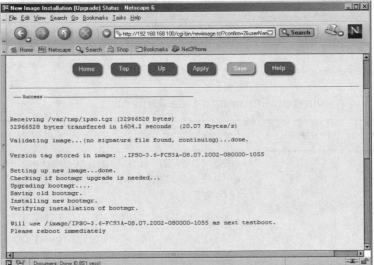

8. When the system comes back up, log in and verify that the new image is running. If you did a test boot, you will want to set the new image as the active image through the Manage IPSO Images screen.

Installing with newimage

If you would prefer to update IPSO versions from the command line, you can use the *newimage* tool. Table 5.2 illustrates the various command-line options you can specify in running the command. If you have the ipso.tgz file loaded on the local system in /var/admin, use **newimage −k −R −l /var/admin** to update the operating system image. After the image is updated, you must reboot to load the new image. You will see the following output:

```
gatekeeper[admin]# newimage -k -R -l /var/admin
Enter ipso image file name [ipso.tgz]:
Validating image...(no signature file found, continuing)...done.


Version tag stored in image:  .IPSO-3.6-FCS3-08.01.2002-181200-1051


Setting up new image...done.
Checking if bootmgr upgrade is needed...


Will use /image/IPSO-3.6-FCS3-08.01.2002-181200-1051 as root for next boot.
To install/upgrade your packages run /etc/newpkg after REBOOT
Please reboot immediately


gatekeeper[admin]# sync; sync; reboot
```

Table 5.2 newimage Command-Line Arguments

Switch for newimage	Description
-k	Upgrades the IPSO image and keep all currently active packages so they will be started upon reboot.
-r <image>	Specifies the image to use on the next boot.
-R	Sets the new image to be used on the next reboot.
-l <path to image>	Tells the newimage command where to find the ipso.tgz file, which contains the new image.
-t <image>	Specifies the image to use for a test boot.
-T	Enables you to perform a test boot with the new image.
-i	Sets the newimage command in interactive mode. Use this option if you need to FTP the file or use the CDROM drive (IP440 only) to upgrade the IPSO image.
-b	Forces upgrade of bootmgr.
-v	Verbose mode for FTP.

Deleting Images

If you don't have enough disk space in /image to load new images, you need to remove old images to make space. The process for deleting images is very simply done through the Voyager Web interface. To delete old IPSO images:

1. Log into Voyager.
2. Click **Config** to bring up the main Configuration window.
3. Click **Manage IPSO Images** under the System Configuration heading.
4. Click the link labeled **Delete IPSO images**.
5. Select the radio button to **Delete** the old images. You may select one or more images to delete as shown in Figure 5.10.

Figure 5.10 Deleting IPSO Images

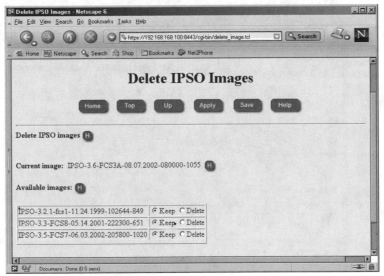

6. Click **Apply** and then click **Save**.

Managing Users and Groups

As with any operating system, one must administer users and groups. On most UNIX systems, the user with unlimited privilege and responsibility is the root user, also known as the *superuser*. In IPSO, the user *admin* takes the place of the root user but has all the same privileges. Whenever you need to make changes to your NSP, you log in as admin because this account has read/write capability to system configuration files and full system access. In this section, we show you how to change the password on your admin account, how to create and delete user accounts, and how to configure groups on your UNIX system. If you're interested in more basic information on user and group concepts, have a look at Appendix A.

Users

To manage users on your Nokia system, log into Voyager and click **Config**. From here, click **Users** under the Security and Access Configuration heading. You should be presented with a screen like the one displayed in Figure 5.11.

Figure 5.11 Managing Users

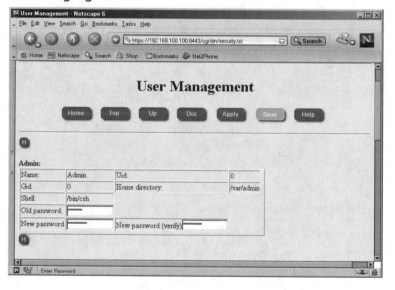

The admin User

As mentioned previously, the admin user is the superuser on the system. If you review some of the settings for admin in the User Management display, you will see that admin has a UID and a GID of 0. *UID* stands for *user ID,* and *GID* stands for *group ID.* These ID values determine that the admin user has superuser privileges on the system. These values mean the same thing on almost all UNIX systems. Other information listed on this page is the host directory, which is /var/admin, and the shell that admin uses—/bin/csh, pronounced "C-shell."

You configure a password for the admin user during the initial configuration of your Nokia platform. If you want to change the password for this user, follow this procedure:

1. From the User Management screen, fill in the Old password, New password, and New password (verify) fields, as shown in Figure 5.11.

2. Click **Apply**.

3. Click **Save** and you will be presented with a login prompt to reauthenticate.

4. Enter **admin** and the new password.

5. Click **Save** again, if the option is still available.

You have the option of accepting or requiring S/key authentication for the admin user on this screen as well. For more information, see the section "Securing FTP" in Chapter 4.

NOTE

Using CLISH, you can change the admin user password with the following command:

Nokia> **set user admin passwd**
Nokia> **save config**

The monitor User

The monitor user is available in IPSO as a read-only user. Once this user is enabled, you can login as monitor through Voyager to view system configuration and resources, but you cannot make any changes to the configuration. This account is predefined in Voyager with the following values:

- Name: Monitor

- UID: 102

- GID: 10

- Home Directory: */var/monitor*

- Shell: */bin/csh*

- Password: None (cannot login)

By default, the monitor user has no password and cannot log into the system. To enable the monitor user visible in Voyager, fill in the new password fields and click **Apply** and then click **Save**.

Other Users

You can create other users to log into the IPSO system and Voyager. If you create a user with UID 0, that user will have read/write access through Voyager and the same permissions that the admin user has in IPSO. Other read-only user accounts can be created too. Simply use a new UID for each new account. To create another user from the User Manager configuration screen:

1. Scroll down to the "Add new user" section and type a username, UID, and home directory for the new user. For another superuser, enter a UID of 0.

2. Click **Apply**.

3. Next enter a password into the New password text boxes for the new user and click **Apply** again.

4. Click **Save**.

Users without admin access will not be able to run the new command-line shell CLISH, but they can log into IPSO and run commands to view system resources and configuration settings. These users will not be able to make any changes that will affect the system. If you would like to give some of these users certain privileges, you could do so by setting up groups, which is discussed in the next section.

You can view the users who are logged into your system with the command *w*. If you type **w** while logged into your Nokia, you should see output similar to the following. This output includes the current time, the time that has passed since the system was last rebooted, the number of users logged into the system, and the system CPU load average over 1-, 5-, and 15-minute intervals.

```
gatekeeper[cherie]# w
10:28PM  up 2 days, 11 mins, 4 users, load averages: 0.03, 0.05, 0.00
USER       TTY FROM              LOGIN@   IDLE WHAT
admin .   d0  -                 Thu10PM 11:09 -csh (csh)
monitor   p0  10.10.10.3        Fri07PM  1:26 -csh (csh)
fwadmin   p1  10.10.10.3         9:01PM     - -csh (csh)
cherie    p2  10.10.10.3        10:28PM     - w
```

Use the following commands to add a new user using CLISH:

    Nokia> **add user** *camon* **uid** *104* **homedir** */var/camon*

    Nokia> **set user** *camon* **passwd**

    Nokia> **save config**

Groups

One way that you can give privileges to users without giving them carte blanche access to your system is to create groups of users. Then you can assign certain permissions to these groups, so that any user who is a member of the group will have the ability to perform certain functions. For example, if you are running Check Point FireWall-1, only admin users can run the programs in $FWDIR/bin. However, if you want to allow a couple of other users the ability to log in and stop or start firewall services or add licenses to the firewall (FireWall-1 4.1 only), you could create an fwadmin group (see the Group Management screen in Voyager in Figure 5.12). After the group is created, you can go into the *cpconfig* utility and set group permissions on the $FWDIR directories. If you have Check Point FireWall-1 4.1 installed, follow these steps to set up group permissions on your Nokia firewall:

1. Log into Voyager and click **Config**.

2. Click **Groups** under the Security and Access Configuration heading.

3. Fill in the Group Name: **fwadmin** under the Add Group Name heading and enter a new GID of **100**. See Figure 5.12 for an example.

4. Click **Apply**. You will now see a new group listed along with the default groups *other* and *wheel*.

5. The next step is to add users to your fwadmin group. To do this, enter an existing user account into the field labeled *Add new member*. For our example, let's add a user called **sysadmin** that was created previously.

6. Click **Apply** and then click **Save**.

Figure 5.12 Group Management

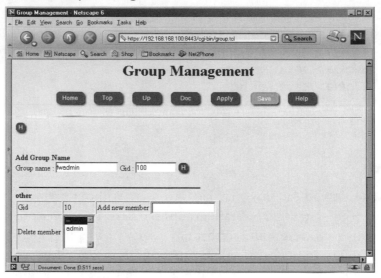

7. Now log into IPSO as **admin** and run **cpconfig**. You will be presented
    with the following options:

    ```
    gatekeeper[cherie]# cpconfig

    This program will let you re-configure

    your Check Point products configuration.



    Configuration Options:
    ----------------------
    (1)   Licenses

    (2)   Administrators

    (3)   GUI clients

    (4)   SNMP Extension

    (5)   Groups

    (6)   PKCS#11 Token

    (7)   Random Pool

    (8)   Certificate Authority

    (9)   Automatic start of Check Point Products


    (10) Exit


    Enter your choice (1-10) :
    ```

8. Enter **5** to configure groups. You will be presented with the following output:

```
Configuring Groups...
=====================
Check Point access and execution permissions
--------------------------------------------
Usually, a Check Point module is given group permission
for access and execution.
You may now name such a group or instruct the installation
procedure to give no group permissions to the Check Point module.
In the latter case, only the Super-User will
be able to access and execute the Check Point module.


Please specify group name [<RET> for no group permissions]:
```

9. Type **fwadmin** and press **Enter**.

10. The system will ask, "Group fwadmin will be used. Is this ok (y/n) [y]?" Press **Enter** to accept the default value *y* for *yes*.

11. The group permissions will then be set on the $FWDIR directories, and you will see the confirmation message, "Setting Group Permissions... Done." on the screen. Then you will be presented with the cpconfig menu again, as in Step 7. Type **10** to exit the configuration tool.

12. You will now be presented with the option of restarting FireWall-1 services. Press **Enter** to accept the default setting *y* for *yes*.

WARNING

With Check Point FireWall-1 Next Generation, this process doesn't seem to work properly. Although the $FWDIR group permissions are changed, a user in the fwadmin group receives errors when trying to run *fw* commands.

In order to set group permissions on files and directories from the command line, use the *chgrp* tool. For example, if you want to set the fwadmin group on all files and directories under the $FWDIR/bin directory, you could change directories into the $FWDIR directory and issue the command *chgrp −R fwadmin bin.* The capital *R* will cause a recursive change on all files and directories under the bin directory, inclusive.

Two groups are created by default on your Nokia Security Platform: the *other* group and the *wheel* group. Any users without full system access, such as monitor, will be members of the *other* group by default. Your admin user will be a member of the *wheel* group. If you want your other users to have the ability to use the *su* command (this command, short for *superuser,* allows users with limited privileges to become the admin or superuser on the system), you will need to add them into the *wheel* group.

> **NOTE**
>
> Use the following syntax in CLISH to add a user to the wheel group:
> Nokia> **add group wheel member camon**
> Nokia> **show group wheel**
> GID   Members
> 0   admin,camon,root

Configuring Static Routes

Almost all administrators need to add static routes into their network, unless they happen to have a very simplified LAN configuration. Nokia makes it very easy to add routes through the Voyager Web interface. Start by clicking **Config**, and then click **Static Routes** under the Routing Configuration heading. Here you have two options for adding routes:

1. You can add routes one by one.
2. You can compile a list of routes and aggregates to add one per line.

If you followed the directions in Chapter 4, you should already have a default route in your Static Routes configuration. To add a single route to the system, fill in the destination network in the *New static route* text box. Also enter the Mask length, Next Hop Type, and Gateway Type fields. Click **Apply** and then fill in the Gateway Address (the next-hop router address), click **Apply**, and then click **Save**.

To add a list of routes at one time, enter routes in the large text box labeled *Quick-add static routes.* The syntax of the routes added here is to have one route per line with a new line at the end of each statement. The statement should include the destination network, mask length, and next-hop router. After you fill in the networks you want to add, click **Apply** and then click **Save**. The routes will be added as shown in Figure 5.13:

```
Example:<destination network>/<mask> <gateway>
172.16.0.0/16 10.10.10.1
172.18.0.0/16 10.10.10.1
192.168.100.0/23 10.10.10.1
192.168.103.0/24 10.10.10.1
10.0.0.0/8 10.10.10.1
```

Figure 5.13 Static Routes Display

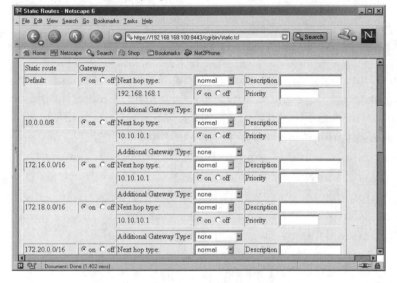

> **NOTE**
>
> You can add and view routes in CLISH as follows:
>   *Nokia>* **set static-route 172.21.0.0/16 nexthop gateway address 10.10.10.1 on**
>   *Nokia>* **show route all**
> To delete the route, use the same command, but change the last word to *off* instead of *on*.

Once the routes are configured, you can perform maintenance on them through this same configuration screen. You can delete a route by clicking **off** next to the network address and then clicking **Apply** and **Save**. You can change a gateway address for a route by clicking **off** next to the gateway address, clicking **Apply**, then selecting **address** for the Gateway Type, then clicking **Apply** again. Finally, fill in the gateway IP address and click **Apply** and then **Save**. You also have the option of writing in a description and/or a priority for each route. To verify that the routing table on the system matches what you see in Voyager, log in and use one of the following options:

- Type **netstat –rn**.
- Type **iclid**, then type **show route** and press **Enter**.
- Type **clish**, then type **show route all** and press **Enter**.

System Backup and Restore

As a systems administrator, you already know the importance of having a good system backup procedure and disaster recovery plan in place should you need to restore important data for your organization. Your Nokias will most likely be some of the most important machines in your network since they are usually placed at key points, you will want to ensure that you are getting backups regularly and that you know how to restore the system if you need to. If you are interested in minimizing downtime when a disaster does strike a highly available Nokia system, Chapter 10 has what you are looking for. In this chapter we show you the utilities available to back up and restore your NSP.

Configuration Sets

Using the Configuration Set Management tool in Voyager, you can make changes to the files that store your current Voyager configuration parameters. The default configuration database is stored in the file /config/db/initial, and a symbolic link file, /config/active, points to this database. Voyager always loads whichever file the /config/active link is associated with. You can use this tool to change that association or to simply make a backup of the current configuration. You also have the option of deleting past configuration sets from this screen.

Follow these steps to make a backup configuration database:

1. Log into Voyager and click **Config**.
2. Click **Manage Configuration Sets** under the System Configuration heading.

3. In the *Save current state to new configuration database* field, type a new name for the current configuration set. In our example, we use the date so we can remember when we made this backup—**config09082002.** (See Figure 5.14.)

Figure 5.14 Managing Configuration Sets

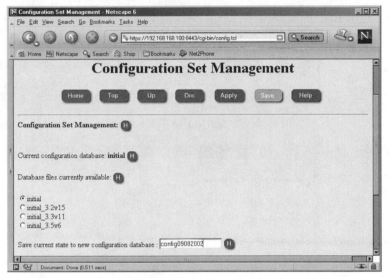

4. Click **Apply**.

5. Now your current config will be listed as *config09082002*, and the active file will now have a symbolic link to this new configuration file. If you only want to make a backup of your existing configuration and do not want it to be the active config, you need to change it back to *initial*. Do this by selecting the radio button next to the **initial** database name.

6. Click **Apply**.

Making Backups

Using the option described in the preceding section, you can save the Voyager settings, but what about backing up the system? The Voyager configuration doesn't include anything from my /var/admin directory or package configuration, such as Check Point FireWall-1. Is there an option for making a full backup?

Yes, the Nokia has a Backup and Restore utility, which allows you to make a default system backup (system files only) and gives you the option to back up home directories and package configuration as well. This backup procedure simply creates a gzipped tarball of all the files you specify on the local system in /var/backup. So you will want to ensure that you have ample disk space on this partition before you begin the process:

1. Log into Voyager and click **Config**.

2. Select the link for **Backup and Restore** under the System Configuration heading. This will bring you to the screen shown in Figure 5.15.

Figure 5.15 Backup Configuration

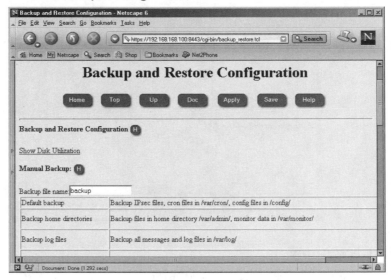

3. Enter a filename such as **backup** in the section marked *Backup file name*. The system will automatically add the current date to the filename, so if you include the date, the filename will be redundant.

4. System files will be backed up by default, including any IPSec files, cron config, and your /config directory. Now you must select from the list of other backup options. This list could be different for you depending on which packages you have in your active configuration. You need to toggle the radio button next to each of these options to **Yes** if you want to back up any of the items in the list that follows. For our example, we select home directories and FireWall-1 NG FP2. These are all set to *No* by default:

■ Backup home directories (*/var/admin* and */var/monitor*) **Yes**

■ Backup log files (*/var/log*) **No**

- Backup */opt/CPfw1-50-02* (Check Point VPN–1/FireWall-1 NG Feature Pack 2) **Yes**

- Backup *hared-50-02* (Check Point SVN Foundation NG Feature Pack 2) **No**

- Backup */opt/ISS* (RealSecure network intrusion detection system Version 6.5) **No**

5. Click **Apply**. You will see the following message on the top of the Voyager screen: *Backup /var/backup/backup_20020908.tgz is running in the background*.

6. When the process is complete, you will see the file in /var/backup as follows:

```
-rw-r--r-- 1 root wheel 136969567 Sep 8 12:19 backup_20020908.tgz
```

You need to refresh the page to see the backup archive listed on the screen. Click **Up** and then click **Backup and Restore** under the System Configuration heading.

7. Click **Save**.

Designing & Planning...

FireWall-1 NG Back Up and Restore Problems

There is a problem with backing up the Check Point FireWall-1 NG FP1 and FP2 packages on IPSO. In FP1, the backup scripts are not present, but you can download a patch that will allow you to make a backup of the Check Point FireWall-1 package only. You can obtain the patch from Nokia by referencing Resolution #10405. You will still need to back up the SVN Foundation manually.

In FP2, the scripts are there, but the SVN Foundation script is corrupt. In order to correct this problem, follow the instructions provided in Nokia Resolution #13387.

Now that you have a backup of system files, you might want to FTP or SCP it off the Nokia to another system for safekeeping. You can use FTP to accomplish this task from within this same screen in Voyager. Scroll down to where it says *Remote Transfer Archive File* and fill in the FTP site information, then choose the backup file that you want to transfer. When you're done, click **Apply** and you will see the following message:

```
Remote Transfer: the ftp is running in the background.
the file transfer might fail, please check /var/log/messages for
    the status of the transfer.
```

This process could take a while because the file is quite large, mostly because we backed up package configuration information. If we had backed up the default files only, the file size would be considerably smaller, as shown in the following output:

```
-rw-r--r--   1 root  wheel      67878 Sep  8 12:31 defaultonly_20020908.tgz
```

NOTE

When making a backup with CLISH, use the following commands:
> *Nokia>* **set backup manual filename** *backup*
> *Nokia>* **set backup manual homedirs** *off*
> *Nokia>* **set backup manual logfiles** *off*
> *Nokia>* **set backup manual** *on*

Now you might be asking, can I schedule regular backups of my Nokia system? The answer is yes. Starting with IPSO 3.5, the ability to schedule backups is built into Voyager with the use of *cron*, which is discussed in detail a little later in this chapter. To schedule a regular backup, scroll down to the section labeled *Scheduled Backup* on the Backup and Restore Configuration screen and select from the pull-down menu one of the following: None (default), Daily, Weekly, or Monthly. See Figure 5.16, where we selected **Monthly** and then clicked **Apply**. Now you are able to select the date, hour, minute, and filename for the monthly backup, as well as the files that you had to choose from when doing a manual backup earlier. When you are finished making your selections, click **Apply** and then click **Save**. The files will be backed up to /var/backup/sched and will be time-stamped. The configuration you specify will be entered into the /etc/crontab file.

You might want to delete backup files from /var/backup occasionally as well, and you can do that by scrolling down to the very bottom of the Backup and Restore Configuration screen. Simply click the **delete** radio button next to the backup filename that you want to remove, and then click **Apply**. See Figure 5.17.

Figure 5.16 Scheduling Backups

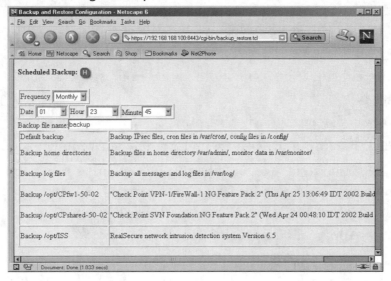

Figure 5.17 Restore from Backup

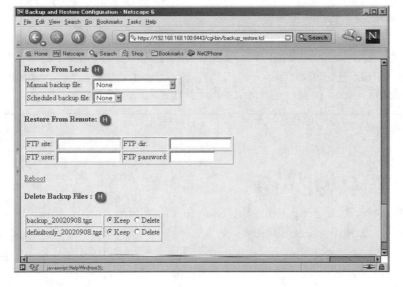

Restoring Backups

You can restore a backup by either using a backup file on the local system in
/var/backup or by using FTP to retrieve the backup file off a remote FTP server.
If you are restoring a configuration from one Nokia to another, ensure that you
have IPSO loaded and the software packages installed before you begin to restore

the configuration files. You should also make sure that you are using the same version of IPSO and the same software package versions that you were using on the system from which you initially took the backup. Follow these steps to restore a backup from a local file:

1. Ensure that the file you want to restore from is in the /var/backup directory.

2. Log into Voyager and click **Config**.

3. Click **Backup and Restore** under the System Configuration heading.

4. Scroll down to the Restore From Local: section (as shown in Figure 5.17) and select the backup file you want to restore from either the *Manual backup file:* or the *Scheduled backup file:* pull-down window.

5. Click **Apply** and then click **Save**.

6. Click the **Reboot** link on the same page.

7. Click the **Reboot** icon and the system will be rebooted with the new configuration.

NOTE

To restore a backup through CLISH, use the following command:
    Nokia> **set restore manual** *backup_20020922.tgz*

System Logging

Choose **System Logging** from the System Configuration heading under the main Configuration screen in Voyager. You will see the default Voyager configuration for system logging that is displayed in Figure 5.18. By default, system logs are stored in a file named *messages* in the /var/log directory on your Nokia system. You can change the logging parameters so that you can accept syslog messages from remote machines, send local logs to a remote machine, and enable logging of Voyager changes through the System Logging configuration interface. If you decide to enable network logging, syslog will use UDP port 514 to transmit the messages. If your log data is traversing a firewall, you might need to open this port for remote logging to operate.

Figure 5.18 System Logging Configuration

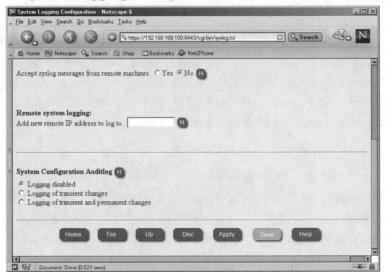

Local System Logging

To view local system logs, click the **Monitor** link in Voyager and select **System Message Log** under the System Logs heading. Here you have the option of searching through the messages file. To view an entire month of data, select the month and click **Apply**. Here you will see system boot messages, crontab messages, SSH key, user logins, and Voyager configuration change messages, among other things. The messages file is rotated monthly, and you can even select past messages files to include in your search criteria.

If you select the option to accept syslog messages from remote machines, your Nokia will begin listening for syslog messages on the network and will log any messages it receives locally, including the hostname of the sending machine in the log entry.

NOTE

To turn on or off the option to accept syslog messages from remote machines through CLISH, use the following commands:

Nokia> **set syslog accept-remote-log** *on*
Nokia> **set syslog accept-remote-log** *off*

Remote Logging

Your Nokia can be configured to send syslog messages to a remote system. This functionality can be useful if you want to have a central syslog server that stores logs. This remote device might even be configured to search your logs for suspicious or unusual activities and generate alerts based on the system logs. Any logs that are sent to a remote syslog server will also be logged locally in the /var/log/messages file. To configure remote system logging in Voyager, follow these six easy steps:

1. Log into Voyager and click **Config**.

2. Click **System Logging** under the System Configuration heading.

3. Enter the IP address of the remote syslog server in the box labeled *Add new remote IP address to log to:*. In Figure 5.19 we have added **10.10.10.1**. Note that Voyager in IPSO 3.4.x does not accept hostnames in the remote address box, only IP addresses. This is an IPSO bug that is fixed in 3.5.

Figure 5.19 Remote System Logging Configuration

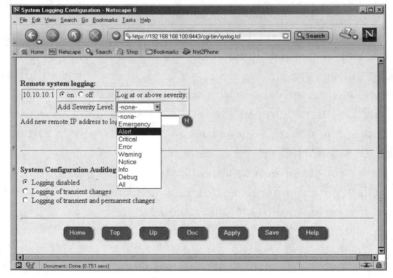

4. Click **Apply**.

5. Now you need to choose the severity level of logs that you want to send to the remote server. Your choices are Emergency, Alert, Critical, Error, Warning, Notice, Info, Debug, and All. The level you choose and all higher levels will be sent to the syslog server.

6. Click **Apply** and then click **Save**. If you enter more than one severity level, the least severe level will be used.

NOTE

Use the following command to enable remote logging through CLISH:
    Nokia> **add syslog log-remote-address** *10.10.10.1* **level** *crit*

WARNING

Be careful not to configure two machines that send syslog data to each other. Doing so will create a logging loop, which is not desirable.

Audit Logs

Using the System Configuration Auditlog option within the System Logging Configuration screen allows you to track the changes that are made to the system configuration. By default, logging config changes is disabled, but you can choose to enable logging for either transient changes only (generated when the Apply button is selected) or for both transient and permanent changes (generated when the Save button is selected).

If you choose to enable configuration logging, you need to specify a file to send these logs to. The default filename is the standard system log file /var/log/messages. You can choose to create a separate file for configuration logs, however, such as /var/log/voyager. Keep in mind that you might need to maintain a new file by rotating it occasionally, especially if you are making a large number of changes to your system.

NOTE

To make changes to the Auditlog configuration through CLISH, use the following commands:
    Nokia> **set syslog filename** */var/log/messages*
    Nokia> **set syslog auditlog** *permanent*

Scheduling Tasks Using cron

UNIX systems have a daemon named *cron* that is used to schedule tasks. If you are familiar with Windows scheduler or *at* commands, think of cron as a similar tool. You can use cron to run any executable file, including shell scripts and other commands, at any time of the day, week, or month, at regular intervals. For example, cron is used to rotate the /var/log/messages file on the first of every month. Tasks that are scheduled through cron are typically called jobs or cron jobs.

The configuration of cron is done through a file called the crontab. Typically, each user on the system can have his or her own crontab file, which will run with whatever privileges that user possesses. Of course, the admin or root crontab file has full privileges, and most system scheduling is done through that file. In IPSO, you can find crontab file in /etc/crontab, which is actually a symlink to /var/etc/crontab. Cron then runs as a daemon and can be viewed with the **ps –aux** command. If you edit the crontab file manually, you need to restart cron (or send it a HUP signal) so that it will load the new configuration file. Alternatively, there is a *crontab* command that you can use to both edit and list the contents of the running crontab configuration. An *–e* switch with the command (i.e., *crontab –e*) will edit the file and update the running cron daemon with any changes you make in real time. Using the *–l* switch allows you to list the file. The syntax of the file is important; each line should have the following values: *minute hour day-of-month month day-of-week command*. Here's a clip of the default /etc/crontab file on IPSO 3.6:

```
#minute hour    mnthday month   weekday user    command
#
5       *       *       *       *       root    /etc/hourly 2>&1 >>/var/
     log/hourly
30      0       *       *       7       root    /etc/weekly 2>&1 >>/var/
     log/weekly
45      23      1       *       *       admin   /etc/backup -f /var/etc/
     sched_backup_vars.sh
15      0       *       *       *       root    /etc/daily 2>&1 >>/var/
     log/daily
45      0       1       *       *       root    /etc/monthly 2>&1 >>/var/
     log/monthly
```

The *2>&1* after each command specifies what to do with standard output and standard error. Basically, this code says to send standard error to standard output and redirect all output to the file specified. The >> means to append to the specified file rather than overwrite it. If no particular action is specified, typically the system messages file will receive this output. It is often useful to redirect this output to /dev/null so that there are no logs generated from the output of the file. One example of this redirection is a FireWall-1 log export command, which would normally show the progression of the export on the command line 1%, 2%, and so on. You would end up with a very large log file if you logged all this output.

Prior to IPSO 3.5, you had to manually edit the crontab file on the system to make changes to cron, but in IPSO 3.5, 3.6 and later, you can schedule cron jobs through the Voyager Web interface (or via CLISH). Click **Job Scheduler** from the System Configuration heading in Voyager, and fill in the requested values in order to schedule a cron job. See Figure 5.20 for an example.

Figure 5.20 Configuring Crontab

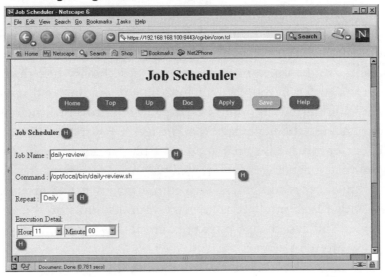

> **NOTE**
>
> To enable a new cron job through CLISH, use the following commands:
>   *Nokia>* **add cron job** *newjob* **command**
> */opt/local/bin/getfw1config.sh* **hour** *23* **minute** *55*
>   *Nokia>* **set cron job** *newjob* **on**
>   Then to delete the job type:
>   *Nokia>* **delete cron job** *newjob*

Summary

In this chapter, we have presented common tasks performed by system administrators on a regular basis in the context of the Nokia Security Platform. It will be necessary for you to perform many if not all of these tasks throughout the duration of your NSP ownership.

Knowing how to properly shut down or reboot your Nokia is very important. If you don't shut down a Nokia system cleanly, you could boot up with a damaged file system, which will require a console connection so that you can run *fsck* to repair the file system. It's simple to reboot or halt your Nokia system properly through the Voyager Web interface.

Nokia packages are additional, optional software packages that run on IPSO, such as Check Point FireWall-1 or ISS RealSecure. A tool is available through Voyager to easily install, upgrade, or remove software packages. It is also easy to back out of new packages simply by toggling the package on or off; thus you can move from one package version to another in no time. If you don't like your latest upgrade to NG FP3, you can back down to NG FP2 without losing any configuration data.

IPSO images are the operating system kernel and binary files that run the system. Voyager provides an interface for installing, upgrading, and removing images for easy administration of the OS. If you prefer to install new images from the command line, use the newimage tool. Images are stored in the /image directory, and the current image is symlinked to the file /image/current. After making changes to the image parameters in Voyager, you need to reboot the NSP.

Another common sys admin task is to administer users and groups. Voyager provides you with a Web interface to manage your accounts on the system from any Web browser. You can change passwords, create new users and groups, and delete accounts through Voyager.

Maintaining network routes can be configured through Voyager as well. Using the Static Routes configuration screen, you can add or remove your default gateway or router and configure static route entries one by one or through an easy quick-add text box where you can enter multiple routes at one time.

Every administrator should plan on getting system backups and have recovery action plans in place in the event of a disaster. Even if you have a simple hardware failure, a backup can make a big difference if you need to rebuild from scratch on a new box. Since your Nokia will usually sit at key points in your network, it is an important box to back up. Voyager provides you with a Web interface for making backups of your system configuration, user home directories, log files, and package configuration. Using this interface, you can FTP the backup files off the Nokia or download them for a restore. Check Point NG FP1 and FP2 backup scripts are missing or corrupted, so if you have these packages, read the preceding section to find out how to back up these important software packages.

Every task covered in this chapter is very important, and system logging is no exception. Fortunately, Nokia's Network Voyager has an administration tool for configuring system logging; you can use this tool to enable remote logging, receive logs from the network, and enable an audit log of Voyager configuration changes. You can monitor system logs via the /var/log/messages file, which is available through the Voyager monitor area, under the System Logs heading.

The final topic we covered in this chapter was configuring cron. Cron is used to schedule tasks for the system to run at specified times. Tasks could include running a custom written shell script to a system binary file. As long as the file is executable, the cron daemon will run the task. The /var/etc/crontab file holds the cron configuration, and it can be edited through Voyager's Job Scheduler link under the System Configuration heading. You can add or delete cron jobs through this interface, which is available in IPSO 3.5 and 3.6. Earlier IPSO releases would require that you manually edit the crontab file using the *crontab −e* command.

Solutions Fast Track

Rebooting the System

☑ It's important to shut down a UNIX system cleanly so that unsaved data is written to the disk and local filesystems are unmounted. If a system is not shut down cleanly, you might need to run */sbin/fsck −y* from the console to correct any file system damage.

☑ Use the command *reboot* to reboot your Nokia system from the command line.

☑ To reboot your system in Voyager, click the Reboot, Shut Down System link from the main Configuration screen.

☑ Use *halt* if you want to shut down the system in order to power down the NSP.

Managing Packages

☑ Packages can be installed or upgraded with ease using the Voyager Web interface. Simply choose the Manage Installed Packages link from the System Configuration heading. From there you can also enable, disable, and remove packages.

☑ Use the *newpkg −i* command to install or upgrade packages from the command line.

☑ It's easy to back out of a package upgrade simply by disabling the new package and enabling the old package through Voyager.

☑ Sometimes certain packages require certain IPSO images. Be sure to read all release notes before you begin.

Managing IPSO Images

☑ IPSO images can be upgraded through the Voyager Web interface by choosing the Install New IPSO Image (Upgrade) link from the System Configuration heading.

☑ Use the *newimage* command to upgrade to a new IPSO image on the command line.

☑ If you are running on IPSO 3.2.1 or earlier, upgrade to 3.3 before moving forward to newer versions. Starting with IPSO 3.4.x, bootmgr is upgraded automatically when needed.

☑ It's easy to back out of an IPSO image upgrade by simply selecting the old image from the Manage IPSO Images link under the System Configuration heading and then rebooting.

☑ The current image is linked to the file /image/current.

Managing Users and Groups

☑ The admin user has full privileges to the Nokia system, just like a root user in most UNIX systems.

☑ The monitor user exists as a read-only user. This user can log into Voyager and view all configuration parameters but can make no changes.

☑ You can create other users on the system. Giving a user a UID of 0 gives the user full privileges, just like the admin user.

☑ You can user Voyager to create groups in which to assign users. A user must be a member of the wheel group in order to use the *su* command on the system.

Configuring Static Routes

☑ Static routes can be added or removed from the Static Routes link under the Routing Configuration heading in Voyager.

☑ You can enter static routes one at a time, or you can enter a bunch of routes all at once using the Quick-add text box. The syntax of this command is *<network>/<bit mask> <next-hop router>/n*.

System Backup and Restore

☑ The default system configuration database is stored in the file /config/db/initial, and a symbolic link file /config/active points to this database. You can make backups of this database through the Manage Configuration Sets link under the System Configuration heading in Voyager.

☑ The Backup and Restore link under the System Configuration heading in Voyager allows you to make backups of system files, log files, user home directories and package configurations.

☑ You can FTP your backup files off the Nokia system or download backup files to restore through the Voyager Backup and Restore configuration tool.

☑ Starting with IPSO 3.5, you can schedule backups through the Voyager Web interface.

System Logging

☑ System logs are stored in /var/log/messages and contain information such as boot messages, SSH key info, user logins, and Voyager configuration changes, to name a few.

☑ You can send system logs to a remote syslog server. Logs are then sent via UDP port 514, and the level of logging you send is configurable in Voyager.

☑ The last setting available in the System Logging configuration screen under the System Configuration heading is Auditlogs, which allows you to log Voyager activities. Transient changes are any changes made when Apply is selected, and Permanent changes are recorded whenever Save is selected in Voyager.

Scheduling Tasks Using cron

☑ Cron is run as a daemon and uses the /var/etc/crontab file to schedule jobs monthly, daily, hourly, and even by the minute.

☑ Starting with IPSO 3.5, you can now schedule jobs with cron through the Voyager Web interface by selecting the Job Scheduler link under the System Configuration heading.

☑ Prior to IPSO 3.5, you had to manually edit cron with the *crontab –e* command.

Frequently Asked Questions

The following Frequently Asked Questions, answered by the authors of this book, are designed to both measure your understanding of the concepts presented in this chapter and to assist you with real-life implementation of these concepts. To have your questions about this chapter answered by the author, browse to **www.syngress.com/solutions** and click on the **"Ask the Author"** form.

Q: Why can't my internal LAN access the Internet? We have a choke router inside the firewall and two separate networks, 172.16.1.0/24 and 172.16.2.0/24, located behind the router.

A: If this is the first time you are connecting your Nokia into this position in your network, you might need to check several things. Start by looking at the physical connections, and ensure that you have a connection to the choke router from the firewall and that the firewall has access to the Internet. If you cannot ping (and firewall policies allow ICMP), check the cabling and speed/duplex settings on the equipment. If the connectivity is OK, make sure that your Nokia has static routes added and saved in the system configuration for these two networks. Verify that you can ping these networks from the firewall.

> The next thing to verify is that all equipment from the workstations to the firewall has the correct default routes configured that will take them to the next hop closest to the Internet. Your workstations should have a default gateway set to the choke router. The choke router should have a default route set to the Nokia. Finally, the Nokia should have a default route configured to your ISP's next-hop router. If everything is configured properly, your workstations should be able to ping the external interface of the Nokia or the ISP router all the way out to the Internet. By following these steps one by one, you should be able to determine the problem with access.

Q: When I use *crontab -e*, I am allowed to run jobs every few minutes if I want to with syntax such as 1,3,5,7,9. Does Voyager or CLISH allow me to do this?

A: No. You cannot schedule jobs more frequently than once per day in Voyager or CLISH without creating a separate job for each. Stick with *crontab -e* if you need this level of granularity.

Q: I noticed *crontab* *–e* dumps me into *Vi*. I hate *Vi*. Are there other editors available in IPSO?

A: No, *Emacs* is not available on IPSO. The line editor *ed* is available if you are brave, however.

Q: If I have a Nokia RemoteLink or VPN220, can I still run current IPSO software on it?

A: Yes, you can run newer IPSO software on these older hardware models. You can even turn your VPN220 into an IP series appliance with full features. See Nokia Resolution #10365 for details. Note that running VPN-1/FireWall-1 NG on hardware with less than 128MB of memory is not supported, however.

Q: I added a static route (or ARP) in Voyager, and it won't show up in the routing table or in Iclid. What's wrong?

A: If the route (or ARP) entry added is incorrect, it will not be displayed. You can troubleshoot this situation either by viewing the forwarding table through the Monitor interface in Voyager or by attempting to add the route on the command line to see what errors are associated with it. It could be that the specified next-hop router is unreachable.

## Chapter 6

Configuring the Check Point Firewall

Solutions in this chapter:

- **Preparing for the Configuration**

- **Configuring the Firewall**

- **Testing the Configuration**

- **Upgrading the Firewall**

☑ **Summary**

☑ **Solutions Fast Track**

☑ **Frequently Asked Questions**

Introduction

The Nokia NSP is, above all else, a firewall platform. Nokia made the choice to bundle Check Point's FireWall-1 with its product both for its stateful and secure technology and for its ease of administration. Nokia developers have been working very closely with Check Point, and in their commitment to further this relationship Nokia platforms have some added features that enhance FireWall-1 performance and its ability to be easily maintained.

You can order a Nokia box with Check Point preinstalled or you can download the installation package from Check Point (with appropriate login ID) and install it yourself. If you need to upgrade your IPSO before installing NG, you need to obtain the IPSO image from Nokia support. It might be necessary to upgrade your boot manager prior to upgrading your IPSO image as well. Please read all release notes prior to installing new packages or images. Nokia recommends that you do not upgrade from 4.1 to NG if you have less than 128MB of memory; instead, do a fresh install.

Nokia's IPSO 3.6 supports Check Point FireWall-1 NG Feature Packs 2 and 3. This chapter shows how to enable and configure your Nokia/Check Point firewall for first-time use. Certain key differences in Nokia's branded version of FireWall-1—differences that make your life as an administrator easier—are discussed. Testing the firewall installation and upgrading the firewall version or service pack are also discussed.

Preparing for the Configuration

Since the Nokia appliance is already hardened, there is very little you need to do to prepare it for firewall installation. You must configure and test networking and DNS and set up the Host Address Assignment through the Voyager GUI, and you might need to upgrade your IPSO and boot manager (see Chapter 5).

Ensure that you have the following ready before you begin configuring Check Point FireWall-1:

- Get your Check Point licenses.
- Configure routing and test network interface cards.
- Ensure IP forwarding is enabled (*ipsofwd on admin*).
- Configure Host Address Assignment.
- Ensure you have at least 128MB of memory and 40MB of free disk space on /opt.

- Read the Release Notes.
- Verify that your IPSO is compatible with VPN-1/FireWall-1 (see Table 6.1).

Table 6.1 FireWall-1/IPSO Compatibility

IPSO Version	VPN-1/FireWall-1 Compatibility
IPSO 3.2.x	4.0 any service pack and 4.1 up to SP2
IPSO 3.3 FCS3	4.1 SP2 and SP3
IPSO 3.3 FCS6, FCS8 (not to be used with IP530)	4.1 SP3
IPSO 3.3E FCS4 (not to be used with IP530)	4.1 SP3
IPSO 3.3.1 FCS7 (IP530 only)	4.1 SP3
IPSO 3.4	4.1 SP4
IPSO 3.4.1 FCS5a	4.1 SP5
IPSO 3.4.1 FCS10-FCS12	4.1 SP5a and SP6
IPSO 3.4.2	NG FP1
IPSO 3.5 FCS3	4.1 SP5a
IPSO 3.5 FCS6-FCS8	4.1 SP5a, SP6 and NG FP2
IPSO 3.5 FCS10	4.1 SP5a, SP6, NG FP2 and FP3
IPSO 3.6	NG FP2 and FP3

For the most recent FireWall-1/IPSO compatibility matrix, look up Nokia Resolution 11253.

Obtaining Licenses

Check Point licenses have changed (again) with the Next Generation release. This means that you cannot use an old 4.1 license when installing NG. If you have 4.1 licenses, don't worry—you can get your 4.1 cert keys upgraded to NG for no additional charge. In order to obtain licenses, you can either go through your Check Point value-added reseller (VAR) or use the Check Point User Center to license your products at http://usercenter.checkpoint.com.

You have two options when it comes to licensing your firewall modules. You can either have them tied to their individual IP addresses (external interface rec-ommended), as with previous versions, or you can tie them all to the management station's IP address. These licenses are called *local* or *central*, respectively. In NG the SecureUpdate management tool can be used to maintain all licenses on the management console.

The management module itself must have a local license based on its own IP address. The nice thing about using central licenses for the enforcement modules is that you can change their IP addresses without needing to replace the license, and you can easily move a license from one module to another.

It is always best to obtain your licenses before you install the firewall software. The program will ask you for your license details during the configuration procedure. If you cannot obtain your permanent license prior to the install, you should ask for an evaluation license. Check Point's eval licenses have full functionality for almost all VPN-1/FireWall-1 features. They are usually valid for one month, and the product is not crippled in any way while running on eval.

Configuring Your Hostname

If you followed the instructions in Chapter 4 for initial configuration of your Nokia Security Platform, you should already have your hostname configured for FireWall-1. If, however, you have jumped to this chapter, you need to know that your VPN-1/FireWall-1 configuration requires that you have your hostname mapped to your external IP address in the Host Address Assignment configuration screen, which you can access from the Voyager main Configuration screen under the System Configuration section. If this function is not configured ahead of time, your license installation will fail.

To add a new hostname, enter either the fully qualified domain name (FQDN) or the simple hostname in the field *Add new hostname*. We are using the name *gatekeeper*, which was the name assigned to this Nokia during initial system configuration. Next click **Apply**, and then type in the IP address associated with gatekeeper. This should be the IP address that you will use if licensing the FireWall-1 product on your Nokia as well, and it is typically the external IP address of the firewall. Click **Apply** again and then click **Save** to complete the host address assignment. See Figure 6.1 for the completed configuration.

Figure 6.1 Host Address Assignment

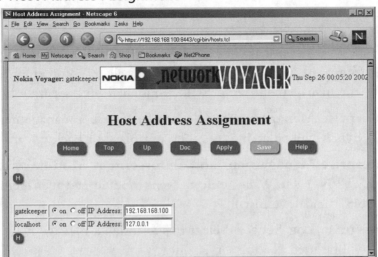

Understanding FireWall-1 Options

The following Check Point Next Generation packages are available:

- **VPN-1 & FireWall-1** Includes FireWall-1 Management module and enforcement point software along with the VPN-1 encryption component.

- **FloodGate-1** Provides an integrated QoS solution for VPN-1/ FireWall-1.

- **UserAuthority** A user authentication tool that integrates with FireWall-1, FloodGate-1, and other e-business applications.

- **VPN-1 SecureClient Policy Server** Allows an enforcement module to install granular desktop policies on mobile users' SecureClient personal firewalls.

- **Reporting Module** An integrated reporting tool that can generate reports, graphs, and pie charts to display information obtained from the VPN-1/FireWall-1 logs.

- **Real Time Monitor** Allows an organization to monitor its VPN connections, Internet connections, and so on.

- **4.1 Backward Compatibility** Allows you to support version 4.1 firewalls from an NG management server.

The VPN-1/FireWall-1 component options are:

- **Enforcement Module** Select this to install an enforcement module only; the management server will be installed on a separate host.

- **Enterprise Management** Select this to install a management server only, which will be acting in either a primary or backup capacity.

- **Enterprise Management and Enforcement Module** Used to install both a VPN-1/FireWall-1 enforcement module and management module (standalone install).

- **Enterprise Log Server** Select this to install a management module that will be used as a log server only.

- **Enforcement Module and Enterprise Log Server** Use this option to install both a VPN-1/FireWall-1 enforcement module as well as a management module that will be used only as a log server.

After the Check Point *cpconfig* utility sets up the type of installation you have chosen, it will run through a number of configuration screens. The screens that you can prepare for in advance are:

- **Licenses** You should read the section on licenses if you need help getting licenses. You will fill in the following fields:

  - **Host/IP Address** The IP address associated with this license or eval.

  - **Expiration Date** The date that the license expires, which may be never.

  - **SKU/Features** The features this license enables (for example, management or 3DES).

  - **String/Signature Key** The license string provided by Check Point to validate the license. This key will be unique for each license and IP address.

NOTE

If you are installing just an enforcement module, you will have no administrators or GUI clients to configure.

- **Administrators** You will need to configure at least one administrator during install.

    - **Administrator Name** Choose a login name for your admin. This field is case sensitive.

    - **Password** Choose a good alphanumeric password. It must be at least four characters long.

    - **Confirm Password** Repeat the same password entered in the previous step.

- **Management Clients** These are the IP addresses of the GUI clients that your administrators will use when connecting to this management module. You might need to configure static IP addresses for your administrators. You can add as many management clients as you'd like or you may enter none, it's up to you. See the following discussion for your Management Client options.

- **SIC Password** If you are installing an enforcement module only, you will be prompted for a password to initialize SIC. This password must also be entered in the configuration for the firewall object in the Policy Editor.

Configuring the Firewall

Next we want to take you through the configuration of Check Point FireWall-1 on your Nokia and introduce you to the way FireWall-1 protects your Nokia during system bootstrap. Before you can start the firewall (*cpstart*) for the first time, you need to have the package enabled in Voyager and run through the Check Point Configuration tool (*cpconfig*). It is during this initial configuration that you determine the type of Check Point installation you want to run on your NSP. You can choose to install a management server and/or enforcement module during this time. This section walks you through each step of the initial configuration screens and gives you some tips for disabling the default and initial policies, which might be problematic when you're doing remote maintenance.

Installing the Package

If you are starting with a fresh Nokia installation and have no previous Check Point packages installed, you need to start by installing the Check Point packages in IPSO. Instructions for installing packages can be found in Chapter 5, but here we guide you through a package installation of NG FP2 on a Nokia using the *newpkg* command. If your Nokia was shipped with the appropriate Check Point packages preinstalled, you should skip to the next section. If you want to upgrade a Check Point package, read the section "Upgrading the Firewall."

Begin by downloading the FP2 wrapper file onto your Nokia into the /var/admin directory. You can download it from Check Point or from one of its resellers. The FP2 wrapper package is simply a .tgz file that starts off by installing NG FP1 (SVN Foundation and VPN-1/FireWall-1) and then upgrades you to NG FP2. Some other packages will be installed as well, including the version 4.1 Backward Compatibility package, Policy Server, FloodGate-1, and Real Time Monitor. When the install is complete, the NG FP2 SVN and FireWall-1 package will be the only ones enabled.

If you're starting with the NG FP3 wrapper package instead, you won't get the other Feature Packs like the FP2 wrapper—just the FP3 version will be installed. The other packages bundled in with the FP3 wrapper include the 4.1 Backward Compatibility package, Policy Server, FloodGate-1, SmartView Monitor, and UserAuthority Server. Regardless of which wrapper package you choose, follow this procedure for installation:

1. Place the wrapper file in /var/admin. The filename will be something like CP_FP2_IPSO.tgz or CP_FP3_IPSO.tgz. Ensure that this is the only package in the /var/admin directory. Do not uncompress or untar the package.

2. From the /var/admin directory, type **newpkg –i**.

3. Choose **4** and press **Enter** at the prompt for installation method. This sequence will install the package from the local file system.

4. Next you will be prompted for the pathname to the package. Enter a single period (.) and press **Enter**. A single period or "dot" indicates the current working directory.

5. Now the install program will find the Check Point NG package and extract the necessary files for installation. You will be prompted with four options—to install, upgrade, skip, or exit. Enter **1** to install. At this time, the packages bundled in the wrapper will be installed. When the process is complete, you will again see the IPSO prompt. You can verify that the packages have been installed by logging into Voyager and viewing the Manage Installed Packages configuration screen.

6. Now you need to log out and log back into your IPSO session. This ensures that you get the new environment variables defined during the package installation. Without having these variables set, you cannot run cpconfig.

7. Run **cpconfig** and install a license. You can skip to the section on cpconfig later in this chapter for more help in this configuration tool.

8. Reboot your Nokia after running cpconfig by typing **reboot**.

Enabling the Package

Check Point packages are enabled just like any other packages on IPSO. In NG, you will always have at least two Check Point packages enabled at any time through the Manage Installed Packages configuration screen, the SVN Foundation, and the VPN-1/FireWall-1 NG package. Only one version of FireWall-1 can be active at any time. If all the Check Point packages are off, you should first enable the SVN Foundation (CPShared) package, then enable the Check Point VPN-1/FireWall-1 package, and then finally enable any other Check Point components (such as backward compatibility, Policy Server or FloodGate-1, and so on).

Follow these instructions to enable Check Point NG FP3 VPN-1/FireWall-1 in Nokia IPSO 3.6:

1. Log into Voyager and click **Config**.

2. Click **Manage Installed Packages** under the System Configuration section.

3. Toggle the **Check Point SVN Foundation** package to **On**.

4. Click **Apply**.

5. Now toggle the **Check Point VPN-1/FireWall-1** package to **On**.

6. Click **Apply** and then click **Save**.

If you need to disable Check Point packages at any time, follow the reverse procedure. Begin by disabling the Check Point VPN-1/FireWall-1 package and then the SVN Foundation. You cannot disable both of these packages simultaneously; you must turn them off one at a time.

Environment and Path

Check Point commands cannot be executed if you do not have the correct environment variables defined in your Nokia login session. Fortunately, during package installation these are configured for you in the file /var/etc/pm_profile. This profile is called from the .profile in your home directory, so whenever you login you will always have the necessary environment to run Check Point commands for installed packages.

Some of the environment variables that are modified when Check Point packages are installed are CPDIR, FWDIR, and PATH. The CPDIR variable tells you where the base SVN Foundation (CPShared) installation directory is located. The FWDIR similarly contains the value of the base VPN-1/FireWall-1 installation directory. An easy way to change directories into the firewall software is to use this FWDIR variable, since the directory names are sometimes quite long and hard to type in without making a mistake. In NG FP3, the variables are defined as follows. You can display the value of any variable by using the *echo* command and including a dollar sign in front of the variable name. For instance, to display the value of the CPDIR variable, type **echo $CPDIR**. The dollar sign ($) in front of a variable means *the value of*:

- CPDIR = /opt/CPshared-50-03

- FWDIR = /opt/CPfw1-50-03

- PATH = /bin:/sbin:/usr/bin:/usr/sbin:/usr/libexec:/etc:/opt/
  CPshared-50-03/bin:/opt/CPfw1-50-03/bin

VPN-1 and FireWall-1 Directory Structure

Within the VPN-1/FireWall-1 package directories, you have several subdirectories, each with its own purpose. Here we would like to highlight some of the most important directories and explain the types of files that you will find in each of them.

$FWDIR directories:

- **bin** Binary files and scripts, such as the *fw, fwd,* and *fwm* binaries and *fwstop/fwstart* scripts, to name a few.

- **boot** Boot configuration files are stored here, including the compiled default filter file.

- **conf** Configuration files, including your objects, rules, and user database.

- **database** Database information.

- **lib** Library files.

- **log** Log files are stored in this directory. On Nokia devices, this is usually a symbolic link to /var/fw/log.

- **spool** SMTP Security Server default spool directory.

- **state** FireWall-1 state information.

- **tmp** Temporary directory where the daemon pid files are located.

Within the conf directory, you will find the objects_5_0.C file, which holds
all your FireWall-1 objects and services. The rulebases_5_0.fws file contains all
your rules, and the fwauth.NDB★ files contain your user database. You'll also find
a gui–clients file here and either a masters or clients file if you have a distributed
installation. The $FWDIR/conf directory is always the most important directory
to back up.

Occasionally you might make changes to the files in the database or lib directory, and you should have a good backup of those as well. Whenever you upgrade
your Check Point software, these files will need to be modified again with those
changes. Sometimes hot fixes that are applied simply replace some files in lib,
such as table.def or base.def.

Your FireWall-1 log files should be maintained on a regular basis. Although
the configuration in the Policy Editor allows you to schedule log switches in
NG, certain log files will not be switched. Even if you are logging to a separate
management server, some log files will be growing in your Nokia's $FWDIR/log
directory. The security server logs such as ahttpd.elg, aftpd.elg, and asmtpd.elg will
be in there, and you'll find that some daemons, such as fwd, will log there as well
(for example, fwd.elg, mdq.elg, and fwm.elg). Most of the files that begin with
fw.★ will be part of the active log files. You could find that if your firewalls have
stopped logging to the management station and the management box isn't listening for incoming connections on TCP port 257 (verify with the command
netstat −an), you might need to run *cpstop* on the management console, move the
$FWDIR/log/fw.★ files, and then run *cpstart* to get things moving again.

The state directory contains the current FireWall-1 state information, and the
files here get updated whenever a policy is installed. At times you might need to
clear out the state directory while the firewall is stopped, to clear a persistent setting. The files in here will be recreated on the next policy install.

IP Forwarding and Firewall Policies

During the Nokia's boot cycle, IP forwarding is disabled. Check Point FireWall-1 will control IP forwarding by enabling it once its services are started. Also during the boot process, the firewall loads a default filter, which blocks all inbound access to the Nokia but allows all outgoing and broadcast packets. This filter is loaded into the kernel before the interfaces of the Nokia are configured. This ensures that there is never a time during the boot process that the machine is unprotected.

When FireWall-1 services start for the first time, a policy cannot be loaded, because the firewall has no saved state. When this happens, it will load an initial policy, which allows a GUI client connection but blocks all other communication. You cannot even ping the device while the initial policy is loaded. If at any other time the system reboots and the firewall cannot fetch a policy either from a management console or from its locally saved state, it will load the initial policy filter. In order to remove either a default or initial filter, you need to type **fw unloadlocal** or **fw unload localhost**, the latter if you have a version of FireWall-1 prior to NG FP2. Use the command *fw stat* to display the current policy that is loaded:

```
gatekeeper[admin]# fw stat
HOST        POLICY       DATE
localhost InitialPolicy 25Sep2002 23:02:21 :   [>eth-s3p1c0]
```

When FireWall-1 is stopped via *cpstop*, IP forwarding is disabled as well. Run *ipsofwd list* to see the current state of IP forwarding. The value of net:ip:forwarding will be 0 if forwarding is disabled and 1 if it is enabled. A filter is not loaded if the firewall services are stopped, so your system could be at risk. Here are some commands you can use to control these settings, with brief descriptions:

- **fwstop –default** Kills all firewall processes and loads the default filter.
- **fwstop –proc** Stops all firewall processes but allows the policy to remain in the kernel for simple accept, drop, and reject inspection.
- **fwstart –f** Starts FireWall-1 services.
- **control_bootsec –r** Removes boot security.
- **control_bootsec –g** Enables boot security.
- **fwboot bootconf** Sets IP forwarding and configures the default filter.

- **comp_init_policy −u** Disables the initial policy.
- **comp_init_policy −g** Enables the initial policy.

The default filter is defined in the $FWDIR/lib directory. In NG FP3, the default filters listed in Table 6.2 are available to choose from in that directory on Nokia. The default default filter (pun intended) is the defaultfilter.boot file.

Table 6.2 Default Filters in $FWDIR/lib

Filter file	Description
defaultfilter.boot	Allows outbound communication (originating from the firewall) and broadcast traffic only.
defaultfilter.dag	Allows outbound communication (originating from the firewall), broadcast traffic, and DHCP.
defaultfilter.drop	Drops everything.
defaultfilter.ipso	Allows SSH, SSL (port 443), and ping inbound and all outbound communication originating from the firewall.
defaultfilter.ipso_ssh	Allows SSH and ping inbound and all outbound communication originating from the firewall.
defaultfilter.ipso_ssl	Allows SSL (port 443) and ping inbound and all outbound communication originating from the firewall.

We personally like the way that the defaultfilter.ipso looks, since it allows SSH and SSL connections to the Nokia while the filter is loaded. Follow this procedure to change the default filter to the defaultfilter.ipso file instead:

1. Log into your Nokia and change directories to **$FWDIR/lib**. From here, copy the defaultfilter.ipso file to **$FWDIR/conf/defaultfilter.pf**.

2. Run **fw defaultgen** to compile the defaultfilter.pf file. The output file will be $FWDIR/state/default.bin. The output of this command is as follows:

```
gatekeeper[admin]# fw defaultgen
Generating default filter
defaultfilter:
Compiled OK.
Backing up default.bin as default.bin.bak
```

3. Copy the **$FWDIR/state/default.bin** file to the **$FWDIR/boot** directory. You can verify that the $FWDIR/boot directory is where the file belongs by printing the file path with the command **$FWDIR/boot/fwboot bootconf get_def**.

Tools & Traps…

Unload InitialPolicy Script

If you are doing a remote upgrade or install, you could run into trouble when you reboot at the end of the installation. Before a security policy is loaded, the system will install a filter, called InitialPolicy, which will block all access to the VPN-1/FireWall-1 host computer (except GUI access). You can log into the console and verify that the filter is loaded with the *fw stat* command:

```
gatekeeper[admin]# fw stat
HOST        POLICY        DATE
localhost InitialPolicy 25Sep2002 23:02:21 :   [>eth-s3p1c0]
```

If you have access to the console, log in as root and unload the filter with the following command:

```
# fw unloadlocal
```

If you do not have access to the console, you could write a shell script to unload the filter and enable it in cron. The various environment variables in /var/etc/pm_profile need to be defined. So, easily enough, we can call the pm_profile file from the unload.sh script. Even before you reboot, you can test that the script works by running it from the command line. Here's a sample unload.sh script that works for FireWall-1 NG FP3:

```
--------------------------------

#!/bin/sh


. /var/etc/pm_profile


$FWDIR/bin/fw unloadlocal

--------------------------------
```

Continued

To enter the script in cron, follow these steps.

1. Verify that you have enabled execute permissions on the file:

```
chmod +x unload.sh
```

2. Edit cron with the following command:

```
crontab -e
```

3. Finally, enter the following line into your crontab file (note this should be one line):

```
0,5,10,15,20,25,30,35,40,45,50,55 * * * * /var/admin/unload.sh >
/dev/null 2>&1
```

This command tells the system to run the unload.sh script every 5 minutes and redirect all output to /dev/null.

Now you can safely reboot the system and log back into it within a 5-minute period from the time it is booted. Don't forget to remove (or at least comment out) the crontab entry once you are back in the firewall.

Running cpconfig

If VPN-1/FireWall-1 NG is installed on your Nokia appliance, but it hasn't been configured yet, you must run cpconfig before attempting to start the new package. If you just received your Nokia fresh from the factory and NG is installed, you still need to run cpconfig before the package will run properly. This is because you must accept the license agreement, choose the components you want to run (management and/or enforcement module), and configure licenses, administrators, GUI clients, and the like.

When you run cpconfig, you must be logged in either through the console or remote login, and your environment variables must be set as described earlier. Then, all you need to do to begin the configuration is to enter the command **cpconfig** and press **Enter**. The very first time the command is run, it will ask you to accept the licensing agreement and then take you through the configuration wizard, prompting you for input at each stage. The configuration options could be a little different depending on your choices along the way, such as whether you decide to install a management module and/or firewall module on the system.

Let's assume that we are installing both management and module on a standalone system. Here is a list of steps to configure your Nokia system:

1. Log into your Nokia and run **cpconfig**.

2. Press **Enter** to read the license agreement, pressing **Spacebar** to continue until you reach the end, and then enter **y** to accept the terms and continue.

3. Next you are prompted for the type of installation you want on your NSP. To run both a management console and firewall module on this box, select option **3**.

4. If this is to be a primary management console (as opposed to a backup), press **Enter** to accept the default value of **1** at this next prompt. You will see some messages about the firewall controlling IP forwarding and loading a default filter. See Figure 6.2.

Figure 6.2 Initial Configuration

```
gatekeeper[admin]# cpconfig


Welcome to Check Point Configuration Program
=================================================
Please read the following license agreement.
Hit 'ENTER' to continue...


This End-user License Agreement (the "Agreement") is an agreement between
you (both the individual installing the Product and any legal entity on
whose behalf such individual is acting) (hereinafter "You" or " Your") and
 Check Point Software Technologies Ltd. (hereinafter "Check Point").
…


Do you accept all the terms of this license agreement (y/n) ? y


Select installation type:
------------------------


(1) Enforcement Module.
(2) Enterprise Management.
(3) Enterprise Management and Enforcement Module.
```

Continued

Figure 6.2 Continued

```
(4) Enterprise Log Server.
(5) Enforcement Module and Enterprise Log Server.


Enter your selection  (1-5/a-abort) [1]: 3
Please select Management type:
-----------------------------


(1) Enterprise Primary Management.
(2) Enterprise Secondary Management.


Enter your selection  (1-2/a-abort) [1]:
IP forwarding disabled
Hardening OS Security: IP forwarding will be disabled during boot.
Generating default filter
Default Filter installed
Hardening OS Security: Default Filter will be applied during boot.
This program will guide you through several steps where you
will define your Check Point products configuration.
At any later time, you can reconfigure these parameters by
running cpconfig
```

Licenses

The license configuration option will be displayed regardless of which modules you have installed. Since we have installed a primary management module, we should be installing a local license that was registered with the local management station's IP address. Follow this step-by-step procedure for adding your license(s). You can see the license configuration input and output outlined in Figure 6.3:

1. When prompted to add licenses, enter **y** for *yes* and press **Enter**.

2. Enter **m** to add the license manually and then press **Enter**. Now you will be prompted for each field of the license. Figure 6.3 shows the following license installed: cplic putlic eval 01Oct2002 dNrP4oprA-3MGjFUa69-PiNHuuHoa-4CyJa5yjk CPMP-EVAL-1-3DES-NG CK-CP. The license components are as follows:

- **Host** The IP address or hostid associated with this license or the word *eval*.

- **Date** The date that the license expires, which may be never.

- **String** The license string provided by Check Point to validate the license. This key will be unique for each license and IP address/host.

- **Features** These are the features this license will enable (for example, management and/or 3DES).

As you can see in Figure 6.3, you also have the option of choosing **f** for [F]etch from file. If you select this option, the configuration will prompt you to enter the filename.

3. Enter the values for Host, Date, String, and Features, pressing **Enter** after each entry.

Figure 6.3 Configuring Licenses

```
Configuring Licenses...
=======================
Host                  Expiration  Signature                    Features


Note: The recommended way of managing licenses is using SmartUpdate.
cpconfig can be used to manage local licenses only on this machine.


Do you want to add licenses (y/n) [y] ?

Do you want to add licenses [M]anually or [F]etch from file: m
IP Address: eval
Expiration Date: 01Oct2002
Signature Key: dNrP4oprA-3MGjFUa69-PiNHuuHoa-4CyJa5yjk
SKU/Features: CPMP-EVAL-1-3DES-NG CK-CP


License was added successfully
```

Administrators

If you have installed a management module, as soon as you enter a license into the configuration program, it will move on to the next setting, which will be to add an administrator. You must define at least one administrator at this time. You can always come back later to add, edit, or delete your administrators. Figure 6.4 displays the steps involved to add your administrator.

> **NOTE**
>
> If you have installed an enforcement module only, you will **not** configure administrators.

It is best to use individual admin usernames instead of a generic username such as *fwadmin*. The problem with using a generic login ID is that you cannot properly audit the activities of the firewall administrators. When you are troubleshooting a problem, it might be important for you to know who installed the last security policy. This becomes more and more important when there are several people administering a firewall system. The fields that you need to fill in are as follows:

- **Administrator Name** Choose a login name for your administrator. This field is case sensitive.

- **Password** Choose a good alphanumeric password. It must be at least four characters long and is also case sensitive.

- **Verify Password** Repeat the same password entered above.

- **Permissions for all Management Clients (Read/[W]rite All, [R]ead Only All, [C]ustomized)**

- **Permission to manage administrators (Yes or No)**

Figure 6.4 Adding an Administrator

```
Configuring Administrators...

===============================

No Check Point Administrators are currently

defined for this Management Station.
```

Continued

Figure 6.4 Continued

```
Do you want to add administrators (y/n) [y] ?
Administrator name: Cherie
Password:
Verify Password:
Permissions for all Management Clients (Read/[W]rite All, [R]ead Only All,
    [C]ustomized) w
Permission to Manage Administrators ([Y]es, [N]o) y

Administrator Cherie was added successfully and has
Read/Write Permission for all Management Clients

Add another one (y/n) [n] ?
```

Setting permissions allows you to define the access level that you will require on an individual basis for each administrator. If you select Read/[**W**]rite All or [**R**]ead Only All, your admin will have access to all the available GUI client features with the ability to either make changes and updates or view the configuration and logs (perhaps for troubleshooting purposes), respectively. You may also choose to customize access so that administrators may be able to update some things and not others. To do this, select **Customized** and configure each of these options. Here are descriptions of each feature listed in Figure 6.5:

- **SmartUpdate** This GUI tool allows you to manage licenses and update remote modules.

- **Check Point Users Database** Allows you to manage users through the SmartDashboard.

- **LDAP Users Database** Allows you to manage LDAP users through SmartDashboard.

- **Security Policy** Allows you to manage the Security Policy tab in the SmartDashboard.

- **QoS Policy** Allows you to manage the QoS (FloodGate-1) bandwidth management policy in the SmartDashboard.

- **Monitoring** Enables access to the Log Viewer, System Status, and Traffic Monitoring GUI clients (a.k.a. SmartView Tracker, SmartView Status, and SmartView Monitor in FP3).

Figure 6.5 Setting Customized Permissions

```
Permissions for all Management Clients (Read/[W]rite All, [R]ead Only
    All, [C]ustomized) c
        Permission for SmartUpdate (Read/[W]rite, [R]ead Only, [N]one) r
        Permission for Check Point Users Database (Read/[W]rite, [R]ead
            Only) w
        Permission for LDAP Users Database (Read/[W]rite, [R]ead Only,
            [N]one) r
        Permission for Security Policy (Read/[W]rite, [R]ead Only,
            [N]one) w
        Permission for QoS Policy (Read/[W]rite, [R]ead Only, [N]one) n
        Permission for Monitoring (Read/[W]rite, [R]ead Only, [N]one) w

Administrator Cherie was added successfully and has
Read Only Permission for SmartUpdate
Read/Write Permission for Check Point Users Database
Read Only Permission for LDAP Users Database
Read/Write Permission for Security Policy
Read/Write Permission for Monitoring
```

Management Clients

The management clients (also called *GUI clients*) are installed on either Windows or Solaris (X-Motif). These clients can be installed on as many desktops as you like, but before they can connect to the management server, you need to enter their IP addresses into the Management Clients configuration tool (see Figure 6.6). You can use this feature, for example, if you install the GUI clients on your own workstation to enable you to control the management server from your PC. This will allow you to connect remotely to manage the Security Policy and view your logs and system status. You do not need to configure any clients at all during the install, but if you are already prepared for this step, you may enter as many clients into this window as necessary. This client info will be saved in a file on your firewall under $FWDIR/conf and will be named *gui-clients*. This is a text file and can be edited directly, or you can bring up this Management Clients window at any time in the future by running cpconfig.

NOTE

If you have installed an enforcement module only, you will not configure GUI clients.

Figure 6.6 Configuring Management Clients

```
Configuring Management Clients...
====================================
Management clients are trusted hosts from which
Administrators are allowed to log on to this Management Station
using Windows/X-Motif GUI.

No Management clients defined

Do you want to add a Management client (y/n) [y] ?
Please enter the list hosts that will be Management clients.
Enter hostname or IP address, one per line, terminating with CTRL-D or
    your EOF character.
192.168.168.3
Is this correct (y/n) [y] ?
```

As you enter GUI clients into this configuration, you type their hostname or IP address, one per line, pressing **Enter** at the end of each. When you are done editing the client list, press **Ctrl + D** to send an end-of-file (EOF) control character to the program to continue.

You are allowed to use wildcards in each GUI client host specification as follows:

- **Any** If you type in the word **Any**, you will allow anyone to connect without restriction (not recommended).

- **Asterisks** You may use asterisks in the hostname, such as 10.10.20.*, which means any host in the 10.10.20.0/24 network; *.domainname.com means any hostname within the domainname.com domain.

- **Ranges** You may use a dash (–) to represent a range of IP addresses, such as 1.1.1.3–1.1.1.7, which means the five hosts including 1.1.1.3 and 1.1.1.7 and every one in between.

- **DNS or WINS resolvable hostnames**

Figure 6.7 displays an example of the configured GUI clients window with various options that you can use for your GUI Client entries. We recommend staying away from using hostnames or domain names, however, since it requires DNS to be configured and working on the firewall. Specifying IP addresses is the best method since it docsn't rely on resolving and will continue to work even if you cannot reach your DNS name servers from the firewall.

Figure 6.7 Management Client Wildcards

```
Please enter the list hosts that will be Management clients.
Enter hostname or IP address, one per line, terminating with CTRL-D or
    your EOF character.
*.integralis.com
1.1.1.3-1.1.1.7
10.10.10.2
10.10.10.3
10.10.20.*
backwatcher.com
noc.activis.com
Is this correct (y/n) [y] ? y
```

Certificate Authority Initialization

Your management server will be a certificate authority for your firewall enforcement modules and will use certificates for Secure Internal Communication (SIC). This is the step in the installation process where the management server's CA is configured and a certificate is generated for the server and its components.

You will be presented with the Random Pool configuration option, where you are asked to input random text until you hear a beep. The timing latency between your key presses will be used to generate cryptographic data, so it is recommended that you enter the data at a random pace, so that some keystrokes are close together and others have a longer pause between them. The more random the key-press intervals, the more unlikely that the input could be duplicated. If the system determines that the keystrokes are not random enough, it will not take them as input and will display an asterisk to the right of the progression bar.

NOTE

The Random Pool configuration screen will also be presented to you if you have installed an enforcement module only so that you can generate an internal certificate for SIC.

Type random characters at random intervals into the Random Pool until the progress bar is full and the message "Thank you!" appears at the bottom of the window, as shown in Figure 6.8. The next step is to initialize the internal CA for SIC. It could take a minute for the CA to initialize. Figure 6.9 displays the messages you will receive on the console while configuring the CA. Press **Enter** to initialize the CA.

Figure 6.8 Random Pool

```
Configuring Random Pool...
============================
You are now asked to perform a short random keystroke session.
The random data collected in this session will be used in
various cryptographic operations.

Please enter random text containing at least six different
characters. You will see the '*' symbol after keystrokes that
are too fast or too similar to preceding keystrokes. These
keystrokes will be ignored.

Please keep typing until you hear the beep and the bar is full.

    [...................]

Thank you.
```

Figure 6.9 Configuring Certificate Authority

```
Configuring Certificate Authority...
======================================
The system uses an Internal Certificate Authority
to provide Secured Internal Communication (SIC) certificates
for the components in your system.

Note that your components will not be able to communicate
with each other until the Certificate Authority is initialized
and they have their SIC certificate.

Press 'Enter' to initialize the Certificate Authority...
Internal Certificate Authority created successfully
Certificate was created successfully
Certificate Authority initialization ended successfully
```

Once the CA is initialized successfully, you will be prompted to enter and send the FQDN of the management server to the internal CA (ICA). This name must be correct for the ICA to function properly and cannot be changed once it is input to the ICA. The following steps can be used to generate the FQDN shown in Figure 6.10 for this cpconfig setting:

1. Type **y** and press **Enter** to define the FQDN now.
2. The current FQDN obtained from the system is displayed. Enter **y** if you want to change it.
3. Enter the value of the FQDN (for example, gatekeeper.nokia.com).
4. Enter **y** if you are sure you typed the value correctly.
5. Now press **Enter** to send the FQDN to the CA.

Figure 6.10 Sending the FQDN to the ICA

```
The FQDN (Fully Qualified Domain Name) of this Management Server
is required for proper operation of the Internal Certificate Authority.

Would you like to define it now (y/n) [y] ?
The FQDN of this Management Server is gatekeeper
```

Continued

Figure 6.10 Continued

```
Do you want to change it (y/n) [n] ?

Warning: The FQDN might be incorrect!
Make sure it contains the host name and the domain name.

NOTE: If the FQDN is incorrect, the Internal CA cannot function properly,
and CRL retrieval will be impossible.

Are you sure gatekeeper is the FQDN of this machine (y/n) [n] ?
Do you want to change it (y/n) [n] ? y

Please enter the FQDN (Fully Qualified Domain Name) of this management:
    gatekeeper.nokia.com

Are you sure gatekeeper.nokia.com is the FQDN of this machine (y/n) [n] ? y

Press 'Enter' to send it to the Certificate Authority...

Trying to contact CA. It can take up to 4 seconds...
 FQDN initialized successfully

The FQDN was successfully sent to the CA
```

Finally, you will be presented with the fingerprint of the management server. This fingerprint is unique to your CA and the certificate on your server. The first time your GUI clients connect to the management server, they will receive the fingerprint so that they can match it to the string listed here and verify that they are connecting to the correct manager. After the first connection, every time the clients connect to the management server, the fingerprint is verified. If the fingerprints don't match, a warning message will be displayed, and the administrator can decide whether or not to continue with the connection. This transaction is displayed in Figure 6.11:

1. When prompted by cpconfig, "Do you want to save it to a file?" as shown in Figure 6.11, type **y** and press **Enter** to save the fingerprint to a file.

2. Type the filename and press **Enter**. The file will be saved in
    $CPDIR/conf.

3. Enter **y** to confirm.

Figure 6.11 Saving the Certificate Fingerprint

```
Configuring Certificate's Fingerprint...

===========================================

The following text is the fingerprint of this Management machine:

CARR HOST MEEK FORD ROOM MATH LAIN HOWE BOY SITU SLUM BALM


Do you want to save it to a file? (y/n) [y] ?


Please enter the file name [/opt/CPshared-50-03/conf]: fingerprint.txt


The fingerprint will be saved as /opt/CPshared-50-03/conf/fingerprint.txt.
Are you sure? (y/n) [n] ? y


The fingerprint was successfully saved.
```

Installation Complete

When the configuration program ends, you might see on the screen a few messages such as "generating GUI-clients INSPECT code" as the system finishes the
installation of the VPN-1/FireWall-1 package. Finally, you will receive the following question: "Would you like to reboot the machine [y/n]?" (shown in Figure
6.12). If you elect not to reboot, you will exit the installation and go back to a
shell prompt. If you choose to reboot, the system will be restarted immediately.

> **WARNING**
>
> If you are remotely connected to this firewall, you will not have access
> after rebooting. The firewall loads a policy named InitialPolicy, which pre-
> vents all access after an install. See the sidebar "Unload InitialPolicy
> Script" for a workaround.

Figure 6.12 Installation Complete

```
generating GUI-clients INSPECT code
initial_management:
Compiled OK.

Hardening OS Security: Initial policy will be applied
until the first policy is installed

In order to complete the installation
you must reboot the machine.
Do you want to reboot? (y/n) [y] ?
```

Getting Back to Configuration

Now that installation is complete, you might need to get back into the configuration screens that you ran through with cpconfig. You can add, modify, or delete any of the previous configuration settings by running cpconfig at any time from the command line. Each screen that you ran through during the initial configuration will now be listed as a menu item, as shown in Figure 6.13.

Figure 6.13 cpconfig

```
gatekeeper[admin]# cpconfig
This program will let you re-configure
your Check Point products configuration.



Configuration Options:
----------------------
(1)   Licenses
(2)   Administrators
(3)   Management Clients
(4)   SNMP Extension
(5)   PKCS#11 Token
(6)   Random Pool
(7)   Certificate Authority
(8)   Automatic start of Check Point Products
```

Continued

Figure 6.13 Continued

```
(9) Exit

Enter your choice (1-9) :
```

Three options listed here did not come up during the initial installation process. Option 4 configures the SNMP Extension. By default, the Check Point module's SNMP daemon is disabled, but if you want to export SNMP MIBS to network monitors, you can use this option to enable SNMP in FireWall-1. Option 5 in the cpconfig output configures a PKCS#11 token that allows you to install an add-on card such as an accelerator card; option 8 allows you to configure the automatic start of Check Point modules at boot time. By default, the Check Point FireWall-1 product will start automatically on reboot.

If you installed an enforcement module only, the cpconfig screens will be a little different. There will be two new choices, which are:

- **Secure Internal Communication** Enables a one-time password that will be used for authentication between this enforcement module and its management server as well as any other remote modules that it might communicate with.

- **High Availability** Allows you to enable this enforcement module to participate in a Check Point High Availability (CPHA) configuration with one or more other enforcement modules. This tab will not show up in your installation since you cannot have a management module installed on an enforcement module in a CPHA cluster.

Testing the Configuration

Now that the FireWall-1 package is configured and you have rebooted your Nokia, it's time to test access to the firewall so you can configure and install security policies. We want to make sure that our firewall is installed and configured correctly, and testing the basic administrative firewall tasks is an easy way to verify that fact. This is particularly important after we have performed an upgrade between major versions (such as 4.1 to NG). We will test GUI client access as well as defining and installing a basic policy. For the sake of completeness, we will test both the pushing and fetching of our security policy.

Testing GUI client access

After you have the Check Point packages installed, enabled, and configured, you can begin configuring a security policy for your Nokia firewall. Even if the InitialPolicy is loaded, you should be able to connect with a GUI client and push a policy. If you have any trouble with this process, unload the default filter with *fw unloadlocal* (prior to NG FP2 the command was *fw unload localhost*). You can run the management clients on the following operating systems:

- Windows 98/ME

- Windows XP (Home or Professional)

- Windows 2000 SP1 or SP2 (Professional, Server, or Advanced Server)

- Windows NT SP6a (Workstation or Server)

- Solaris 8 (32 or 64 bit—note that running the GUI on Solaris requires a Motif license)

If you are running a firewall prior to NG FP3, you will be logging into the Check Point Policy Editor to manage security policies. In NG FP3, the name of the editor has been changed to *SmartDashboard*. The FP3 SmartDashboard doesn't look much different from the FP2 interface, so we will use the FP3 smart clients in our examples. On Windows, begin by going to **Start | Programs | Check Point SMART Clients | SmartDashboard NG FP3**. You will be presented with a login prompt like the one in Figure 6.14.

Figure 6.14 SmartDashboard Login

To log in the first time, enter your username, password, and management server IP address. If you are connecting to the Nokia as the management server, enter the IP address of the interface that is closest to you (it could be the internal IP or SSN IP) in the Management Server box. As the client connects, you will be presented with the management server's fingerprint that was generated during the initial configuration procedure. You should match the fingerprint in the client to the fingerprint on the management server to verify that you are connecting to the correct machine (see Figure 6.15). If it matches, click the **Approve** button to continue logging into the management server.

Figure 6.15 Fingerprint Identification

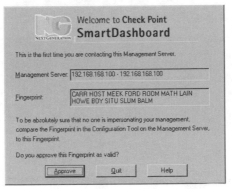

If the fingerprint changes because you reinstalled the management server software, put in new hardware as a replacement for the old management server, or regenerated the ICA certificate, you will receive a warning similar to the one displayed in Figure 6.16. Again, you should verify the fingerprint before accepting the new one.

Figure 6.16 Fingerprint Warning

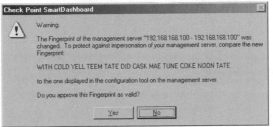

As long as the fingerprint remains the same, you will get no message after the first acceptance. Behind the scenes, Check Point will verify that the fingerprint matches. After you pass authentication and accept the fingerprint, you will see the SmartDashboard window, as shown in Figure 6.17. From here you can view and manage your network objects and policies. Initially, you will have a single object configured to represent your firewall, which NG creates for you during installation. See Figure 6.18.

Figure 6.17 Check Point SmartDashboard

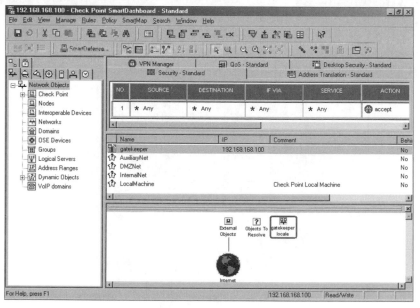

Figure 6.18 Check Point Gateway Object

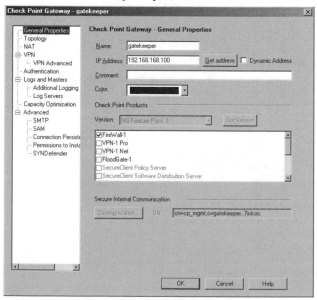

NOTE

In NG FP2 and FP3, you can now select a check box to log into your management clients in demo mode. Previously, you would need to log in with the management server field set to *local to run the demo. Also new in FP3 is the ability to select a management server from a pull-down list. This is a really nice feature if you normally manage multiple management servers, since each time you type in a new server, it is added to the list.

You should verify that your firewall object is configured properly before you try to push a policy. To edit your firewall object, click **Manage** in the main menu and select **Network Objects**. Highlight the firewall object and click **Edit**. Check that the correct IP address is entered in the General Properties tab. The IP entered here should correspond to the external IP address of your firewall, which is the same IP address that you use for a local license on the firewall. Modify the Check Point products installed to include the options that the installation didn't select for you, such as VPN-1, FloodGate-1, and so on. Also verify that the Topology tab is configured with the correct information about your firewall.

NOTE

If you have a distributed installation, you need to create the firewall object for you Nokia. It will not be created for you as it was in our previous example.

When you are finished editing your firewall object, click **OK**. Now you can begin creating all the other network objects that you will need to use in your Security Policy. Using these network objects, you will create a rule base in the Security tab of the SmartDashboard. Here we put in a simple "accept-all" policy to show you the procedure. Do not use an accept-all policy on your firewall, since a policy like this will provide you with no protection.

Begin by clicking the **Rules** menu option and select **Add Rule | Top**. This will enter the default rule, any source, destination, or service to drop without logging. Right-click the **Action** cell and select **Accept**. Then right-click the Track cell and select **Log**.

Now choose the **File** menu and **Save** the policy. The policy is named *Standard* by default and is defined in Figure 6.17.

Pushing and Fetching Policy

Now you are ready to test pushing a policy to your Nokia firewall. From the SmartDashboard, click the **Policy** menu and choose **Install**. Your objects, rules, and users will be saved at this time. If this is the first time you are installing a policy, you will receive a warning message like the one displayed in Figure 6.19 until you click the box to stop showing the message. This message simply informs you that there are some rules that are defined through the Global Properties that can be configured through the Policy menu. These rules are "implicit" rules and are not visible in your Security Policy window. You can make these rules visible by selecting **Implied Rules** from the **View** menu. Check the box so that you don't see this message again, and click **OK** to continue.

Figure 6.19 SmartDashboard Warning

Next you will receive a policy install window where you need to select the type of policy you will install on certain Check Point objects (see Figure 6.20). If you have multiple firewalls, they will all be displayed in this window. If you are installing to a standalone Nokia, accept the default values and click **OK** to begin the installation process. (By *standalone* we mean a VPN-1/FireWall-1 management server and enforcement module installed on a single platform—in other words, the opposite of a distributed installation.)

Now your management server will verify the rule base, compile the security policy, and push the policy to the firewall module. An installation process status window will be displayed, similar to the one in Figure 6.21. Now you must wait for the installation to complete. When the installation is done, the Close button will light up and the status will change to a green check mark if the install was successful. There could be warnings associated with the policy installation, and in that case a red exclamation point (!) will accompany the check mark, as shown in Figure 6.22. This installation window is new in NG FP3.

Figure 6.20 Policy Installation Targets

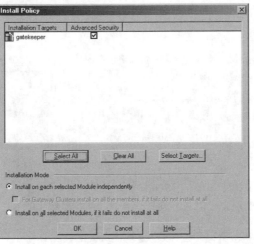

Figure 6.21 Installation Process

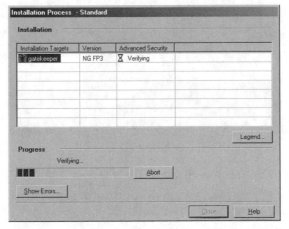

If you receive warnings or errors on the installation, you can view these messages by clicking the button labeled **Show Warnings**, as displayed in Figure 6.22. If you have not yet configured antispoofing on your gateway's interfaces, you will always receive these warnings on a policy install. You could also have a warning about your license, if it will expire in less than a week. See the errors from the install in Figure 6.23.

Figure 6.22 Installation Succeeded

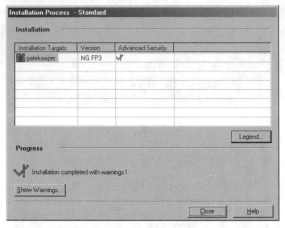

Figure 6.23 Verification and Installation Errors

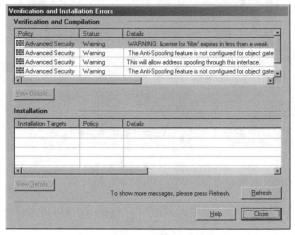

Other status options may be displayed in the Installation Process window. On this page Check Point provides a Legend button that pops up a quick explanation on each of the possible status icons you could receive (see Figure 6.24).

If the policy installation was successful, you are done. You can continue to modify and install your policy as many times as is necessary to completely define a security policy for your organization. If policy installation fails for some reason, try some of these steps:

- Verify that the firewall process is running on the module with the command *ps –auxw | grep fw*.

- Try unloading the policy from the console with the command *fw unload-local*, then try reinstalling the policy from the management server.

- Ensure that there is network connectivity between the management server and the module. Check cables and test with ping.

- Check that SIC is configured properly. Look at http://support.checkpoint .com/kb/docs/public/firewall1/5_0/pdf/sic.pdf for assistance.

Figure 6.24 Status Icon Legend

Once you are set up to push a policy successfully, you will want to verify that the firewall can fetch a policy from the management station. The Nokia will attempt to fetch a policy on system startup or whenever the firewall module is restarted. To force the Nokia to fetch a policy, use the *fw fetch* command. Available switches for this command are listed in Table 6.3. Type **fw fetch localhost** to load the last policy installed or **fw fetch master1** to fetch from the management host defined as master1 in the $FWDIR/conf/masters file.

Table 6.3 fw fetch Syntax

Switch	Description
-n	Fetches a policy from the management server and only loads the policy if it is different from the current policy loaded.
-f <filename>	Fetches a policy from the management server listed in *<filename>*. If no filename is specified, uses the $FWDIR/conf/masters file.
-i	Ignores the SIC information, such as SIC names.

Configuring & Implementing…

FireWall-1 Command Line

The following are some other useful FireWall-1 commands that you might find handy while configuring Check Point on your Nokia firewall. Some of these have been discussed throughout the chapter:

- **cpstop** Stops all Check Point products and the SVN Foundation.
- **cpstart** Starts the SVN Foundation and all Check Point products.
- **cplic print** Prints the currently installed licenses.
- **cplic put** Adds a license.
- **fw tab –t connections –s** Lists the number of connections in the FireWall-1 connections table.
- **fw ver** Displays the version of VPN-1/FireWall-1. Use the *–k* switch to see the kernel version.
- **fw stat** Lists the currently loaded policy, date the policy was last installed, and the interface and direction that the security policy is enforcing.
- **fw unloadlocal** Unloads the current security policy so that no policy is loaded.
- **fw load** When run on the management console, this can push a policy from command line to a remote module.
- **fw lichosts** Displays the hosts that are protected by your firewall, when a limited license is installed.
- **fwstop –default** Stops all VPN-1/FireWall-1 services and loads the default filter into the kernel.
- **fwstop –proc** Stops all VPN-1/FireWall-1 services, but keeps the policy loaded in the kernel. Only simple accept, drop, and reject control decisions will be made.
- **fwstart –f** Starts the VPN-1/FireWall-1 services.

Upgrading the Firewall

This section is dedicated to upgrading your FireWall-1 software on your NSP. We'll start by assuming that you are running FireWall-1 4.1 SP-6 on IPSO 3.4.1 FCS10 or later. If you are on a prior version of FireWall-1 4.1, you should start by upgrading your IPSO to the latest 3.4.1 and then upgrading to SP-6. If you are on FireWall-1 4.0, you need to upgrade to 4.1 before upgrading to NG. Don't get overzealous; be careful and take small steps, and you will be better off in the long run. You can upgrade from 4.1 SP-6 to NG FP1, FP2, or FP3. We recommend that you first go to the FP2 bundle (which actually installs the FP1 packages as well) before moving on to newer Feature Packs.

The first thing you should do once you are on 4.1 SP-6 is to run your configuration through one of the upgrade verification tools that Check Point provides. This might catch errors that could cause the upgrade to fail or cause the resulting configuration to be unusable after the upgrade. There is a tarball named upgrade_verifiers_NG_FP2_nokia.tgz for IPSO 3.4.x and 3.5 and associated release notes. You should only run this on your Nokia if you have a management server installed. This script checks the $FWDIR/conf directory on your management console. Download this bundle to your Nokia management server and gunzip and untar it into its own directory. You can obtain this file from www.checkpoint.com/techsupport/downloadsng/utilities.html#upgrade_verify:

1. If the upgrade_verifiers_NG_FP2_Nokia.tgz file is in your /var/admin directory, create a subdirectory and put it in there: **mkdir upgrade_verifiers; mv upgrade_verifiers_* upgrade_verifiers; cd upgrade_verifiers**

2. Now run **gunzip *** to uncompress the file.

3. Extract the tarball with the command **tar –xvf upgrade***.

4. Run the pre_upgrade_verifier script with the following syntax: **pre_upgrade_verifier –p $FWDIR –c 4.1 –t NG_FP2 –f upgrade.txt**.

5. Look into the upgrade.txt file to determine what you might need to change before beginning the upgrade process.

Remember to read any release notes before you begin the upgrade procedure. You could have certain configuration options that require special attention before you begin upgrading. Here's a brief list of some common configuration issues that you will need to resolve in 4.1 before you install NG FP2 or later:

- Disable all FWZ configurations. NG FP2 and later no longer support FWZ for VPNs.

- Disable objects that have certificates configured for Hybrid IKE. You might even be better off to delete these objects and recreate them once you've upgraded to NG.

- Disable any SKIP or manual IPSec VPN configurations. Only IKE is supported in NG FP2 and FP3.

- Ensure that your firewall object names match exactly the hostname of the firewall modules. This name mapping should be in the hosts file on both the management and firewall modules as well. You cannot change the hostname or object name once you have upgraded to NG due to the certificates' dependence on this information.

Upgrading from 4.1 SP6 to NG FP2

If you have a separate management server, always make sure that you upgrade that management server before you upgrade any firewall modules. Once you are confident that you are ready to upgrade to NG, download the NG FP2 or FP3 wrapper package to your Nokia and follow the instructions provided. Here we use the NG FP2 wrapper for demonstration, and we recommend that you go to FP2 before FP3 to ensure that your configuration is merged successfully at each step. You can follow this procedure whether your Nokia is a standalone or distributed installation:

1. Since you are on IPSO 3.4.1, the first thing you need to do is upgrade your IPSO image to the latest 3.6 release. See instructions on upgrading IPSO images in Chapter 5.

2. Start now with the wrapper package for NG FP2 named CP_FP2_IPSO.tgz. Ensure that this is the only package in your /var/admin directory before you begin. Then run **newpkg –i** from the /var/admin directory.

3. Press **4** and then press **Enter** to install from the local file system.

4. When asked to enter a pathname to the package, simply enter a single dot (**.**) and press **Enter**.

5. Now choose **2** and press **Enter** to upgrade from an old package.

6. Choose the **FireWall-1-strong.v4.1.SP-6 - Check Point FireWall-1 (Strong) Version 4.1 SP-6 (Wed May 15 16:10:58 IDT 2002 Build 41617)** package from the list of packages you can upgrade from. In our list it is number 1, so we choose **1** and press **Enter** to continue.

7. Next the upgrade program will verify that you really want to perform this upgrade with the following question: "Do you want to upgrade from FireWall-1-strong.v4.1.SP-6 to CP_FP2_IPSO? [y/n]." Enter **y** for yes and press **Enter** to continue. As the packages are being upgraded and installed, you will receive a lot of messages on the console. There is no more text for you to input at this timc. All you can do is sit patiently and wait for the upgrade to complete. You will see a message that the WebTheater service is no longer supported and that it will be deleted. You will also see a notice that the system failed to find an Internal CA in objects_5_0.C file, but it will be created after cpstart. You can safely ignore both messages. The following packages are installed while you wait:

   - NG FP1 SVN Foundation
   - NG FP1 VPN-1/FireWall-1
   - NG FP2 SVN Foundation
   - NG FP2 VPN-1/FireWall-1
   - NG FP2 Backward Compatibility with 4.1 package
   - NG FP2 Policy Server
   - NG FP2 FloodGate-1
   - NG FP2 Real Time Monitor

8. When the newpkg program exits, you will be brought back to a shell prompt. Both the SVN Foundation and VPN-1/FireWall-1 packages are already enabled in Voyager. You need to log out and log back into the Nokia in order to obtain the latest environment variables. So, type **exit** and then log in again.

9. Run **cpconfig**. If you need help with any of the options here, read the section on cpconfig earlier in this chapter. You need to add a new license because 4.1 licenses will not function on NG.

10. **Reboot**. When the system comes back up it will not load the last policy you had installed in 4.1. It will load the defaultfilter policy instead. You need to push the policy to the firewall the first time after the upgrade.

11. Log into your management server from your NG FP2 Policy Editor Management Client. Accept the fingerprint and verify that your policy appears to be intact after the upgrade.

12. Select **Install** from the **Policy** menu to push a policy.

13. Test communication through your firewall. You might need to reconstruct VPN settings and set up Hybrid IKE again to get things working the way they were prior to the upgrade.

NOTE

If you receive a verification error that says "Missing IP protocol for user defined service MSExchange-DirectoryRef," simply delete this service from the **Manage | Services** window and restart the installation.

If you upgraded from 4.1 directly to FP3, you might need to configure interfaces in the Topology tab on your Check Point Gateway object before you can install a policy.

Upgrading from NG FP2 to NG FP3

The upgrade procedure for FP3 is very simple. You begin the same way you started out with the FP2 upgrade—by downloading the FP3 wrapper package called CP_FP3_IPSO.tgz. You can run this wrapper to upgrade from 4.1 SP-6, NG FP1, or NG FP2 or to install NG FP3 from scratch on your Nokia firewall. We took you through the procedure of a fresh install at the beginning of the chapter. To upgrade to FP3 instead, run *newpkg −i* as you normally do to install a new package, but when prompted whether to install or upgrade, select **2** and press **Enter** to upgrade from an old package.

After upgrading to FP3, the FP3 SVN Foundation and VPN-1/FireWall-1 packages will already be enabled in Voyager. All you need to do is exit your login session and log back in to obtain the correct environment variables. Run cpconfig and if there is nothing new to configure, exit cpconfig and reboot. When the system comes back up, the InitialPolicy will be loaded, which means that you need to push a policy after the upgrade.

Backing Out from NG to 4.1

If you need to back out from a recent upgrade for some reason, the procedure on a Nokia is quite simple. First you need to disable any NG components such as Policy Server and FloodGate-1 and **Apply** and **Save** your changes. Next disable NG VPN-1/FireWall-1 and **Apply** and **Save**, and then finally disable the NG SVN Foundation package and **Apply** and **Save**.

Now you can enable the old 4.1 package and **Apply** and **Save** your changes. Then you must reboot the box. When the box comes back up, the FireWall-1 services will not be started. You must log into Voyager and go to the **Check Point FireWall-1** configuration screen found under the Security and Access Configuration heading. Click the radio button next to **Start FireWall-1 automatically at reboot?** to **On**, then **Apply** and **Save**. Finally, log into the Nokia and run **fwstart** from the command line. The firewall will load the last 4.1 policy you had configured, pick up where you left off before the upgrade, and start automatically on the next reboot. You can go back into Voyager and delete any disabled packages for cleanup if you don't want to save them for another try later.

Summary

All FireWall-1 administrators with Nokia firewalls need to know basic tasks such as installing and upgrading the Check Point FireWall-1 software packages. If you never upgraded your firewall, you could be at risk if there are known vulnerabilities in that release that have been resolved in newer patches. In this chapter we have provided the tools necessary to complete these tasks so that you can continue to secure your organization with Check Point FireWall-1 on Nokia.

Preparation is always key to a successful upgrade or install. With FireWall-1, you need to obtain licenses, configure a hosts entry, and possibly upgrade the IPSO image on your Nokia before you can begin with Check Point. It's also very important to read all release notes available before you install new software.

Once you have the software installed on IPSO, you then need to enable it. If you are running Check Point NG, you will first need to enable the SVN Foundation, **Apply** and **Save** your configuration, and then enable the VPN-1/FireWall-1 packages. When you enable packages through the Manage Installed Packages configuration screen, the file /var/etc/pm_profile is updated with appropriate environment variables. This means that you will need to log in again to the Nokia after the packages are enabled to receive the correct shell environment. The next step to configuring the firewall is to run cpconfig. The first run of this utility will prompt you for the type of install (standalone or distributed), licenses, administrators, management clients, ICA initialization, SIC password (firewall module only), and then finally to reboot. You can always reconfigure your firewall at any time by running cpconfig again, which will provide you with a menu to choose the option you want to edit.

After configuring Check Point, you need to verify that you can log in with the management clients and push a policy. You should also test fetching a policy to ensure that the firewall will operate properly during a reboot. If you have any problem doing these things, verify that the firewall is running on the module with the command **ps –auxw | grep fw**, try unloading the policy from the console with the command **fw unloadlocal**, ensure that there is connectivity between the management server and the module by checking cables and testing with ping, and check that SIC is configured properly.

Once you have a running FireWall-1 installation, you eventually need to upgrade your firewall software to stay up to date. Whenever you are upgrading the firewall in IPSO, you must first upgrade your IPSO image to one compatible with the new software. The next step is to get the new firewall package downloaded to your Nokia, then run *newpkg –i* to start the upgrade. Choose the option to upgrade from an old version (as opposed to install, which will not copy over your configuration), and then choose the old FireWall-1 package that you are upgrading from. If you're upgrading from 4.1 to NG, run your configuration through an upgrade verifier utility provided by Check Point to see if there are any configuration issues that you can sort out before you upgrade the management server. The recommended upgrade path is to go from 4.1 SP-6 to NG FP2 via the wrapper package (which installs FP1 first) and then to NG FP3.

Solutions Fast Track

Preparing for the Configuration

- ☑ Get licenses ahead of time and read the release notes.
- ☑ Make sure Host Address Assignment is configured along with proper networking (interfaces, routes, and IP forwarding).
- ☑ Verify IPSO compatibility with the version of FireWall-1 you are installing.

Configuring the Firewall

- ☑ If you're installing NG FP1, you must start with the SVN Foundation and then install the VPN-1/FireWall-1 package.
- ☑ If you're installing NG FP2 or FP3, use the bundled wrapper install files.
- ☑ Use *newpkg −i* to install packages.
- ☑ Ensure that the packages are enabled in the Manage Installed Packages configuration screen.
- ☑ Run cpconfig to finish the Check Point FireWall-1 configuration. This will prompt you for the type of installation (management and/or firewall module), license key, administrators, management client IP addresses, and ICA/SIC initialization.
- ☑ Reboot your Nokia after running cpconfig for the first time, before attempting to start FireWall-1.

Testing the Configuration

☑ Log into the management server running on your Nokia via the SmartDashboard (a.k.a. Policy Editor)

☑ Push a policy to your Nokia.

☑ Fetch a policy from your Nokia.

Upgrading the Firewall

☑ Use the upgrade verifier utilities provided by Check Point to check your configuration for possible problems upgrading from 4.1 to NG.

☑ Upgrade your IPSO image before upgrading the Check Point FireWall-1 software.

☑ The recommended upgrade path is to go from 4.1 SP-6 to NG FP2 via the wrapper package (which installs FP1 also) to NG FP3.

☑ Backing out of an upgrade is as easy as disabling the new packages, enabling the old packages, and rebooting.

Frequently Asked Questions

The following Frequently Asked Questions, answered by the authors of this book, are designed to both measure your understanding of the concepts presented in this chapter and to assist you with real-life implementation of these concepts. To have your questions about this chapter answered by the author, browse to **www.syngress.com/solutions** and click on the **"Ask the Author"** form.

Q: I installed NG FP1 Primary Management Module on a Nokia appliance, but I can't log in with the Check Point NG management clients. What am I doing wrong?

A: Your management clients must be on the same build as your management module. Verify that your IP address is listed in the gui-clients file and upgrade your management clients to FP1.

Q: I just upgraded one of my 4.1 firewall modules to NG, and it's not able to fetch a policy. What can I do?

A: Verify that you have changed the module's version to NG in its workstation object and that you have initialized SIC. You might have to push the policy the first time after an upgrade.

Q: I keep receiving the error "h_slink: link already exists." Is something wrong?

A: This message is listed in the release notes, which states that it can be safely ignored.

Q: During firewall-to-firewall IKE negotiations, the Check Point NG FP2 firewall changes the subnet mask to something other than what I had configured. This was causing the VPN to fail. What is the firewall doing?

A: There is a configuration setting in objects_5_0.C by default that allows the firewall to calculate the subnet to use for IKE negotiations when there are multiple consecutive subnets in the encryption domain. This also causes a problem if you add a new network object to the domain, which is consecutive with an existing network object already in the domain, and then your firewall changes the subnet it uses for the VPN and causes a failure. This is mostly a problem if you are establishing VPNs to other non-Check Point devices. Check Point has provided this procedure to shut off this behavior in FireWall-1:

1. Run **dbedit**, and log onto the management server locally using the admin username and password.

2. Issue these commands: **modify properties firewall_properties ike_use_largest_possible_subnets false update properties firewall_properties quit**.

3. Open a policy editor GUI, and install the policy.

4. Stop the firewall module (**cpstop**), and clear the contents of $FWDIR/ state (back up the files in another location; however, the firewall should recreate the files automatically when we start it back up), then restart it (**cpstart**). After it restarts, again go to the policy editor and install a policy to it so it can regain its state.

Q: What are the differences between state synchronization in 4.1 and NG if I'm using VRRP for failover?

A: In FireWall-1 4.1 you could create state synchronization between two firewalls by setting up a sync.conf file, which contained the IP address of the other module, and by setting putkeys between these two modules. In NG, you must configure the two firewalls as members of a gateway cluster. Synchronization is then configured through the cluster object, and the sync.conf file is no longer used.

## Chapter 7

System Monitoring

Solutions in this chapter:

- **Static Monitoring**
- **Dynamic Monitoring**
- **Using the Iclid Tool**

- ☑ **Summary**
- ☑ **Solutions Fast Track**
- ☑ **Frequently Asked Questions**

Introduction

Apart from the ease with which Voyager allows system configuration, it also allows the administrator to look inside the inner workings of the IPSO operating system to monitor various aspects of the Nokia appliance. While it is running, the operating system collects a wealth of information about dynamic data such as running processes, as well as CPU and memory usage. In addition, the operating system can also be queried for static data, such as interface configuration and status, or the kernel-forwarding table. This information gives a snapshot of the overall status and health of the Nokia appliance. To truly make sense of this data, one needs to have some indication of what his or her Nokia appliance looks like under normal conditions.

Static and dynamic monitoring features enable you to manage and maintain system availability. In some network environments, fault tolerance and network resiliency are critical elements within the organization. Nokia appliances offer a way to monitor state information for each interface that can help determine which Nokia appliance (in a high-availability setup) has failed and which Nokia appliance has been promoted to primary or demoted to backup status. Having access to this information is important in troubleshooting system and network problems.

Monitoring features can also be used to help troubleshoot potential routing issues with dynamic routing protocols with RIP, BGP, OSPF, or VRRP. Almost all network administrators and engineers experience some type of routing problem in their networks. These problems include routes not being advertised correctly, a firewall blocking routing updates, or unauthorized changes to the network. The Voyager monitor features make it easy for you to display specific statistics such as the contents of IP routing tables, caches, and databases. Information provided can be used to determine resource utilization and solve network problems. You can also display information about node reachability and discover the routing path that your device packets are taking through the network.

As you might expect, Voyager has two divisions in its main monitoring screen: static and dynamic. Later in the chapter we show you exactly what you will see from the various options given in each section.

Static Monitoring

The information obtained from the static monitoring features in Voyager is no different from the traditional *show* commands performed on most routers. As a matter of fact, the Nokia platform also has a command-line interface, known as *Iclid,* or the *IPSRD CLI Daemon*, which has an interface very similar to Cisco's IOS.

Voyager's static monitoring features are discussed in this section. These features provide relevant information at a given point in time that can assist in troubleshooting potential routing issues and aid in problem analysis.

Routing Protocols

The IPSO platform supports various protocols such as OSPF, BGP, RIP, IGRP, VRRP, PIM, DVMRP, and IGMP. Let's take a look at some of these in detail.

Open Shortest Path First

Open Shortest Path First (OSPF) is a link-state protocol that is used to distribute routing information within a single autonomous system (AS). OSPF uses a link-state algorithm in order to build and calculate the shortest path to all known destinations. In a link-state protocol, each router actively tests the status of its link to each of its neighbors, then sends an update to its neighbors accordingly. Each router uses this link-state information to build a complete routing table. This method is much faster than using distance-vector protocols (which do not scale well in large routing environments), especially in case of changes in the link state. Thus, OSPF is often used in large-scale networks to help improve overall routing and performance.

IPSO provides monitoring features that allow you to monitor OSPF configuration and state. Figure 7.1 provides a summary of the OSPF configuration. This information can be useful for troubleshooting OSPF issues.

Figure 7.1 OSPF Summary

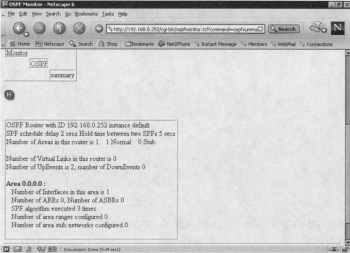

Figure 7.2 shows monitoring information for the OSPF database. OSPF routers use a database to help make routing decisions (calculating the shortest path) and track the state of other OSPF routers in the area.

Figure 7.2 The OSPF Database

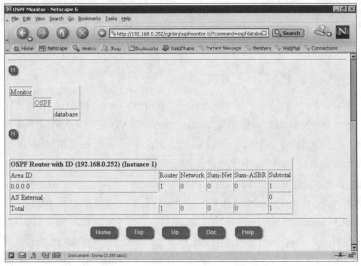

Figure 7.3 shows some OSPF errors. OSPF errors allow you to identify specific errors in OSPF such as mismatched Hello intervals and mismatched area IDs.

Figure 7.3 OSPF Errors

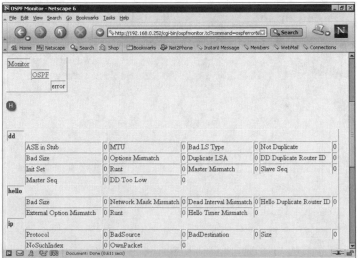

Figure 7.4 shows the OSPF neighbors screen.

Figure 7.4 OSPF Neighbors

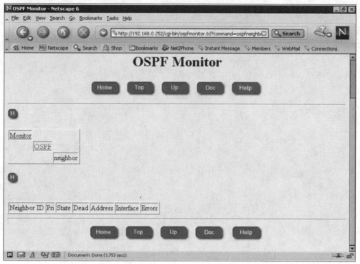

Border Gateway Protocol

The *Border Gateway Protocol (BGP)* is a routing protocol that is used to exchange routing information with other routers on the Internet and between ISPs. BGP is known as a very robust and scalable protocol that uses defined policies to determine routes. When a TCP connection between BGP neighbors is first established, the neighbors exchange full routing information. Moreover, periodic updates are sent only when changes to the routing table are detected, thus reducing unnecessary overhead on the routers. Figures 7.5–7.9 show the BGP monitor screens.

Figure 7.5 The Main BGP Monitor

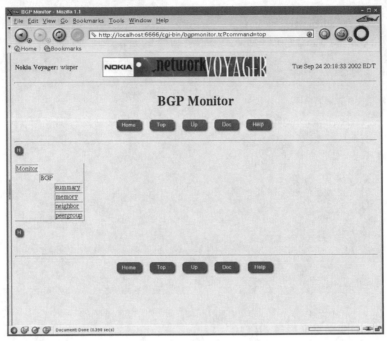

Figure 7.6 BGP Summary

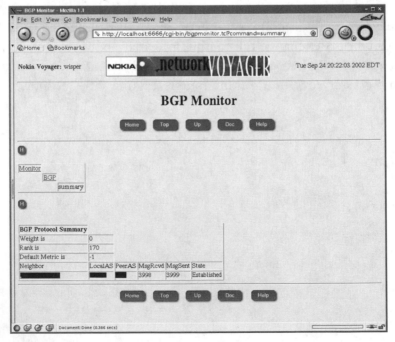

Figure 7.7 The BGP Memory Monitor

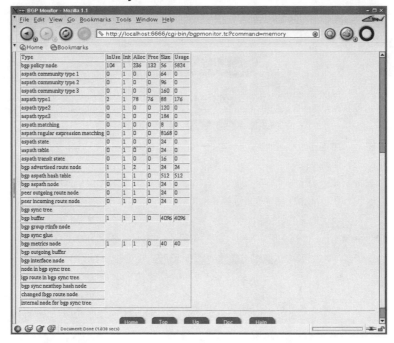

Figure 7.8 BGP Neighbors

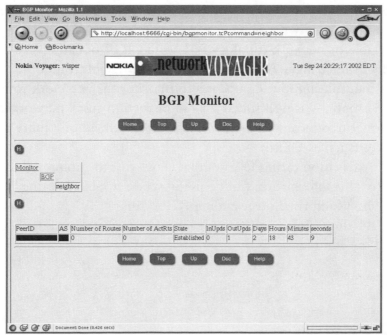

Figure 7.9 BGP Peergroups

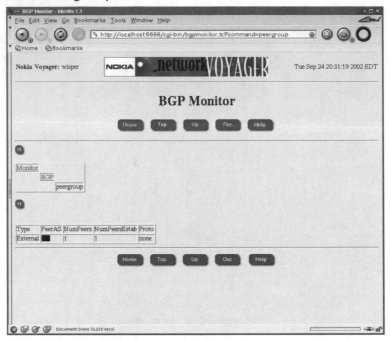

Routing Information Protocol

Routing Information Protocol (RIP), a distance vector protocol, is one of the more common and easily implemented routing protocols. Whenever a change to the routing table or network topology is detected, RIP updates its entire routing table to reflect the changes. After updating its routing table, the router immediately begins transmitting routing updates to inform other network routers of the change. RIP simplicity is well suited for use in flat and small networks that do not have enough redundant paths to warrant the overhead of a more sophisticated protocol (such as OSPF)

IPSO provides monitoring features that allow you to monitor RIP configuration and state. This information can be useful when troubleshooting RIP issues. Figure 7.10 shows information regarding RIP errors.

Figure 7.11 shows information regarding RIP packets—a summary of packets received and transmitted.

Figure 7.10 RIP Errors

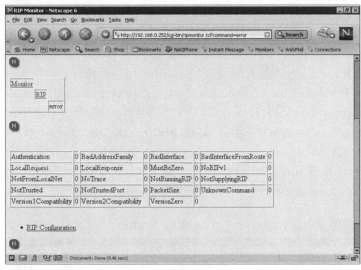

Figure 7.11 RIP Packets

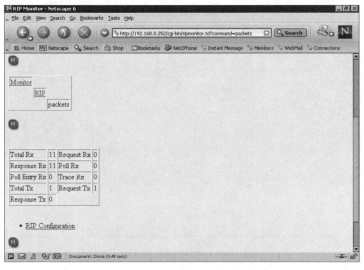

Virtual Router Redundancy Protocol

Virtual Router Redundancy Protocol (VRRP) uses an election protocol that
dynamically assigns routing responsibilities for a VRRP router. VRRP is designed
to eliminate single points of failure. In a typical VRRP high-availability environment, there are two routers. The router controlling the IP addresses associated

with the virtual router assumes Master status, and the other VRRP router assumes Slave status. Any of the virtual router's IP addresses on a LAN can then be used as the default first-hop router for internal hosts. If the VRRP router in Master state fails, a VRRP router in Slave status is promoted to Master status. In the IPSO implementation of VRRP, primarily two parameters, the priority and the priority delta, are used during the election process for the virtual router. Typically, the VRRP router with the highest priority is designated as the master. Figure 7.12 depicts Virtual Router ID (VRID) 45 in Master state with a priority of 100. The effective priority is also an indication of Master status. It indicates that VRID 45 has taken control over the virtual IP address (10.10.100.253) and that all LAN traffic is traversing through that VRRP router. Figure 7.13 shows the corresponding slave router with an effective priority of 95.

Figure 7.12 The VRRP Interface in Master Status

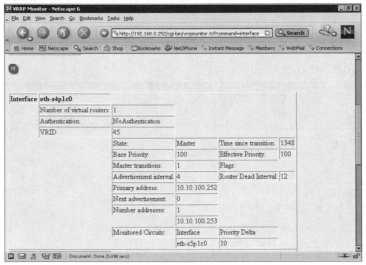

NOTE

If a virtual router is in "initialize" state for longer than a 20-second interval, check the VRRP configuration. Typically, the initialize state indicates that something in the VRRP configuration, such as the backup IP address, is invalid.

Figure 7.13 The VRRP Interface in Slave Status

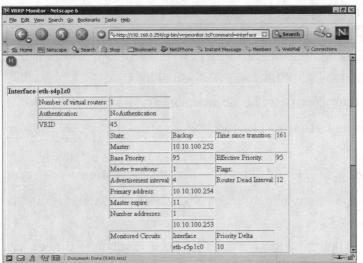

It should be noted that Nokia uses both VRRP version 2, an RFC proposed standard, and VRRP Monitored Circuit (MC), a Nokia extension to the RFC. VRRP MC was created to enhance the performance of VRRP. VRRP version 2 should only used if you must establish VRRP between a Nokia Appliance Platform and a platform from another vendor or if you do not have an extra IP address to use for the monitored circuit implementation.

Resource Statistics

IPSO provides resource statistics about the file system and other attributes of the platform. Figure 7.14 shows the Resource Statistics screen, which has the following elements:

- **Total Uptime** Shows the total time the system has been up and running.

- **Total User Time** Shows the total time spent executing in user mode.

- **Total System Time** Shows the total time the system spent executing on behalf of the processes.

- **Major Page Faults** The number of times data was not present in memory and was retrieved from disk.

- **Minor Page Faults** The number of times a memory page had been marked as invalid but had not yet been swapped out to disk.

- **File System Writes** The number of times the system wrote data from the application address space into the kernel file system cache.

- **File System Reads** The number of times the system read data from block devices into the kernel cache, then copied data from the kernel's cached copy into the application address space.

- **Message Writes** The number of times the system writes to the kernel.

- **Message Reads** The number of times the system reads from the kernel.

- **Signals Received** The number of times a signal was received.

- **Total Swaps** The number of times a process was swapped out of main memory.

- **Voluntary Context Switches** The number of times a task or process causes the scheduler to switch to another process.

- **Involuntary Context Switches** The number of times a task or process decides to switch to another process by itself. This could occur when a timer interrupt signals that the current process is hogging the CPU.

Figure 7.14 Resource Statistics

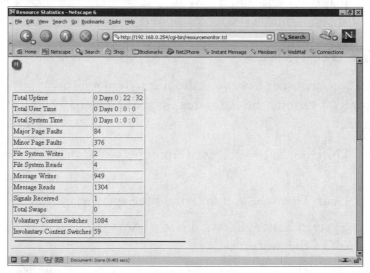

Forwarding Table

The *forwarding table* is essentially the kernel's routing table. The kernel maintains a routing information database, which is used in selecting the appropriate network interface when transmitting packets. If you look closely at the forwarding table in Figure 7.15, you can determine what IP address range has been assigned to each interface on the router. For instance, network 10.10.100.0/24 is directly connected to interface eth-s4p1c0; likewise, network 192.168.0.0/24 is directly connected to interface eth-s5p1c0. When the kernel routes a packet, it attempts to find the most specific route matching the destination.

Figure 7.15 A Forwarding (Routing) Table

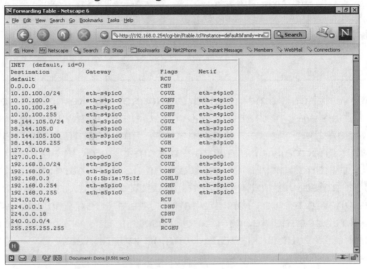

Each route has different attributes that are described in the column. The following is a short list of some of these flags and their meanings:

- **U** Up; the route is active.

- **H** Host; the route destination is a single host.

- **G** Gateway; send anything for this destination on to this remote system, which will figure out from there where to send it.

- **S** Static; this route was configured manually, not automatically generated by the system.

- **C** Clone; generates a new route based on this route for machines we connect to. This type of route is normally used for local networks.
- **L** Link; the route references an Ethernet hardware address.

Hardware Monitoring

Hardware monitoring allows you to monitor the system characteristics of elements present in your system. You can monitor the temperature of the hardware, the status of each device slot in use, and the watchdog timer. Each hardware element provides information about the overall health of the IPSO platform. Often, faulty hardware can lead to errors at the software or operating system level. IPSO provides some tools for early detection of such errors that are discussed in this section.

NOTE

The IPSO watchdog timer is used to monitor the kernel for general health. When we say that the watchdog timer is *tickled* by the kernel, we simply mean that the kernel queried the timer to indicate that the kernel is operating normally. If the kernel becomes stuck in an interrupt, for example, waiting for I/O to complete on a faulty hard drive, the watchdog timer will not receive its expected *tickle* and assumes the kernel is unable to run. This is a fatal system error, and the watchdog timer will reboot the device in such cases. In this way, the watchdog timer prevents your Nokia from hanging indefinitely.

System Status

System status provides you with an overall health check of your platform. It provides status regarding the temperature and watchdog timer. In Figure 7.16, the overall state of the router is good; a green LED indicates "good" status.

The watchdog timer is used to detect system hangs. Figure 7.16. shows the watchdog timer in reset mode, so when the watchdog timer detects a hardware problem or when the timer expires, the watchdog timer resets the system. In this example, it appears that the watchdog timer was *tickled* by the kernel over 900 times. The last system reboot was done manually, either by the *shutdown* command or by power-cycling the device.

Figure 7.16 System Status

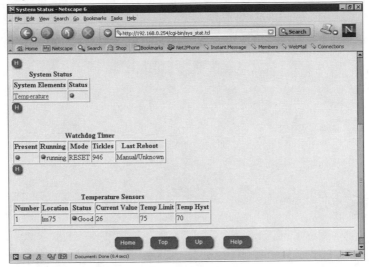

The IPSO platform implements an internal temperature sensor. Limits can be set on these temperature sensors through the *overtemperature shutdown register* and the *hysteresis (HYST) register*. Each value can be set and read to half-degree accuracy. An alarm is issued so that when the temperature gets higher than the overtemperature shutdown value, it stays on until the temperature falls below the hysteresis value. The host can query the LM75 sensor at any time to read the temperature.

If you look at Figure 7.16, you will see that the current temperature value is 26 (degrees Celsius) with a temperature limit of 75 degrees Celsius. Whenever the IPSO platform gets above 75, alarms are generated until the temperature value falls below the hysteresis value of 70.

Slot Status

The Slot Status monitoring page, used to monitor the status of the Nokia router's PCI slots, provides some general details regarding the PCI device driver. Typically, quad-Ethernet cards are inserted into the slots (depending on the model of Nokia platform) for network expansion. Figure 7.17 shows that Slot 2 is in use because it displays a green LED.

Figure 7.17 Slot Status

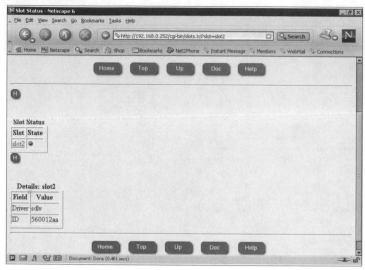

Dynamic Monitoring

Dynamic monitoring information is retrieved from your Nokia platform to give you near-real-time information. Dynamic monitoring presents you with statistical information about memory, CPU utilization, processes, disk space, swap space, and log messages generated by the IPSO platform. In addition, the dynamic monitoring feature in Voyager offers critical, real-time information about network interfaces. This information allows you to track interface usage and link state. The information obtained from the dynamic monitoring features in Voyager is no different from some traditional UNIX operating system commands and *show* commands performed on most routers.

System Utilization

The System Utilization monitor provides vital information about the operating system. More specifically, this monitor can provide indications as to which system resources could be limiting overall system performance. Often, system performance depends on how efficiently the resources are allocated.

CPU and Memory Utilization

CPU and memory are two of the most important system resources from a performance perspective. IPSO reports CPU utilization in three separate load averages that together form an estimate of overall CPU usage. The three load averages report the average number of processes in the kernel run queue (waiting for CPU time so they can execute) during the last minute, the last 5 minutes, and the last 15 minutes. In Figure 7.18, you will see that there was a peak during the 5-minute interval. High load averages (usually anything over 2 in all three fields) indicate that the system is under a continuously heavy load.

Figure 7.18 CPU and Memory Utilization

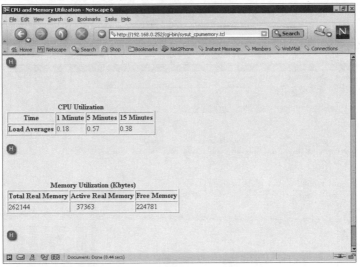

Memory utilization can also be observed through this Voyager screen. On most UNIX machines, the *vmstat* command accomplishes the same thing. In Figure 7.18, you will see that there is approximately 224,781 kilobytes of free memory. The free memory is the memory that's available to the operating system; the active memory is the memory that's currently in use by the operating system.

Disk and Swap Space Utilization

IPSO allows you to monitor and track system disk usage. The output found in Figure 7.16 reports four file systems:

1. **/dev/wd0f** Mounted at root; 83% capacity.

2. **/dev/wd0a** Mounted at config; 0% capacity.

3. **/dev/wd0d** Mounted at var; 2% capacity.

4. **/dev/wd0e** Mounted at opt; 19% capacity.

Voyager allows you to monitor the total number of kilobytes on each disk as well as the percentage of file system storage in use and what portion of the file system is available. In Figure 7.19, the root file system /dev/wd0f is at 83 percent capacity. Although this looks bad, remember that in IPSO the root partition is mounted read-only, so this figure should never rise above 83 percent. Dynamic configuration files and logs are stored in the /config and /var partitions, and optional user software is stored in /opt, so these three partitions are more important to watch.

Figure 7.19 Disk and Swap Space Utilization

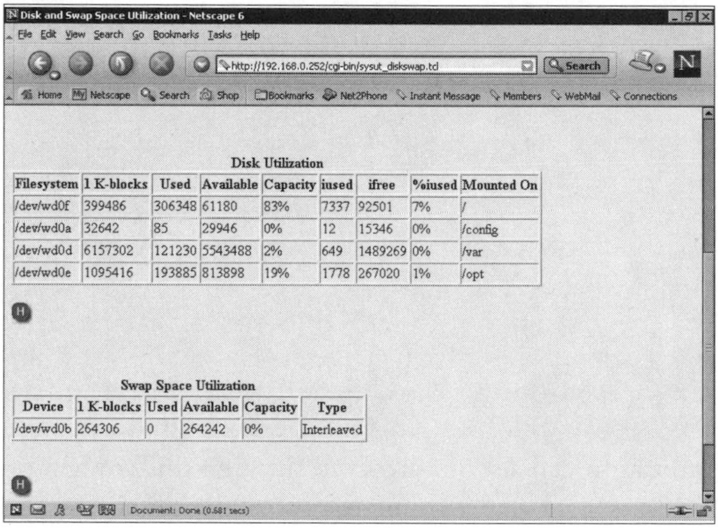

IPSO also shows you the inode usage statistics on its hard drive partitions. An *inode* is a structure on disk that uniquely identifies a file; in other words, every file on your hard drive has an inode associated with it. Filenames are merely a convenience to the user; the operating system references all files by inode number. A limited number of inodes are available in each partition (hence a limited number of files), and although this number is quite large, it can be exceeded if you have a large number of small files on a disk partition. It is even possible to run out of inodes while still having plenty of free disk space, which is why you should watch these numbers in addition to raw disk space. If you ever do run out of inodes, normal users will not be able to create files, but all is not lost. IPSO reserves 5 percent of the total inodes exclusively for the superuser, ensuring that you can recover your system. In Figure 7.19, you can see that the root partition has the highest percentage of inodes used, at 7 percent.

Swap space is the space on a disk used as the virtual memory extension of a machine's real memory. Swap space allows the operating system to pretend that it has more memory than it actually does. Memory in the IPSO operating system (and most other operating systems) is divided into fixed-sized chunks called *pages*. Pages that the operating system has not accessed recently or that are somehow deemed unimportant are "swapped out" of memory until they are needed later, whereas needed pages can be "swapped in" to memory. The term *page fault* refers to the operation of going to disk to get a memory page that is needed by a running process.

Figure 7.19 shows the disk partition (/dev/wd0b) that holds the system swap area. Currently, the operating system is using zero swap space with over 264,000 kilobytes available. The type *interleaved* refers to how the swap space is allocated on the disk and applies only if there is more than one swap partition.

> **NOTE**
>
> It is important to delete old IPSO packages from the IPSO platform as file system capacity approaches high percentages. If packages or files are needed, it is suggested that they be archived off the IPSO platform for later use. In addition, log files can take up unnecessary space locally on a file system. An alternate option is to log syslog remotely to a syslog server. (See Chapter 5 for details on remote logging.)

Process Utilization

Each task or thread of execution in an operating system is known as a *process*. Each process is assigned a *PID*, or *process identifier*, used by the kernel to uniquely identify a particular process for tracking and reporting purposes. Each process utilizes a certain percentage of CPU and memory usage; thus managing CPU and memory resources must be done by monitoring and controlling processes.

In Figure 7.20, look at the process assigned PID 269, the /bin/xpand daemon. IPSO uses this process to handle requests from Voyager. In this example, the process was started at 6:59 A.M. and has been running for 0:00:58 seconds.

Figure 7.20 Process Utilization

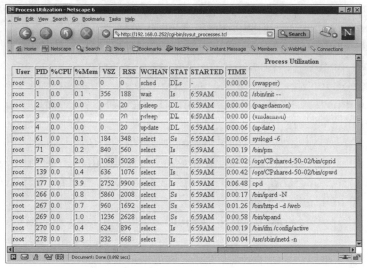

NOTE

You can find additional information regarding these parameters (and others) by reading the *ps* man page online at the following Web site: www.freebsd.org/cgi/man.cgi?query=ps&apropos=0&sektion= 0&manpath=FreeBSD+2.2.6-RELEASE&format=html

The following are the parameters IPSO displays when it monitors process utilization:

- **User** The user who executed or initiated the process.

- **PID** The unique number assigned to a process; the process identifier.

- **% CPU** The percentage of CPU the process is utilizing while active.

- **% Memory** The percentage of memory the process is utilizing while active.

- **VSZ** The virtual size of the process.

- **RSS** The resident page set size in kilobytes.

- **WCHAN** The wait address. The event on which a process waits.

- **STAT** The process state.
- **STARTED** The time the process was started by the user.
- **TIME** The amount of time the process has been running.

Current and Historical Network Activities

The information found in the "Current and Historical Network Activities" section of Voyager provides trend reporting and some level of forecast analysis for you to become proactive with monitoring. This data may help you forecast additional bandwidth needs, memory requirements, and other hardware and software requirements based on statistics generated by IPSO. The information found in these log reports will help you identify and track potential problems over a given period of time (hours, days, weeks, and months). This section discusses some of the reporting features and information that IPSO makes readily available to you.

Monitor Report Configuration

IPSO provides you with the ability to configure report options to meet your network and reporting requirements. You have the option to disable particular network logging options. In addition, you are able to control the interval at which data is collected for reporting. Figure 7.21 shows the report configuration screen.

Figure 7.21 Monitor Report Configuration

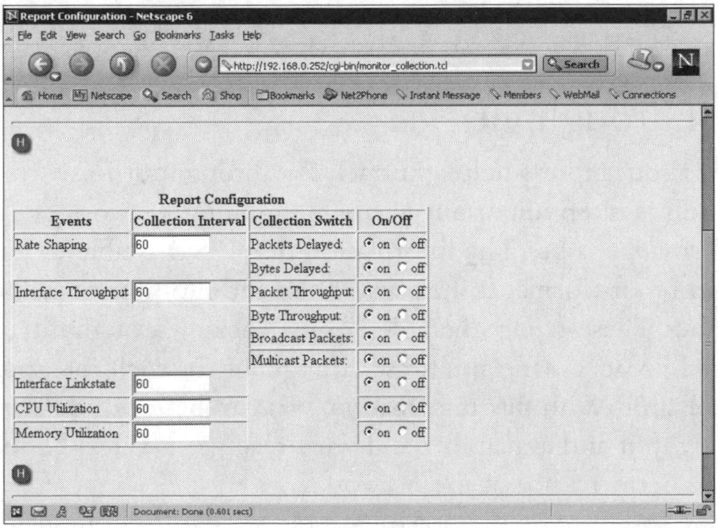

Rate-Shaping Bandwidth Reports

The rate-shaping bandwidth reports provide you with information about specific bandwidth utilization. *Traffic shaping* allows you to implement a specific policy that controls the way data is queued for transmission through traffic prioritizing.

IPSO provides reporting information for all aggregates, indicating rate-shaping information for packet and byte delays. Here the term *aggregates* refers to the totals for each event. Figure 7.22 shows the configuration screen for these reports.

Figure 7.22 Rate-Shaping Bandwidth Report Configuration

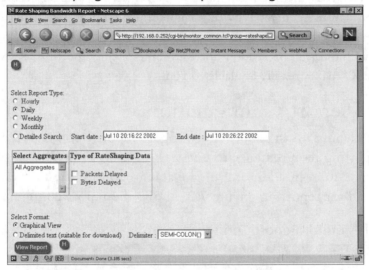

Interface Throughput

Interface throughput reports help you track the throughput for each interface. This information is often important in troubleshooting network congestion and network performance issues. The information that IPSO is able to generate can be presented in report format to help you track and monitor overall traffic management statistics. These reports help determine packet throughput, byte throughput, and broadcast and multicast throughput for each interface over a given period of time. With this information, you can better understand how to optimize throughput and availability and what changes need to be made to improve overall performance in the network.

You are able to create reports for each interface by the hour, day, week, or month, with a *detailed search* option that allows you to specify start date and end date as search criteria. These options are shown in Figure 7.23.

Figure 7.23 Interface Throughput Report Configuration

Figure 7.24 shows a graph generated from the interface throughput report configuration page, which shows hourly statistics. This graph shows the packet throughput for the interface chosen in the configuration screen. As you can see, there are two peak periods reaching approximately 2800 packets per hour.

Figure 7.24 Interface Throughput Data Graph

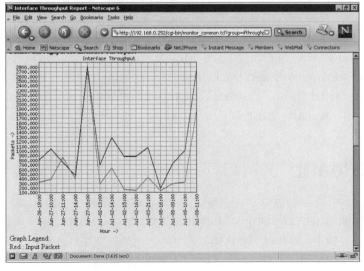

Interface Link State

The *interface link-state* report provides you with information regarding the link state for each interface. The information generated can help determine if an interface is experiencing problems (Layer 1 or Layer 2); often interfaces start exhibiting problems by generating link errors. This information helps you determine if new hardware is needed or whether or not the interface has been configured properly. Figure 7.25 shows the interface link-state report configuration screen.

Figure 7.25 Interface Link-State Configuration

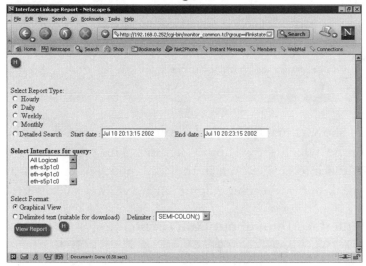

The information in Figure 7.26 is a report generated from the page shown in Figure 7.25. It summarizes and tracks the state of a particular interface during a specific time interval (hour, day, week, or month). This graph indicates that the link state (based on daily statistics) for interface eth–s5p1c0 was up 100 percent of the time.

System Health

The "System Health" section of Voyager's monitor provides you with invaluable information regarding the status of the IPSO platform. Often, you are unaware of symptoms that can be telltale signs that something is happening or about to happen. This section discusses some IPSO monitoring features that can better assist you in identifying performance and system issues with your Nokia appliance.

Figure 7.26 An Interface Link-State Report

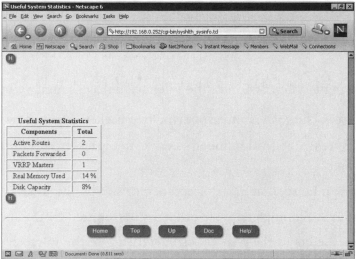

Useful System Statistics

The Useful System Statistics page provides a snapshot of the IPSO unit (see Figure 7.27). It shows you how many active routes were detected, the number of packets the operating system forwarded, the number of VRRP routers in master state, your real memory utilization, and your disk capacity. Having this type of information in one location is very convenient.

Figure 7.27 Useful System Statistics

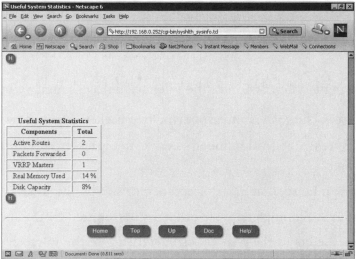

Interface Traffic Statistics

The Interface Traffic Statistics page reports the status for each physical and logical interface on the IPSO platform. The information provided in the summary shown in Figure 7.28 is polled from the operating system to report near-real-time statistics. When you're troubleshooting network issues, it is important to determine whether or not an interface is dropping packets, is sending and receiving packets properly, or is generating errors. In addition, it is important to differentiate the physical interface from the logical interface. The term *physical interface* refers to the hardware device itself, whereas the term *logical interface* refers to the software processes determining whether or not an interface is usable. The physical link needs to be up before the software can activate the logical interface.

Figure 7.28 Interface Traffic Statistics

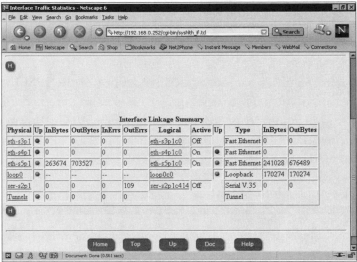

The following is a description of the interface linkage summary in Figure 7.29:

- **InBytes** The total number of error-free packets received by the interface.

- **OutBytes** The total number of error-free packets transmitted by the interface.

- **InErrs** The total number of errors received by the interface.

- **OutErrs** The total number of errors transmitted by the interface.

- **Type** Refers to the physical characteristics of the interface.

Figure 7.29 Interface Queue Statistics

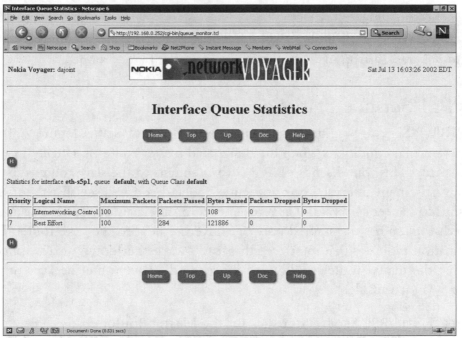

Interface Queue Statistics

The Interface Queue Statistics page provides information regarding packet flow for each interface. A router is a shared resource in your network, and many of the problems that occur in the network are often related to the allocation of a limited amount of shared resources (buffer memory and bandwidth, for example) to competing users, applications, and service classes. Interface queuing allows you to manage the flow of packets by creating policies and priorities. Figure 7.29 shows interface queuing statistics for the interface eth-s5p1c0.

The Interface Queue Statistics page is summarized by the following:

- **Priority** Refers to the order in which packets are queued and processed.

- **Logical Name** Refers to the class of service delivery.

- **Maximum Packets** Refers to the maximum number of packets that can be processed.

- **Packets Passed** Refers to the number of packets sent through the interface.

- **Bytes Passed** Refers to the number of bytes sent through the interface.
- **Packets Dropped** Refers to the number of packets dropped.
- **Bytes Dropped** Refers to the number of bytes dropped.

VRRP Service Statistics

The VRRP Service Statistics page is used to view VRRP status. Figure 7.30 depicts normal conditions when the designated master router is actually in Master state. This router sends VRRP advertisements to the slave router during the advertisement interval. Look at Figure 7.30 and you will see that the interface eth-s5p1c0 has sent over 1300 advertisements to the slave router, whereas interface eth-s4p1c0 has transmitted only one advertisement to the slave router. This information indicates that interface eth-s4p1c0 was either down or disconnected and that the master router could not fail over to the slave router because the slave router was unavailable.

Figure 7.30 VRRP Service Statistics for the Master Router

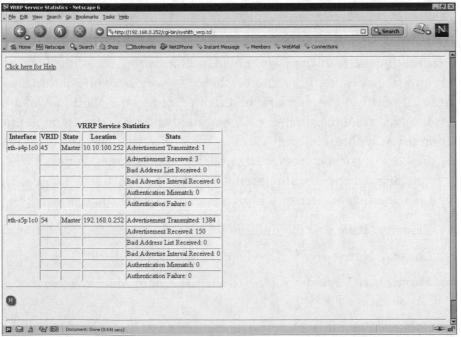

The Location column refers to the IP addresses for each interface of the master router—the IP address that is bound to the physical interface (10.10.100.252 and 192.168.0.252). If the slave router is promoted to master status, this column will refer to the IP addresses of that particular router (10.10.100.254 and 192.168.0.254) , as shown in Figure 7.31.

Figure 7.31 VRRP Service Statistics for the Slave Router

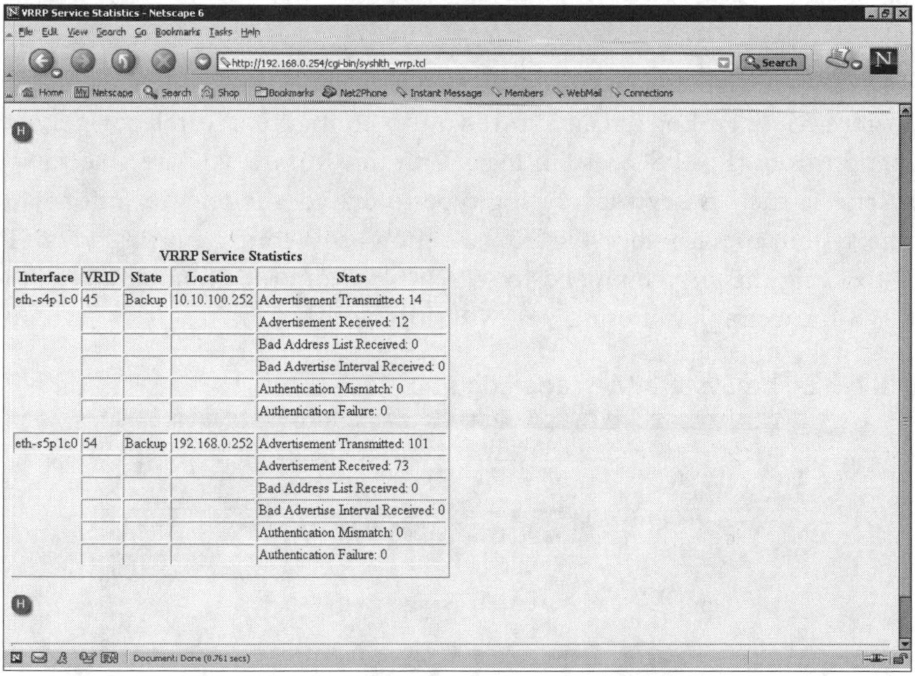

VRRP exchanges can be authenticated to guarantee that only trusted VRRP routers can communicate with each other. By default, such authentication is disabled. Any positive number in the Authentication Mismatch field indicates that either the password or the authentication key does not match between VRRP routers. The Authentication Failure field indicates the number of times authentication failed due to mismatch in passwords or authentication keys.

System Logs

System logs are a good source of information about the IPSO platform. Like most UNIX systems, IPSO can generate a considerable amount of log data, some interesting and some not so interesting. Nevertheless, this information is a critical component for monitoring the overall health of your Nokia appliance. At times, you could find reviewing large amounts of log data annoying or impossible, and you might neglect reviewing logs for that reason. However, when system problems arise, you could be left wondering what occurred and why.

IPSO helps ease the burden of sorting through tons of data by providing reporting features with specific search criteria. This helps you extract "interesting" data from the IPSO platform logs for a given time period. This section discusses some of the reporting IPSO provides for reviewing system logs.

Message Log

The System Message Log screen allows you to configure a search for pertinent information from the IPSO system logs. With this feature, you are able to specify search criteria such as keywords or log type to extract the relevant information from the system message logs. Figure 7.32 shows this configuration screen. This is similar to using the *grep* command to search files from the command line. (See Chapter 8 for examples of using *grep* with log files.)

Figure 7.32 The System Message Log

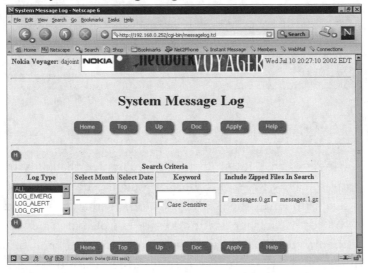

Figure 7.33 shows a message log report generated from July 10 log data in the file /var/log/messages.0.gz. The report searched this entire compressed file for all the log entries dated July 10.

Figure 7.33 A System Message Log Report

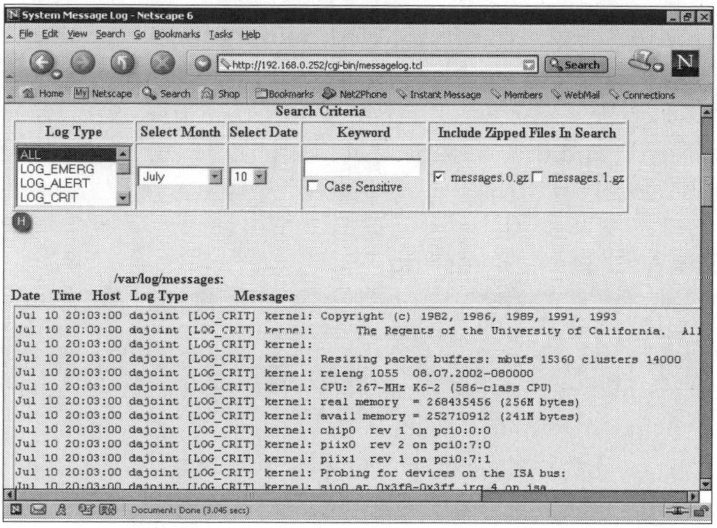

Web Server Access Log

The Web server access log records accesses to the Voyager interface via HTTP or HTTPS. It is important to know who accessed (or attempted to access) the configuration setup. Figure 7.34 shows output from the Web server access log that shows login by IP address, username, time, and date. In addition, the Web server access log provides some information as to what configuration settings the user changed.

Figure 7.34 A Web Access Log File Report

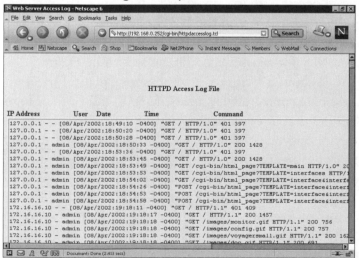

Web Server Error Logs

Web server error logs assist you in troubleshooting process errors with your Apache Web server. These error logs provide specific information regarding the time and day the error occurred, the type of error (notice, error, or critical), the location of the error, and the message that was generated. Figure 7.35 captures a portion of the Web server error log generated by IPSO.

Figure 7.35 A Web Server Error Log

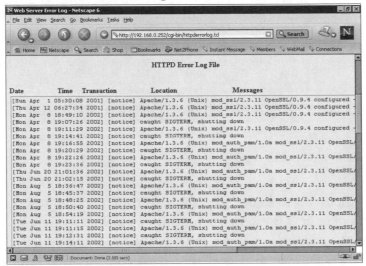

User Login/Logout Activity

The User Login/Logout Activity report provides you with an audit trail that tracks login and logout activity on the IPSO platform. You can track the login and logout activity for each specific user account or by using the *all* option, which reports activity for all user accounts, as shown in Figure 7.36.

The login and logout activity report tracks information by user account, source IP address or terminal device, time of login, and time of logout. This information can be used in conjunction with other information to monitor overall user activity on your Nokia device. Often this information can be used to determine system misuse. For instance, if you detected someone trying to exploit an FTP vulnerability on your Nokia firewall, you could use the information from the login and logout activity report to provide relevant information. Figure 7.37 shows a successful login attempt with admin privileges, executing an FTP session on July 2 at 12:18 from source IP address 192.168.0.3.

Figure 7.36 User Login/Logout Activity

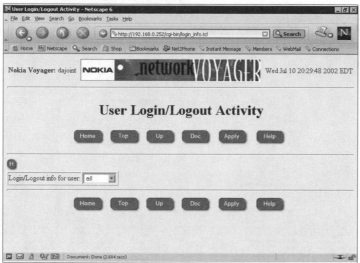

Figure 7.37 A User Login/Logout Activity Report

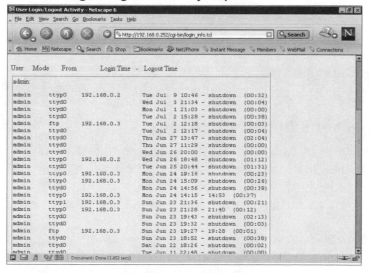

Management Activity Log

The management activity log also monitors and tracks user login activity as well as provides specific details regarding changes made to the IPSO configuration. For example, Figure 7.38 presents a section of log file showing that interface eth-s4p1c0 was turned off by someone who logged in as admin, and that this change occurred on July 13 at 15:46:03.

Figure 7.38 A Management Activity Log

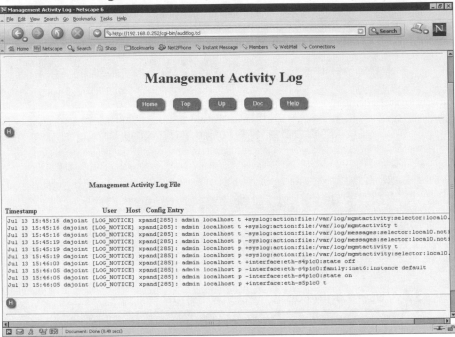

Management Activity Logging

It is important to have the tools and information readily available to track changes made to the system configuration. That information should include time stamps and username information with a brief description of what that user changed while accessing the system configuration.

Routers and firewalls are a critical part of network infrastructures. If a router goes down or becomes unavailable due to configuration errors, many organizations will experience disruption in service and will lose the ability to communicate with key business entities within their network and outside the organization. It is recommended that you create an account for each user who will be making configuration changes (see Chapter 5 for details). After creating an account for each user, enable management activity in Voyager's System Logging configuration. In the "System Configuration Auditlog" section, enable logging of transient and permanent changes.

Using the Iclid Tool

The *Iclid* (IPSRD CLI Daemon) *utility* is a command-line tool that allows you to view information related to the IPSO platform. The command-line interface is very similar to Cisco's IOS and is useful in situations that require troubleshooting to address an immediate issue. Let's take a closer look at some of the commands available through Iclid.

From the command line, you must type **iclid** to enter the Iclid shell. Figure 7.39 captures the main Iclid commands (*exit, get, help, quit,* and *show*), accessed through the Help (?) key. This Help key can be used anywhere in Iclid to provide command completions, as can the Tab key:

- **Exit or Quit** Exits the Iclid utility.
- **Get** Retrieves detailed and raw information from IPSO.
- **Help** Displays help information.
- **Show** Shows categorized system information.

Figure 7.39 The Iclid Help Display

Figure 7.40 captures all the arguments that can legally follow the *show* command. Simply press the **Tab** key to have Iclid display the command completions that are available.

Figure 7.40 The Iclid show Command

The *show interface* command shows the number of network interfaces installed on the IPSO platform and indicates whether or not the interface is up or down, with corresponding IP address and mask. Figure 7.41 shows that only interface eth-s5p1c0 is up.

Figure 7.41 The Iclid show interface Command

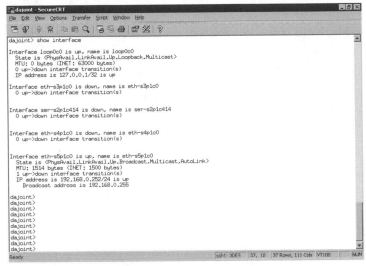

The *show route* command displays the active routes configured in IPSO. This information should be consistent with the output from *netstat –rn*. (See Figure 7.42.)

Figure 7.42 The Iclid show route Command

Figure 7.43 captures the possible completions for the *show ospf* and *show rip* commands. If network or routing issues arise, Iclid provides a convenient and fast interface for retrieving routing information for each specific protocol.

Figure 7.43 The Iclid show ospf and show rip Command Completions

For example, *show ospf* will show OSPF summary information, whereas *show ospf neighbor* will show all neighbor information for a particular router.

NOTE

You can retrieve Iclid information from the command line by using the *echo* command. *echo* is a UNIX command that tells the shell to display a particular value, as shown in Figure 7.44.

Figure 7.44 Running Iclid With the echo Command from the Command Line

Summary

As networks become more complex and diverse, you will need to have tools readily available to track the overall health of your network and Nokia devices. More specifically, you will need to be able to identify changes in the overall performance of your network over a given period of time. It is important to measure and baseline network performance under normal load conditions. These normal indicators allow you to more accurately identify problematic areas when they arise. Voyager's collection of static and dynamic monitoring features gives you the tools you need to measure baseline and abnormal performance from IPSO.

Nokia provides you with many tools and features for monitoring overall system and router performance through the Voyager interface. It should be noted that performance problems are not just network related; application and operating system issues can contribute a great deal to the degrading of network performance, and Voyager helps you there as well. A proactive approach should be taken to get the most out of the monitoring tools IPSO provides. Proactive monitoring helps identify problem areas and symptoms before they get out of control. This is one of the most critical aspects of monitoring: detecting the "early warning" signs. Once those problem areas and symptoms have been identified, you can devise a response or remediation strategy to correct the issue. It could be something as simple as upgrading the memory on your Nokia appliance or replacing a network interface card.

It is important to have tools available to track changes made to the system and router configuration. IPSO allows you to track user login and logout activity as well as any configuration changes made by each user. This functionality provides the necessary audit trail that links individual users to actions taken on the system. However, if individual accounts are not created for each user, it will be difficult to hold individuals accountable or link a particular person to a specific action taken on a system.

Finally, the Iclid tool provides a Cisco IOS-like shell that can be used to quickly monitor or display routing and network information. Iclid is much more convenient than lynx to use over a console connection, and it provides plenty of functionality for those who actually *enjoy* spending time at a command prompt.

Solutions Fast Track

Static Monitoring

☑ Static monitoring can be used to troubleshoot potential routing issues with OSPF, BGP, RIP, and VRRP.

☑ The forwarding (routing) table can be viewed through Voyager.

☑ Static monitoring allows you to monitor hardware aspects of the IPSO platform, including the temperature of the unit.

☑ System resources such as system uptime and total number of page faults can be displayed through Voyager.

Dynamic Monitoring

☑ Dynamic monitoring polls IPSO frequently for real-time monitoring information.

☑ The system logs that IPSO produces provide critical information about access times and user activity on the system.

☑ Dynamic monitoring information allows you to monitor disk space, swap space, memory usage, and system process utilization.

☑ Dynamic monitoring provides text-based or graphical reports on interface link state and interface throughput.

☑ You can monitor useful system statistics such as the total number of packets forwarded and the number of active routes from within the dynamic monitor.

☑ You can search system log files for specific information or specific date ranges from within the dynamic monitor.

Using the Iclid Tool

☑ You can use the **?** or **Tab** keys to display all possible command completions from within Iclid.

☑ Iclid automatically moves to the next page within 30 seconds if no action is taken. This usually happens when an Iclid command has more output than can fit on the screen. You can use **Ctrl + S** or **Ctrl + Q** to temporally defeat the timing issue.

☑ Iclid can be used to display the routing table from the kernel.

☑ Iclid can be used to display information regarding configured interfaces.

☑ You can display information on dynamic routing protocols from within Iclid.

Frequently Asked Questions

The following Frequently Asked Questions, answered by the authors of this book, are designed to both measure your understanding of the concepts presented in this chapter and to assist you with real-life implementation of these concepts. To have your questions about this chapter answered by the author, browse to **www.syngress.com/solutions** and click on the **"Ask the Author"** form.

Q: Is there a way to reset the various counters I see in Voyager?

A: The only way to reset the monitoring features in IPSO is to reboot the router.

Q: If firewalls are running in High-Availability mode and the firewall daemon dies on the master firewall, will VRRP transition to the slave firewall?

A: No. VRRP only monitors the link of the interfaces. If the firewall daemon dies, VRRP will not transition to the slave firewall. The VRRP monitoring information will still show the primary firewall as master.

Q: What are some of the advantages for using bandwidth tools and interface-queuing techniques?

A: These features help improve overall performance on the network by prioritizing traffic. In general, these network performance tools optimize bandwidth utilization by managing the delivery of packets based on policies and class of service. More specifically, interface queuing dictates what packets are queued and which are sent out first.

Q: Is there a way to create a user account that only allows access to IPSO monitoring information and no configuration settings?

A: Yes. With IPSO you can create a monitor account that only permits access to IPSO monitoring information. See Chapter 5 for more details.

Q: Is it possible to use IPSO monitoring information to find information relating to a security breach?

A: The IPSO monitoring information is intended to provide you with information regarding the overall health of the platform. However, IPSO does provide relevant information that can be used to track user access times and user activity.

## Chapter 8

Advanced System Administration

Solutions in this chapter:

- **Understanding the Boot Manager**
- **Using CLISH**
- **Troubleshooting**

☑ **Summary**

☑ **Solutions Fast Track**

☑ **Frequently Asked Questions**

Introduction

Despite the fact that Nokia has worked hard (and has mostly succeeded) at making Voyager the focal point of system configuration and monitoring, at times it is not adequate, and sometimes when power users want to stray from its grip and drop into the more familiar and powerful command shell. IPSO 3.6 has made this switch much easier with the addition of *CLISH*, the new Nokia command-line configuration shell.

Let's talk first about the IPSO boot sequence and how to use the boot manager. When things really go badly, we talk about how you can use system debugging tools to assist your interaction with Nokia support.

The IPSO command shell is simply the UNIX C-shell, or csh, so it is possible to write shell scripts using the shell built-in commands and system binaries. The shell and system binaries provided are based on those from FreeBSD 2.2.6, so if you need a command reference, you can use those UNIX manual pages, which you can find on the Internet. A good, useful subset of the FreeBSD base installation is part of the IPSO operating system. One section is devoted entirely to using the CLISH shell, new in IPSO 3.6.

Using the shell means you have access to all your familiar UNIX commands: *vmstat*, *netstat*, *ifconfig*, *tail*, *grep*, *df*, and many others. Various other useful utilities, such as Perl and the Bash shell, have been ported to IPSO. (See Appendix B for details on getting and installing these packages.) We will talk about some of the most useful commands for troubleshooting and show you when you might want to use them. In those rare cases where we must use Voyager, we will stick to the lynx interface, to remain as close as possible to the command line.

Understanding the Boot Manager

The Nokia *boot manager* is a small program that runs just after system startup but before the operating system kernel is loaded into memory. Its main function is to load the kernel from disk into memory, which then handles normal system startup and initialization. Nokia's boot manger has gone through several changes over the years and has been present on the system hard drive, a specially formatted diskette drive, or (most recently) in flash memory, the latter to ease upgrades and provide some measure of resiliency in the event of a hard disk crash. The boot manager will, if left unattended, simply bootstrap the system with the default kernel image, but it can be interrupted and given options from a rudimentary command shell. This functionality is typically useful, for example, to boot into "single-user" or nonnetworked mode for system maintenance.

The boot manager in the IP300, IP500, and higher series allows you to do various things that would be impossible if your Nokia device were already booted fully. Chief among these tasks are the following:

- You can perform a factory default installation.
- You can boot from an alternate kernel and/or an alternate device.

The boot manager in the IP400 series of Nokia appliances is limited to allowing you to perform a factory default install, and then only from a boot diskette.

Single-User Mode

Before we can begin discussing the boot manager, you need to understand a system mode called *single-user mode*. This mode of operation is used frequently for performing system maintenance (such as upgrading the boot manager, for example) and is considered "safer" for such actions because it is nonnetworked and has fewer services running. The normal mode of operation of your Nokia appliance is called *multiuser* or *networked* mode. Your Nokia will boot into multiuser mode by default if it is allowed to boot unattended. Single-user mode must be forced at the boot manager prompt. The procedure for entering single-user mode differs depending on the model of Nokia you are using.

The IP440

To get your IP400 series appliance into single-user mode, reboot or power-cycle it from a console connection. When you see the boot: prompt, you must enter **–s** and press **Enter** within 10 seconds or the device will boot into its normal multiuser mode of operation. Once the boot process into single-user mode is complete, you will be asked to **Enter pathname of shell or RETURN for sh:**. Just press the **Enter** key to get a command shell. To exit, simply type **exit** or press **Ctrl + D** (hold down the Control key as you press the **D** key). This key combination causes you to leave single-user mode and restart the system.

The IP300 and IP500 or Higher Series

On an IP500 or higher series device, you will see the text *Entering autoboot mode. Type any character to enter command mode* during the startup sequence, at which point you can press any key before the 5-second timeout to get to the boot manager prompt. To get into the boot manager on an IP300 series device, wait until you see the *Verifying DMI Pool Data* line in the boot sequence, then press the number **1** to start loading boot manager. At this point, the procedure is identical to the IP500 series: Just wait until you see *Type any character to enter command mode*, then press any key before the 5-second timeout to get to the BOOTMGR[0]> prompt. Now type **boot –s** and press **Enter**. Again, after the system boots, it will ask you to *Enter pathname of shell or RETURN for sh:*. Press the **Enter** key to get a command shell. To exit single-user mode, type **exit** or press **Ctrl + D**. Either choices causes you to leave single-user mode and restarts the system.

In both cases, pressing any key before the configured timeout period at the boot sequence prompt will stop the timer and keep you in the boot manager until you exit or resume the boot sequence manually. We discuss booting manually in the section "Boot Manager Commands" later in the chapter.

NOTE

It is also possible to enter single user mode from a running system. Type **kill –TERM 1** (you must be logged in as admin on a console for this to work) to send the *init* process a TERM signal and force entry into single-user mode. The same thing can be accomplished by typing **shutdown now** from a console login.

Understanding the IPSO /image Directory

Nokia has devised a clever way of saving old IPSO images and file systems and making them available after upgrades in the event a downgrade is ever necessary. As we discussed in Chapter 2, the file /image/current/kernel points to the kernel image that is booted by default when your Nokia system is left to start unattended. In practice, there is more going on under the hood than merely a symbolic link to a kernel image file.

Let's take a look at the directory structure of /image in detail. In Figure 8.1, we see that /image/current is actually a symbolic link to the directory IPSO-3.5-FCS6-05.02.2002-024900-1005, which itself contains almost an entire IPSO file system tree. Executing the *uname –a* command shows us that this is indeed a Nokia with IPSO 3.5 FCS6 installed and running. Executing a **cd /image/IPSO-3.5-FCS3-03.26.2002-011300-976** command places us in the previous IPSO's file system tree, so we can see our previous kernel image file as well as the /bin, /usr, /sbin, and /etc directories of the old IPSO. So where do the current system's /bin, /usr, /sbin, and /etc directories point? To the corresponding directories in the /image/current directory, of course. If you execute an *ls –l /etc* command, we see that /etc is merely a symbolic link to /@sys/etc. We would see a similar pattern for /bin, /usr, /sbin, /web, and /dev. @sys is merely Nokia's link to whatever directory /image/current points to. To see this, type **ls –l /@sys**, which shows exactly the same output as when we executed *ls –l* from the /image/current directory.

Figure 8.1 A Trip Through the IPSO /image Directory

Boot Manager Variables

Now we have enough background information to talk about how IPSO's boot manager works. The boot manager operates by referencing some user-definable variables that are given sensible defaults when your Nokia device is shipped. Table 8.1 lists each variable and its purpose. This section discusses how to change the value of these variables.

Table 8.1 User-Definable Boot Manager Variables

Variable Name Value	Meaning	Factory Default
autoboot	Do we wait for *bootwait* seconds at the boot manager prompt during startup before continuing unattended?	Yes
boot-device	Device to load the boot-file from	wd0
boot-file	Kernel image path	/image/current/ kernel
boot-flags	Flags to pass to the kernel	-x
-x	Do not identify the flash disk as wd0	N/A
-d	Enter the kernel debugger as soon as possible during startup	N/A
-s	Single-user mode; admin password may be needed if console is marked "insecure" in /etc/ttys	N/A
-v	Verbose mode	N/A
bootwait	The amount of time to wait at the boot manager prompt for user input before continuing	5 seconds

NOTE

If you set autoboot to *No*, your Nokia device will stop at the boot manager prompt during startup and wait indefinitely for your keyboard input. In this case, you would need to manually enter the *boot* command from a console connection to get the system up and running.

Boot Manager Commands

Once you are at the boot manager prompt, you can enter various commands. Here is a list of those commands with sample uses:

- **printenv** Prints all variables and their values to the screen.
- **showalias** Shows alias list in volatile memory. Eight aliases are available.

- **sysinfo** Shows CPU, memory, and device information.

- **ls** The syntax of this command is ls *device path*; this will view the contents of a directory given by *path* on the device *device*. For example, *ls wd0 /image/current* will list the contents of the currently active IPSO directory tree.

- **setenv** This command is used to set environment variables. The syntax you should use is setenv *name value*. For example, to change the default 5-second boot timeout to 10 seconds, enter **setenv bootwait 10**.

- **unsetenv** This command unsets or clears the environment variable given to it by name. So, for example, *unsetenv boot-file* clears the boot-file variable. Note that unsetting autoboot will not clear it but will set it to *No*. Similarly, unsetting *bootwait* will set that variable to 0.

- **set-defaults** Resets the given environment variable back to its default value, so *set-defaults bootwait* would set bootwait back to 5 seconds. If you use set-defaults with no arguments, the system resets all the boot manager environment variables to their default values.

- **setalias** Used to set an alias. An alias allows you to substitute one name for another. The syntax for this command is *setalias <name device>*, where *name* is the alias you want to create, and *device* is the name of the device you want to alias. Note that *disk* is a predefined alias for *wd0*.

- **showalias** Displays a list of all the currently defined aliases.

- **unsetalias** Used to delete or undefine an alias. The syntax for this command is *unsetalias <name>*, so the command *unsetalias disk* deletes the alias named *disk* that you defined earlier.

- **halt** Used to halt the system, which is typically followed by the system being powered off. Note that *halt* can also be used from a multiuser or single-user shell and is the safest way to power off your Nokia device, since it makes sure that all mounted file systems are unmounted.

- **help** Show help for the various boot manager commands.

- **boot** The *boot* command is used to boot the system manually. It allows you to specify that you would like to boot from a specific device, with a specific kernel image, using explicit kernel flags. It is sometimes useful to restore a system that has been rendered unbootable by a failed upgrade or corrupt kernel image. The syntax of the boot command is boot <*boot-device*> <*boot-file*> <*boot-flags*>. For example, typing **boot wd0 /image/current/kernel.old** would boot the kernel named *kernel.old* in the /image/current directory on device *wd0*. Typing just the word **boot** here has the same effect as if you had typed **boot wd0 /image/current/kernel** (/image/current/kernel always points to the kernel image of your most recently installed IPSO). Typing **boot –s** boots your Nokia into single-user mode.

- **install** Performs a factory default installation. This command is discussed later in the section.

- **passwd** Normally, access to the *install* command in the boot manager is open to anyone with physical access to your Nokia appliance; no password is necessary. If you are not confident in the physical security measures at your workplace, it is probably a good idea to set a password for access to this command. The first time you use *passwd*, it will prompt you for a new password twice. Once the *install* password has been set, you will be prompted for the current password before being allowed to change it again.

WARNING

Be careful! If you lose or forget the *install* password, in order to get access to it again you will have to remove your hard drive(s), reboot your Nokia appliance, change the install password, reinstall your hard drive(s), and reboot again. Some older appliances without the boot manager in flash memory must be returned to Nokia to have the password reset.

Reinstalling or Upgrading the Boot Manager

Reinstalling or upgrading your boot manager is sometimes necessary. Reinstalling your boot manager is usually something your support provider will ask you to do in rare circumstances—perhaps to rescue a system after a failed IPSO upgrade. Manual upgrade of your boot manager is needed only when you upgrade IPSO from version 3.2.1 to version 3.4 and later. Starting in IPSO version 3.3, the boot manager is upgraded automatically for you if needed, so we recommend upgrading to version 3.3 first, before going to any later version. You must be in single-user mode to reinstall or upgrade your boot manager. The procedure is outlined here:

1. Download the boot manager specific to your hardware model and IPSO version on a workstation or laptop that has network connectivity to your Nokia appliance. To find the correct boot manager image file, go to http://support.nokia.com, log in, and follow the Release Notes and Software Download link for the version of IPSO you are interested in. The link to the boot manager image is under the heading Boot Manager Upgrade Images for the IP300 or IP500 and later series and under the heading Boot Floppies for the IP400 series. Note that you do not have to upgrade the boot diskette on an IP400 series device sunless you want to perform a factory-default install.

2. Transfer the image file you just downloaded to your appliance using FTP or SCP, remounting your root partition read/write with the command **mount –uw /**.

3. Now log into your Nokia, and check the md5 hash of the downloaded image with **md5 <*path to downloaded image file*>**. The correct hash is displayed on Nokia's Web site, just below the image download link.

4. For the IP300 and IP500 or higher series, copy the downloaded image file to /etc/nkipflash.bin.

5. For the IP400 series, copy the image to a diskette using the UNIX **dd** command. On your Nokia device itself, you would place a diskette in the drive and run the command **dd if=<** *image path*> **of=/dev/rfd0**.

6. Type **reboot** and follow the preceding instructions for getting your device into single-user mode.

7. Since the IP400 series of devices uses the boot diskette as its boot manager, you are done. The boot diskette will automatically start the factory-default install process. (See the next section for details.)

8. If you have an IP300 series device, use the following commands to install or upgrade your boot manager:

   ■ Install: **/etc/install_bootmgr wd0 /etc/nkipflash**

   ■ Upgrade: **/etc/upgrade_bootmgr wd0 /etc/nkipflash**

9. If you have an IP600 or IP700 series model, use the following commands:

   ■ Install: **/etc/install_bootmgr wd1 /etc/nkipflash**

   ■ Upgrade: **/etc/upgrade_bootmgr wd1 /etc/nkipflash**

10. Reboot with the command **reboot**. Your Nokia device should stop at the boot manager prompt just after it restarts, because all its boot manager environment was wiped clean by the upgrade or install. Simply type **set-defaults** at the boot manager prompt to get them back to their default values.

11. Proceed with your IPSO upgrade using the boot manager's **install** command or use **newimage** from a shell prompt. If you were just reinstalling a previous boot manager version, bring up the system manually with the boot manager's **boot** command. (See the next section for the specifics of the boot command.)

Performing a Factory-Default Installation

You might find it necessary to reinstall IPSO as thought it just came from the factory—perhaps if you are configuring a previously used Nokia device or have a damaged installation. As discussed earlier, the boot manager's *install* command (or the boot diskette on an IP400 series model) accomplishes this task. This procedure will reformat and repartition your hard drive, so make sure that you have performed appropriate backups before starting. The procedure is as follows:

1. Set up an FTP server and make sure the Nokia appliance you are reinstalling has physical network connectivity to it. Test your FTP server from another host to make sure it works. The IP400 series has the capability of pulling the required files from its CD-ROM drive instead of from an FTP server.

2. Download the necessary IPSO package (ipso.tgz) and whatever other packages you want (such as FireWall-1) from either Nokia or Check Point's support site. Place the packages on your FTP server or burn them onto a CD (IP400 series only).

3. Get to the boot manager prompt as described in the "Single-User Mode" section. On an IP400 series device, you have to boot from either the boot diskette provided with your appliance when it was shipped or create a new boot diskette with the correct boot manager for the version of IPSO you are reinstalling. *The boot diskette will automatically start the reinstall procedure when you boot with it in the drive, so skip to Step 7 at this point.*

4. Use the boot manager's *printenv* command to see the version of your boot manager, and make sure it is compatible with the version of IPSO

you are installing. Use the guidelines in the section "Reinstalling or Upgrading the Boot Manager," if necessary.

5. Type **install** and press **Enter** from the boot manager prompt.

6. Enter the install password, if you set it up previously.

7. Follow the prompts, which will have you enter your device serial number, specify both your IP address and the IP address of your FTP server, and specify the username and login for your FTP server. You have the option of getting the required files from a CD-ROM drive on the IP400 series.

8. Once IPSO has been transferred and installed on your Nokia, reboot with the **reboot** command.

9. After a reboot, you will be back at the Hostname? prompt, as if this were a freshly unpacked box. Refer to Chapter 3 for the new install procedure.

Using CLISH

Command-line configuration before IPSO 3.6 was always a very difficult proposition on Nokia firewalls, given the way IPSO handled system configuration. As we discussed in Chapters 2 and 4, any changes you make to configuration files in /etc are lost at the next reboot, and changes made with standard UNIX tools such as ifconfig might not last even 5 minutes due to system daemons such as *ifm* and *pm* that monitor interfaces or critical processes and restart or reconfigure them on the fly, according to the settings in /config/active. The usual way to make system configuration changes was to edit the /config/active file, then synchronize it with the relevant configuration file in /etc with the **_xlate* series of commands. This method was imperfect, however, because anyone starting up Voyager would not see your changes and could override them accidentally unless a reboot was done after every change. The *dbset* command could also be used to make changes from the command line, but very few of the *dbset* command sequences were documented by Nokia, at least for public consumption.

User demand and the need for a scriptable interface that could enable remote configuration changes caused Nokia to release the *Command Line Interface Shell*, or *CLISH*, starting in IPSO 3.6. CLISH provides a simple command-line interface to *all* Voyager configuration options, either through a shell-like environment or from a file containing CLISH command sequences. If you are familiar with the secure, remote command execution capabilities of SSH, you will see the potential that exists for a remote Nokia management tool. In this section, we talk about how to enter and use the CLISH shell interface to make permanent system changes, without going near Voyager.

CLISH Basics

To enter CLISH, type **clish** and press **Enter** from a command prompt. You will see a Nokia> prompt, ready to accept commands. Although CLISH comes with a large reference guide, it really is not necessary for most commands. Simply press the Help (**?**) key at the CLISH prompt and a basic help screen will appear (see Figure 8.2).

Figure 8.2 The CLISH Help Screen

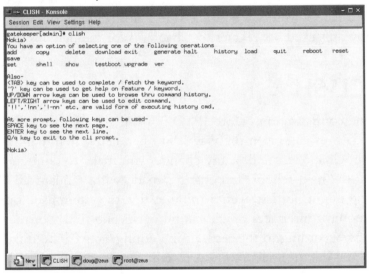

The help operator (?) can even be used in the middle of a command string, to give context-sensitive help on the argument you just typed and what needs to follow. Some of the other nice features CLISH offers are Tab completion of commands, command history perusal with the Up and Down Arrow keys (both of which work much like the Bash shell), basic command-line editing with the Right and Left Arrow keys, and C-shell style history search with the ! operator. Pressing **Ctrl + u** will erase the current line; pressing **Ctrl + c** will abort the current command. **Quit** or **exit** causes you to leave CLISH, although this step is unnecessary if you just want to execute a shell command or two. In that case, type the **shell** command to spawn a subshell directly from CLISH; when you are done entering commands, type **exit** to get back to the CLISH prompt.

If you want to see what commands are available from one of the main sections shown on the basic help screen, type that command and press **Tab**. You will see a list of valid command arguments that can follow whatever you just typed. For example, if you want to see what the *show* command has to offer, type **show** and press **Tab**. You will see something like the screen shown in Figure 8.3. (Notice the *More* reminder at the bottom of the screen; it indicates there are more completion choices, which you can access by pressing the **Spacebar**.)

Figure 8.3 Show Command Completions in CLISH

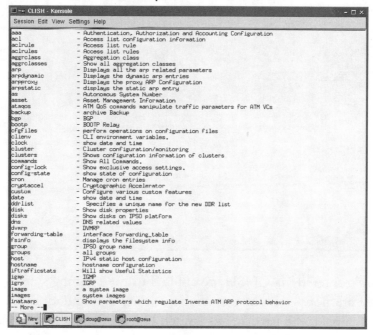

If you press **q**, you are put back at the *show* command you just typed, with a trailing space added for whatever you want to type next. You only ever need to type just enough of the command or argument for it to be unique before pressing the **Tab** key again, so type **fowar**, press **TAB**, and then press **Enter**. When you press Tab, the phrase *forwarding-table* is completed for you and is then displayed (see Figure 8.4). To get this command with the least amount of typing, you could have simply typed **sho** and pressed **Tab**, then typed **fo** and pressed **Tab**, then pressed **Enter**.

CLISH also has the capability to execute just one command or multiple commands from a file in *batch mode*. To execute just one command, type **clish −c "command"** from a shell prompt. To execute more than one command, place the commands (one per line) in a text file and execute them by typing **clish –f commandfile.txt**. The same file can be loaded and executed from within CLISH as well. From a CLISH prompt, type **load commands commandfile.txt**.

Figure 8.4 CLISH Display of the Forwarding Table

Commands entered via CLISH are applied to the running system immediately, but they are not persistent across reboots. Any configuration changes you make must be *saved* to be permanent—much like the Voyager apply/save semantics. To permanently save all your configuration changes from within the interactive shell, type **save config**. To save your configuration changes to a separate file named *configfile.txt*, type **save cfgfile configfile.txt**. This will be a full-blown valid system configuration file and is saved in /config/db with all the other system configuration files. Beware that the new configuration file is linked to /config/active once it is saved, effectively altering your system's active configuration. This might not be immediately obvious and is not documented. If you are using the one-off command form or the batch file form of CLISH, add the switch –*s* to the command to force a configuration save after the command or batch file executes, as in **clish –s –f commandfile.txt** or **clish –s –c "set vrrp accept-connections on"**.

In general, CLISH commands are formatted as *operator feature argument(s)*, where *operator* is usually one of *show*, *set*, *add*, or *delete*. Yes or no arguments are generally specified *yes* or *no* on the command line, similarly for *on* or *off*. If you know a feature name, using the word *default* for the argument always sets the system default value, even if you don't know what it is. This can be a good way to get your system back to normal if you enter a strange setting by mistake.

If you maintain a Nokia system for which there are more administrators besides yourself, it is helpful to block other administrators' ability to make configuration file changes. To do this, enter CLISH and type **set config-lock on**. Make your changes, then type **set config-lock off** to release the lock. You will get an error message if you try to lock the configuration when someone has already locked it.

Troubleshooting

When things go wrong, it is nice to know that you have a fully functional operating system under the hood that can help you get enough information to solve problems yourself or at least to help your support provider fix the problem. This section discusses the various command-line utilities that IPSO provides for performing things such as recovering lost passwords, log management and searching, packet sniffing, and memory usage collection. Many of these commands are merely simple UNIX commands that we use together in the way that they were intended, and some are creations of Nokia that allow you to gather information for them, should the need arise.

Managing Logs

The IPSO operating system provides several command-line utilities and many log files that can be used to troubleshoot problems or monitor user or process behavior. Most of the log files created and maintained by IPSO are in the /var/log directory, although some are in other subdirectories of /var. Check Point FireWall-1 logs are kept in /var/fw/log. We talk about some of the most useful utilities and log files in the following sections.

Searching and Displaying Log Files

Figure 8.5 shows the contents of the /var/log directory. The most useful file here is the one named *messages*. This is the global system log, sometimes called the *syslog*, and is preconfigured for you through settings in /etc/syslog.conf. Notice that, in addition to a messages file (which is text and can be displayed as such), there are seven files, named messages.0.gz through messages.6.gz. These are the compressed system logs for the past seven months. Every month, a system cron job runs that truncates the /var/log/messages file after compressing and saving it to /var/log/messages.0.gz. The old messages.0.gz file becomes messages.1.gz, and so on, until messages.6.gz is deleted and replaced by messages.5.gz. So IPSO will keep seven months' worth of archived logs for you while keeping your logs from growing uncontrollably and using up all the space in the /var partition. This process is known as *log rotation*. IPSO rotates some other logs in /var/log as well, including the HTTP access and error logs and the wtmp log that contains user login and logout times. Some log files are rotated more frequently; the system audit logs, for example, are rotated once per day because they have a tendency to grow in size very quickly. This is another nice feature of IPSO; not all UNIX operating systems do this for you.

Figure 8.5 Listing of the /var/log Directory

You can use the *more* command to page through a text file one screen at a time with the Spacebar, and you can combine *gzip* and *more* to display the compressed logs, without permanently decompressing the gzipped archive. *Tail* is useful to watch logs in real time, and *grep* is a powerful search tool. For firewall logs, the Check Point *fw* command can be quite useful and is typically much faster and more responsive than Check Point's log viewer GUI. The following are some basic examples of using these commands; refer to the online man pages at www.freebsd.org/cgi/man.cgi?manpath=FreeBSD+2.2.6-RELEASE for detailed information on these and many other IPSO commands. Documentation for Check Point's *fw* command can be found in the *FireWall-1 Reference Guide* available at www.checkpoint.com/support/downloads/docs/firewall1/4_1/CPRef.pdf (support login required):

- **more /var/log/messages** Pages through /var/log/messages one screen at a time.

- **gzip –cd /var/log/messages.6.gz | more** Decompresses /var/log/messages.6.gz and sends the output through a pipe to *more*.

- **tail –f /var/log/httpd_access_log** Watches the HTTP access log in real time.

- **grep –E '\<10\.100\.6\.1\>' /var/log/messages** Displays all the lines in /var/log/messages that contain the IP address 10.100.6.1. (The \< and \> character sequences are necessary so you don't match IP addresses such as 110.100.6.11).

- **grep –E –v 'LOG_INFO|LOG_NOTICE' /var/log/messages | more** Prints all the lines in /var/log/messages that do *not* contain the strings LOG_INFO or LOG_NOTICE and pages through the output.

- **grep 'LOG_CRIT' /var/log/messages | grep –E –v 'FW-1|ex_expire' | more** Displays all the lines in /var/log/messages that contain the string LOG_CRIT but do *not* contain the strings FW-1 or ex_expire and pages through the output.

- **fw log –nft** Displays the firewall logs in real time.

- **fw log –nft | grep –i 'icmp' | grep –i 'drop'** Displays in real time firewall log entries for the service icmp that are dropped by the firewall. (The *-i* tells the system to do a case-insensitive string match.)

- **fw log –nft | grep –E '\<10\.100\.6\.\1\>' | grep –v 'domain'** Shows all real-time firewall log entries containing the IP address 10.100.6.1 but that are *not* DNS traffic.

NOTE

Remember that under normal firewall operating conditions, your firewall logs are sent to your management console (in a distributed Check Point installation), which in many networks is a Windows NT or 2000 server, not your Nokia box. The *fw log* commands will not display anything on a firewall module, since there are no logs to display. The *fw log* commands work on Windows NT or 2000, but the *grep* portion of those commands does not. We recommend installing the excellent free software package Cygwin (see www.gnu.org/philosophy/free-sw.html for what the term *free software* means) on your Windows management station in that case, because it will provide you with a Bash shell and all the familiar UNIX text-processing utilities, including *more*, *tail*, and *grep*. The *fw log* command is much less useful without these utilities, especially in high-traffic environments. You can get a Cygwin net installer from www.cygwin.com/setup.exe. The Cygwin package even includes the latest OpenSSH server and clients, which can greatly ease remote administration of a Windows server.

Automating SCP Log Transfers

Sometimes it is necessary to transfer log files to another host because either your /var partition is out of space or you want to get a log file to another workstation for detailed analysis of some kind. It is possible to use FTP to transfer log files from your Nokia device, but this process suffers from several problems:

- The transfers are in plain text and can be sniffed, including usernames and passwords.

- Automating FTP is more involved than automating SCP transfers.

- You must remember to use ASCII or binary mode to transfer files to a remote host, depending on the file type (for example, uncompressed text versus compressed binary files).

SSH, specifically SCP, addresses all these problems. It provides for secure, encrypted file transfers using RSA or DSA authentication. Once the procedure has been automated, it is a simple matter to schedule transfers using cron. Here are the steps you need to take to set up this type of authentication.

First, you must generate public and private RSA keys for the user who will be transferring the log files from the Nokia device. We assume that this is user admin, since this will be the most common case, although you only need an unprivileged user who has read access to the required log files at a minimum. Note that we use CLISH and lynx to generate the appropriate SSH keys; you could use the *ssh-keygen* command to generate a public/private key pair from the command line, although the keys generated by *ssh-keygen* will not be visible in Voyager if you do so. CLISH is a good option for generating the public and private keys, because it is simple to use and any changes you make while in CLISH can be written to the global configuration file /config/active. We recommend generating version one and two keys because doing so will support the widest range of SSH servers.

The CLISH commands are as follows:

```
Nokia> set ssh identity v1 user admin size 1024 passphrase ""
Nokia> set ssh identity v2 dsa user admin size 1024 passphrase ""
Nokia> save config
Nokia> quit
```

Figure 8.6 shows a CLISH session that generates SSH version one and version two key pairs for the admin user, followed by a listing of the /var/admin/ .ssh directory, where you can see the key pairs listed.

Figure 8.6 Generating SSH Key Pairs in CLISH

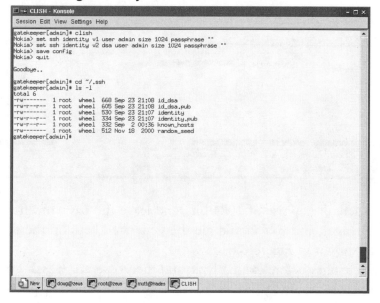

Here are descriptions of the files listed in Figure 8.6:

- **identity** RSA (SSH version one) private key file.
- **identity.pub** RSA (SSH version one) public key file.
- **id_dsa** DSA (SSH version two) private key file.
- **id_dsa.pub** DSA (SSH version two) public key file.

If you must use lynx to generate the SSH keys because you are using an IPSO version prior to 3.6, open up a lynx session and select the **Config** link on the opening screen. From there, navigate to **SSH (Secure Shell) | Go to the key pairs page | View/Create Identity Keys for User 'admin'**. You should be at the screen titled SSH Identity Keys For admin, as shown in Figure 8.7.

Figure 8.7 Generating SSH Keys in lynx

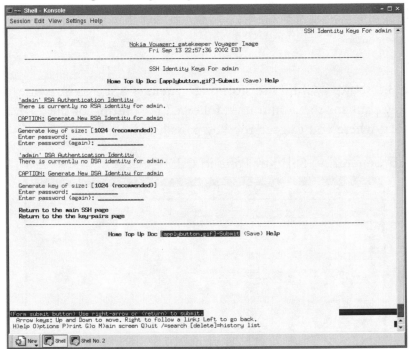

Keep the default key size of 1024 bits, and leave the password fields empty. Apply your changes, and you should see the generated keys on the screen after a brief pause, as shown in Figure 8.8.

Save your changes before exiting lynx, and then type **cd ~/.ssh**. You should see the SSH key files listed after you type an **ls –l**. Note that the two public key files are just ASCII text, so you can use *cat* to view their contents (see Figure 8.9).

The next step is to copy the two public key files /var/admin/.ssh/identity .pub and /var/admin/.ssh/id_dsa.pub to the remote host that will be accepting your transfers. You can copy the files to a diskette or use SCP to transfer the files. It is even possible to completely avoid a file transfer and cut and paste the public key text if you have a session to each host open in a console window or xterm. Both keys should be appended to the end of .ssh/authorized_keys in the user account that will be accepting the log transfers. Be careful not to overwrite this file if it exists, because it could contain other public keys from other SSH clients and removing them will disable logins for those hosts. Once this is done, you should test connectivity from your Nokia device to the host with the SSH server. Assuming the remote host has an IP address of 10.100.6.153, and you copied the public key files to dmaxwell's user account, for example, you can type **ssh dmaxwell@10.100.6.153** to open a remote session. The first time you connect, you will be prompted to accept the host key for 10.100.6.153, which, when accepted, will be appended to your ~/.ssh/known_hosts file. You should connect and be dumped into a command shell as user dmaxwell without being prompted for a password, since the SSH client and server have authenticated each other with your public and private keys.

Figure 8.8 Generated SSH Keys

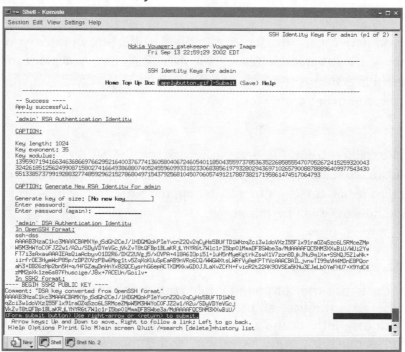

NOTE

You can read more about the basic theory behind public-key cryptography in Chapter 10 of *Check Point NG Next Generation Security Administration*, published by Syngress Publishing, ISBN 1928994741.

Figure 8.9 SSH Keys in /var/admin/.ssh

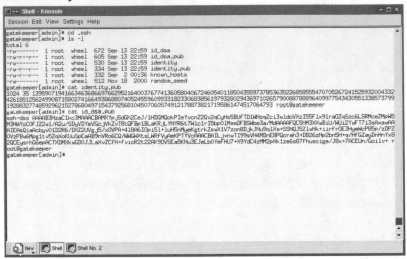

Once you have cached the server's host key by logging in once, you can initiate unattended, encrypted file transfers with SCP. Assume you want to transfer all the firewall logs from your Nokia to the remote SSH server. You would use the following command to do so:

```
scp /var/fw/log/*log dmaxwell@10.100.6.153:
```

Note the trailing colon (:); this is necessary because SCP expects a target path specifier. In the command, the colon is shorthand for *Place the file in the home directory of the user dmaxwell.* All files matching the pattern *log in your /var/fw/log directory will be transferred.

WARNING

Do not attempt the command while your management station is running, because the firewall processes have the log file opened for access continuously. Either run *fwstop* first, or perform an *fw logswitch* command, followed by an *fw logexport,* and compress your firewall logs before transferring them.

Recovering Passwords

Any good firewall administrator's toolbox should have the answer to the question, "What do I do if I lose or forget the admin password?" Nokia has a procedure that allows you to reset the admin password if you have local console access. Here are the steps involved:

1. Boot into single-user mode from a directly attached console connection. In IPSO version 3.4.x and later, the console is considered "secure," so you will not be prompted for a password if you boot into single-user mode from the boot manager prompt. (See the section "Single-User Mode" earlier in this chapter.)

NOTE

For this procedure to work, you must boot into single-user mode from the boot manager prompt.

2. You will not be able to change the admin's password in lynx, because you need the old admin password to even start lynx. Nokia has an executable that will allow you to temporarily change the admin's password. Run **/etc/overpw** from the single-user shell. Follow the prompts (see the code that follows).

3. Type **reboot** or **Ctrl + D** and allow the system to come up into full multiuser mode. *If your version of IPSO is 3.5 or greater, skip to Step 7.*

4. In IPSO 3.4, a bug prevented the *overpw* command from working correctly, and it assigned an empty password to the admin user. You will not be prompted for an admin password in this case when the system comes up, enabling you to get to a command shell, but you still will not be able to log into Voyager because it does not accept empty passwords.

5. A fix for this situation is to run the command **dbpasswd admin *newpassword "''"***, where *newpassword* is your new password and the trailing "''" specifies the old, empty password.

6. Run the command **dbset :save** to save the new password to the active configuration file.

7. Once this procedure is complete, you should be able to use Voyager or lynx again to set a new, permanent admin password.

Here is what the above procedure looks like when run through on IPSO 3.6:

```
Enter pathname of shell or RETURN for sh:
# /etc/overpw
    This program is used to set a temporary admin password when you have
    lost the configured password.  You must have booted the machine into
    single user mode to run it.  The configured password will be changed.
    Please change the temporary password as soon as you log on to your
    system through voyager.


Please enter password for user admin:
Please re-enter password for confirmation:
Continue? [n] y
Running fsck...
/dev/rwd0f: clean, 65453 free (2461 frags, 7874 blocks, 0.6%
    fragmentation)
/dev/rwd0a: clean, 36154 free (42 frags, 4514 blocks, 0.1%
    fragmentation)
/dev/rwd0d: clean, 5802929 free (625 frags, 725288 blocks, 0.0%
    fragmentation)
/dev/rwd0e: clean, 902680 free (992 frags, 112711 blocks, 0.1%
    fragmentation)


    Admin password changed.  You may enter ^D to continue booting.
    THIS IS A TEMPORARY PASSWORD CHANGE.
    PLEASE USE VOYAGER TO CREATE A PERMANENT PASSWORD FOR THE USER ADMIN.
```

Using tcpdump

We saw above how *grep* and other command-line tools can be quite useful in foraging through firewall log files, but sometimes you need to see a more detailed view of network traffic. This is where *tcpdump* comes in. It is a network sniffer that can be used to display packet header information from various levels of IPSO's TCP stack.

The most basic use of *tcpdump* is to examine all the traffic across a network interface. It will show you a decent level of detail by default. The syntax for this task is *tcpdump —i <interface name>*. So, for example, if your Nokia's internal (physical) interface was named eth-s1p3, you would use **tcpdump —i eth-s1p3** to see all the traffic coming across that interface. This command usually gives you too much information, however, so *tcpdump* will accept Boolean expressions on its command line that will filter the output. You can specify hosts, ports, or protocols as part of the expression.

The easiest way to learn is to see some examples of *tcpdump* in use. Table 8.2 shows the most common *tcpdump* command line arguments, whereas Table 8.3 shows some useful command sequences you can try yourself. If you would like more information, the man page for *tcpdump* is one of the few available in IPSO. Don't forget that you can always use *grep* with the output of *tcpdump*, as we did with the log files earlier.

Table 8.2 tcpdump Command-Line Arguments

Option	Meaning
-a	Converts numeric addresses to names.
-c <number>	Stops after processing <number> packets.
-e	Displays the Layer 2 header information.
-i <interface name>	Listens on interface <interface name>.
-n	Don't convert numeric addresses to names.
-q	Prints less information.
-r <filename>	Reads packets from file <filename>, which was created with the —w option.
-S	Prints absolute, as opposed to relative, TCP sequence numbers.
-v, -vv, -vvv	Various levels of output verbosity, in increasing order.
-w <filename>	Writes output to the binary file <filename>.

Table 8.3 tcpdump Examples

This Command...	Will Show You...
tcpdump —i eth-s1p3 host 10.100.6.153 and not port 80	All the traffic to or from the host 10.100.6.153 that is not on port 80 over the interface eth-s1p3.

Continued

Table 8.3 tcpdump Examples

This Command...	Will Show You...
tcpdump –i eth-s1p3 src host 10.100.6.153 and tcp dst port 22	All the TCP traffic to port 22 from the host 10.100.6.153 over the interface eth-s1p3.
tcpdump –i eth-s1p3 –w vrrp.out proto vrrp	All the VRRP traffic across the interface eth-s1p3. This will be written to the binary file *vrrp.out.*
tcpdump –i eth-s1p3 –r vrrp.out	All the data from the file *vrrp.out*, collected above.
tcpdump –i eth-s1p3 udp port 500	IKE key negotiation across the interface eth-s1p3.

In the commands described in Table 8.3, the output file generated by the *–w* switch is not a text file and can only be read by *tcpdump* or some other software written to parse the binary file format. If you want to save text output, redirect the standard output of these commands to a text file, as in *tcpdump –i eth-s1p3 host 10.100.6.153 and not port 80 > tcpdump.txt*. Figure 8.10 shows the output of an SSH session from my workstation at 10.100.6.153.

Figure 8.10 Output of tcpdump –i eth-s1p3 host 10.100.6.153 and port 22

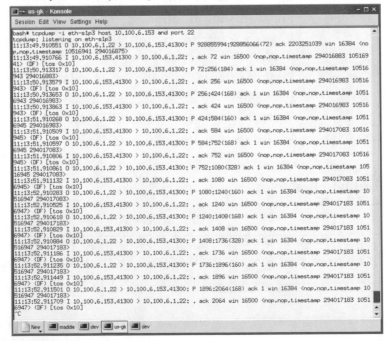

Let's analyze one of the lines in this output so you get an idea of what the information actually means. You should have a basic understanding of how TCP/IP works to get the most out of *tcpdump*.

```
11:13:49.910766 I 10.100.6.153.41300 > 10.100.6.1.22: . ack 72 win 16500
    <nop,nop,timestamp 294016883 10516941> (DF) [tos 0x10]
```

The first part, 11:13:49.910766, is a time stamp, which is as accurate as the IPSO kernel's internal clock. The part 10.100.6.153.41300 > 10.100.6.1.22 says that this packet came from 10.100.6.153, port 41300, and went to 10.100.6.1, port 22. The period (.) after the colon indicates that no TCP flags were set in this packet. We could see an S (SYN), F (FIN), P (PUSH), or R (RST) here as well. The string ack 72 means that this packet had a piggybacked ACK on it, for the 72nd data byte. win 16500 says that our available receive buffer is 16,500 bytes. The string <nop,nop,timestamp 294016883 10516941> describes various TCP options; the *nop* is a "no-op," used as padding. The only TCP option set in this packet is the timestamp option. The two numeric values are the timestamp value and timestamp echo reply. The (DF) means the "don't fragment" bit is on, and [tos 0x10] is the IP Type of Service option. In this case, 0x10 is the Minimize Delay option.

NOTE

An excellent reference on the inner workings of TCP/IP can be found in Richard Steven's book, *TCP/IP Illustrated*, Vol. I, ISBN 0201633469.

Troubleshooting Flows

Firewall *flows* are a feature Nokia added to the IPSO operating system to specifically work in conjunction with and increase the throughput for certain types of FireWall-1 traffic. To understand how flows work, we need to understand how IPSO and FireWall-1 normally work together to inspect and route packets at the kernel level.

The traditional name for the path that packets take through the IPSO kernel is *slowpath*. First, a packet comes in via a network interface and gets a kernel route lookup at the device driver level. It is then passed up to the FireWall-1 kernel module, where it is checked against the connection table. If the packet is not in the table, it gets checked against the firewall rule base. Assuming that the packet is part of an existing connection or is accepted by the rule base, it gets passed back down to the network interface device driver (now as an outbound packet), where it gets another route lookup. Then the connection table/route lookup process is repeated again, before the packet is sent on to its destination. This means that two connection table lookups and three routing table lookups for every packet. Nokia found that the bottleneck in this *slowpath* process was the connection table lookups, which are very slow compared with packet routing.

In an attempt to increase FireWall-1 throughput, Nokia implemented what is essentially a copy of the connection table at the device driver level. In what Nokia terms *flowpath*, incoming packets now get a connection table lookup at the same time they get a routing table lookup from the network interface device driver. The connection table lookup is done with the cached copy, not the FireWall-1 copy. If the packet matches an established connection, it is immediately forwarded on to its destination. If the packet does not match a connection table entry, it is passed up to the FireWall-1 kernel module, where it continues with the *slowpath* process as normal. Changes to the FireWall-1 connection table (for example, for new connections) are immediately propagated to the cached copy so that it is always up to date. This process results in a throughput increase for firewall traffic, with the best performance increase seen with small (64-byte) packets that are part of long-term, existing connections (such as large FTP or SCP transfers, for example). Nokia claims a four-fold increase in throughput in the best case, with performance gains decreasing as the packet size increases. A small amount of overhead is incurred when a new connection is established, because of the need to update the cached copy of the connection table, but this overhead is offset by the performance gains described, so throughput actually increases, even if only slightly, in almost all cases.

Firewall flows do have some limitations, however. Flows are not used at all for encrypted, ICMP, multicast, or authentication (security server) traffic. If you want to increase throughput of your VPN traffic, install a hardware accelerator. The combination of flows and a hardware VPN accelerator is the reason that Nokia's IP series devices attain such high firewall throughput numbers (refer back to Chapter 1). Note that NAT and antispoofing configuration data *is* cached by flows.

NOTE

Do not confuse Nokia's *flowpath* with Check Point's *fastpath*, which is a way to avoid connection table lookups in older FireWall-1 versions by assuming that all non-SYN packets were part of an existing connection and could be accepted without a connection table lookup. You could implement this at a global level by checking off the *fastpath* option in the version 4.0 policy editor. Although this feature resulted in some performance improvement, it was woefully insecure. Nokia's flows are a way to get an increase in throughput without any loss of security, since every packet gets the required connection table lookup.

There have also been problems with the implementation of flows in older versions of IPSO. The tool was introduced in IPSO 3.3 and has been enabled by default in all IPSO releases since then. Several Nokia knowledge base articles detail kernel panics that cause reboots when flows are enabled and certain conditions are met in FireWall-1 versions 4.1 SP2, SP3, and SP5. You should read Resolutions 4352 and 8731 in Nokia's knowledge base if you are using any of these versions. There are generally three solutions in each case:

1. Apply a hot fix or upgrade your particular FireWall-1 version, either of which can be downloaded from Check Point's support site. If you are on SP2 or SP3 now, SP4 will fix this problem. If you are on SP5 now, there is a hot fix available.

2. Upgrade to the latest FireWall-1 version and service pack available for your version of IPSO. At the time of this writing, this is SP6, with an OpenSSL hot fix. This is recommended because the latest service pack always includes past bug fixes and almost always fixes other bugs or security problems. Remember that not all versions of IPSO support all versions of FireWall-1, so you might need to upgrade your IPSO as well. (See Chapter 5 for details.)

3. Disable flows with the *ipsofwd slowpath* command. Nokia recommends this as a last resort.

You can always check whether flows are enabled with the *ipsofwd list* command:

```
usgk[admin]# ipsofwd list
net:ip:forward:noforwarding = 0
net:ip:forward:noforwarding_author =
net:ip:forward:switch_mode = flowpath
net:ip:forwarding = 1
usgk[admin]#
```

You can see in this case that flows are enabled by looking at the net:ip: forward:switch_mode line, shown in bold type. If flows were disabled, the word *flowpath* would be replaced by *slowpath*.

Configuring & Implementing…

Understanding How IPSO Handles IP Forwarding

If Check Point's FireWall-1 is not installed on your Nokia appliance, IP forwarding is enabled by default, since most people would be using it as a router in that case. If FireWall-1 is installed, IP forwarding is disabled by default and, unlike other platforms supported by Check Point, the *cpconfig* utility *cannot* be used to control IP forwarding. The state of IP forwarding (either enabled or disabled) during the operation of the firewall is given by a few simple rules:

1. If your Check Point firewall is unable to load a policy from a management console when it starts and no previously loaded policy is stored on the firewall (which would be in $FWDIR/state), the system will load a default filter that blocks all inbound network connections. This includes the case where you unload your security policy with the *fw unload-local* (NG FP2 or later) or *fw unload* commands.

2. If FireWall-1 starts and loads a policy successfully, IP forwarding will be enabled.

3. When FireWall-1 is stopped with *fwstop* or *cpstop*, IP forwarding will be disabled.

To manually enable IP forwarding, perhaps for network testing after an *fw unload* command has been issued, use the following command: *ipsofwd on admin.*

To manually disable IP forwarding, use the command *ipsofwd off admin.*

The *admin* in both commands specifies the user who is changing IP forwarding. You can see the current forwarding value, the status of Nokia's flows, and the last person who changed the state of IP forwarding using the command *ipsofwd list.*

Using ipsoinfo

The term *ipsoinfo* refers to the command that Nokia provides you to assist Nokia or your support provider in troubleshooting, should the need arise. It is similar in some respects to Check Point's *cpinfo* (or *fwinfo*), but *ipsoinfo* includes much more information. In fact, if the *cpinfo* command is found when the *ipsoinfo* command is run, it includes the *cpinfo* output in the file it generates. All you need to do to run the command is type **ipsoinfo** and press **Enter** when logged in as the admin user; after a while, the command will complete and leave a tarred, gzipped file named ipsoinfo-hostname-mm.dd.yyyy-time.tar.gz in the /var/admin directory. Be warned that this file can be quite large and can take some time to generate. If you extract it (either with WinZip after offloading it or with tar and gzip), it will contain the following files and directories:

- A system summary file
- A *dmesg* output
- A *cpinfo* output, if that command is present
- The ipsctl.log file, which tracks changes made through *ipsctl*
- The contents of the /var/etc, /var/log, /var/crash, and /var/tmp directories
- The contents of the /opt and /config/db directories

As you can see, this file will give you or your support provider lots of information about your system configuration—enough to recreate it exactly, if that is necessary. Figures 8.11 and 8.12 give you an idea of what the *ipsoinfo* process entails, with and without *cpinfo*, respectively. *cpinfo* does not come bundled with your Check Point software; you must download it from www.checkpoint.com/techsupport/downloading/utilities.html.

Using dmesg

The *dmesg* command outputs several screens of useful data, normally just the console messages printed by IPSO during its boot sequence. However, it also prints the most recent console errors on your running system. Figure 8.13 shows a partial output of the *dmesg* command on a smoothly running system—meaning that it has had no console errors that have displaced this information. In IPSO, the boot-time *dmesg* output is always saved in the file /var/run/dmesg.boot, so you can always look there if need be. You can see that your CPU type and speed, total RAM, and device probing results are all part of this output.

Figure 8.11 ipsoinfo Run With cpinfo

Figure 8.12 ipsoinfo Run Without cpinfo

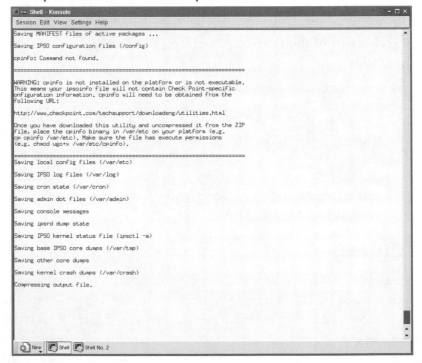

Figure 8.14 shows the partial *dmesg* output of a system experiencing many console errors, in this case on a Nokia system with Firewall-1 installed. This

particular error message indicates a synchronization problem with Nokia flows and Check Point's state tables, for which a hot fix is available. These errors also appear in this system's log file, /var/log/messages, as critical errors.

Figure 8.13 Output of dmesg Command Showing Boot Sequence

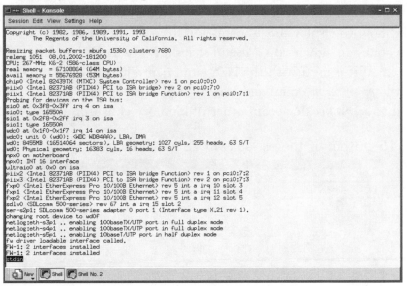

Figure 8.14 Output of dmesg Command Showing Console Errors

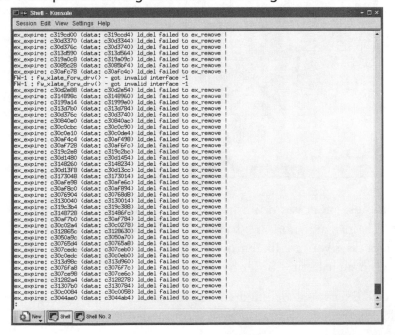

Memory and Processes

In this section, we discuss memory and process monitoring from the command line. It is useful when you are troubleshooting any system to have a good grasp of what the system processes are actually doing behind the scenes, so we will tell you what some of IPSO's system daemons do. Where appropriate, we discuss CLISH and how to display this information from a CLISH shell.

The *ps* command gives you a useful snapshot of what is happening on your Nokia system, if it is used with the right arguments. Figure 8.15 shows the output of the *ps -auxwm* command, which displays statistics about all processes running on your Nokia device, in order of memory consumption.

Figure 8.15 Output of the ps -auxwm Command

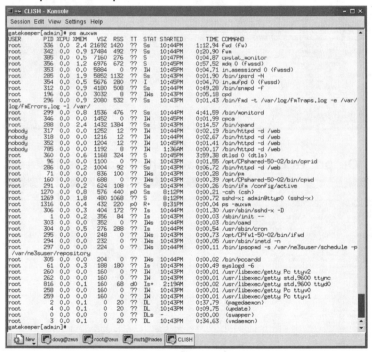

What do these processes do? Some, like *csh,* have obvious functions, but others, like */bin/pm,* are more mysterious. The following is a list of the most important processes you are likely to see running on your Nokia appliance. They are presented in alphabetical order by process name:

■ **cron** Executes scheduled commands as configured per user in a crontab file. The system crontab is in /etc/crontab.

- **csh** The default command shell run when you log into IPSO remotely or via serial console. This can be changed; see Appendix B for a list of shells available on IPSO.

- **fmd** The Fault Management daemon.

- **getty** Monitors serial ports for user logins.

- **httpd** The Apache HTTP daemon as used by Voyager.

- **ifm** Monitors all interfaces for changes and maintains consistency with /config/active.

- **ifwd** Monitors network interfaces for changes and reloads the firewall security policy so that it enforces the policy on the new interfaces. Nokia recommends disabling this daemon on firewalls in its final interface configuration. This can be done through Voyager in the Check Point configuration section. *ifwd* can be useful on systems with hot-swappable NICs, such as the Nokia 600 or 700 series devices.

- **inetd** A daemon that listens for network connections for the servers it has enabled in its configuration file, /etc/inetd.conf. In a default Nokia installation, the only network server enabled is Telnet.

- **init** The first process started by the kernel after system boot. It starts all the *getty* processes that listen for console logins and also starts the *inetd* process that listens for network logins.

- **ipsrd** The IPSO routing daemon. It modifies routing tables after dynamic routing protocol updates or static route changes.

- **monitord** Collects real-time statistics on interfaces and routing.

- **pagedaemon** Manages the movement of memory pages into and out of main memory.

- **pccard** The PC Card Daemon. Handles the insertion and removal of PCMCIA cards.

- **pm** A daemon that monitors certain critical processes and restarts them if they die.

- **rcm** Controls the system's run level (single- or multiuser).

- **snmpd** A daemon that responds to queries via SNMP.

- **sshd-x** Secure Shell daemon. Listens for incoming secure shell connections.

- **swapper** Manages the system swap space.

- **syslogd** Daemon that logs system messages.

- **update** This daemon flushes file system caches to disk periodically.

- **mdaemon** Memory daemon. It manages virtual memory.

- **xpand** Implements operating system changes to the global configuration file /config/active.

Sometimes during testing or network troubleshooting, it is useful to have a historical view of process and memory data. If you simply need a synopsis of memory and swap space usage at any given moment, you can use the command *vmstat –ism | more* to get very detailed memory and swap statistics, including how much memory each process in your system is using (see Figure 8.16). This form of *vmstat* is actually run as part of the *ipsoinfo* command.

Figure 8.16 Partial vmstat –ism Output

Look at the *vmstat* output. If the MemUse or HighUse column is greater than the Limit column for any of the categories, you might need to upgrade your physical memory.

If you want to know which processes are routinely hogging your memory, CPU, or swap space, you can use the following script, written by Nokia and available in Nokia's knowledge base as Resolution 11093. It is designed to be run periodically from *cron* and determine which processes are using the most memory and swap space. When run, it appends its output to the file /var/admin/vmstatmon.out. Here is the *crontab* entry you should use:

```
0,5,10,15,20,25,30,35,40,45,50,55 * * * * /var/admin/scripts/vmstatmon.sh
```

You can insert this line into the admin user's *crontab* using the *crontab* −*e* command, which opens a *Vi* editing session for you, or using Voyager or lynx if you are using IPSO 3.6. It is possible to use CLISH or Voyager to schedule cron jobs, but we recommend against using either one of them, since the interface is rather clumsy and doesn't appear to support schedules of finer than once per day without adding a separate job for each time increment.

Make sure to save the following script as /var/admin/scripts/vmstatmon.sh, and make it executable with *chmod +x /var/admin/scripts/vmstatmon.sh:*

```csh
#!/bin/csh
source /var/etc/pm_cshrc
# This program will monitor the usage of the swap file over time
# and list the top 10 processes hogging memory
# Save the output to this file
set output=/var/admin/vmstatmon.out
# Number of processes to report on
set processnum=10
################# main program begin
# print the date
echo ooooooooooooooooooooooooooooooooooooooooooooooooooooo >>! $output
date >>! $output
echo " " >>! $output
# print the swap file usage
pstat -ks >>! $output
echo " " >>! $output
# print the top process hogs
ps auxmw | head -${processnum} >>! $output
```

Figure 8.17 shows the output of this script.

Figure 8.17 Output of vmstatmon.sh

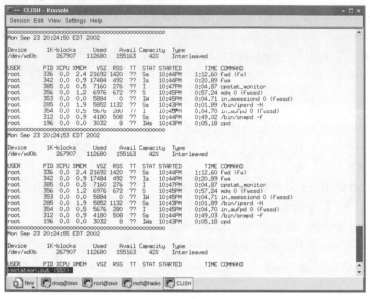

Designing & Planning…

Understanding IPSO Memory Allocation

The IPSO kernel allocates itself a fixed amount of RAM at system startup. This memory is reserved solely for the kernel's use and is *hardwired*, which means that it can never be swapped out to disk, unlike memory pages allocated to user processes. Just how much memory gets allocated depends on how much total RAM your system has. Approximately one-third of the total physical memory is reserved for the kernel's use, down to a minimum of 32MB. Applications (referring to processes in kernel stack and kernel module(s), if any) are each allowed to use up to 60 percent of the memory allocated to the kernel.

For example, on an IP330 with 64MB of RAM, the kernel will reserve the minimum of 32MB for itself, since one-third of 64 is approximately 21. Of that 32MB of kernel memory, 60 percent, or about 19MB, is available to any one application. The situation improves somewhat on an IP440 with 256MB of RAM; now the kernel reserves 85MB for itself and allows any one application to use up to 51MB.

Continued

Why is this important? Because the Check Point inspection engine is implemented as a kernel module and needs kernel memory for its many state tables. In Check Point FireWall-1 version 4.1, the firewall kernel module didn't need much memory (relative to the amount reserved by the kernel itself), so a system with 64MB of RAM would run FireWall-1 just fine. Check Point NG requires more kernel memory and will run only adequately on systems with at least 128MB of RAM. You might have had to increase the amount of memory allocated to the firewall kernel module at some point, if you had a firewall with a large number of concurrent connections passing through it. You can see just how much memory the Check Point firewall module has allocated and is using by executing the command *fw ctl pstat*. The relevant section of the output is the one titled "Hash kernel memory statistics".

Note that IPSO imposes a maximum of 512MB for the kernel address space, regardless of system RAM available. This means a maximum of 170MB is available for any single application process.

Summary

The IPSO boot manager is a valuable tool, knowledge of which is a large part of troubleshooting problems from boot failures to lost administrative passwords. Nokia puts the boot manager in flash memory in all its currently produced devices, although it has been on the system hard drive or even on a diskette in the past. The boot manager's main function is to load the IPSO kernel into main memory, and it does this if left to function unattended. If the boot sequence is interrupted, however, the boot manager gives you access to a rudimentary command shell, from which you can set and clear environment variables that control its function. The boot manager itself can be upgraded or reinstalled if the need arises.

Also extremely useful and new in IPSO 3.6 is the Command Line Interface Shell, or CLISH, which gives you the functionality of Voyager from a command shell. CLISH can be used in shell mode to enter interactive commands, or it can be used in batch- or single-command mode. Changes to the global configuration file /config/active can be made by saving your changes from the CLISH shell, much like the Save button in Voyager. It is possible for administrators to get exclusive access to the CLISH shell if they maintain a Nokia appliance with other administrators.

Nokia appliances can provide high levels of firewall throughput when *flows* are enabled. The biggest performance gain is seen in long-lasting connections with small packet sizes, such as large FTP transfers. *Flows* are enabled by default in IPSO 3.3 and later and can be disabled if needed with the command *ipsofwd slowpath*.

Troubleshooting problems can be made easier with the right command-line tools; anything that can be seen or done from a GUI interface such as Voyager or the Check Point log viewer is also possible from the shell. Managing and searching log files, in particular, benefits from the flexibility that tools such as *grep* offer. If your disk runs out of space or you need to more closely examine a log file, SSH (SCP) can be used to initiate secure, unattended log file transfers to remote hosts.

Other tools IPSO offers to make your life as an administrator easier include *ipsoinfo, dmesg, ps, vmstat,* and *tcpdump*. The *ipsoinfo* command is used to collect detailed system data for troubleshooting by your support provider or Nokia, whereas *dmesg* will show you boot-time messages or frequent console errors. The commands *ps* and *vmstat* can be used to diagnose memory or swap space problems, and *tcpdump* provides for detailed network packet header analysis.

Solutions Fast Track

Understanding the Boot Manager

☑ The boot manager is responsible for loading the operating system kernel into memory.

☑ Nokia's boot manager is kept in flash memory, but it has been on the hard drive and diskettes, the latter in the IP400 series only.

☑ Single-user mode can be accessed through the boot manager with the *boot −s* command.

☑ You can change the operation of the boot manager by changing the value of various environment variables with the *setenv* command.

☑ The *set-defaults* command sets all the environment variables back to their default values.

☑ You might have to upgrade your boot manager prior to upgrading your IPSO version.

☑ You can upgrade or reinstall your boot manager from single-user mode.

☑ You can perform a factory-default installation using the *install* command or a boot diskette on the IP400 series of devices.

Using CLISH

☑ CLISH has all the functionality of Nokia's Voyager, from a command-line interface.

☑ CLISH can be run in shell mode or batch mode or used to execute single commands.

☑ CLISH provides context-sensitive help with the ? key and command completion with the Tab key..

☑ Remember to save your configuration changes with the *−s* flag or the *save config* command.

☑ It is possible to block other administrators from making changes with CLISH with the *set config-lock on* command.

Troubleshooting

- ☑ Most of IPSO's system log files are kept in /var/log, except for firewall logs, which are in /var/fw/log.

- ☑ IPSO rotates system logs monthly so that they do not grow uncontrollably in size.

- ☑ *grep*, *more*, *tail*, and *gzip* can be used together to provide powerful log searching capabilities.

- ☑ SCP can be used to automate the transfer of log files in a secure way.

- ☑ It is possible to recover a lost admin password with the */etc/overpw* command.

- ☑ *tcpdump* can be used to show detailed packet-level data moving across a network interface.

- ☑ Firewall flows are enabled in IPSO 3.3 and higher, providing for increased FireWall-1 throughput for certain kinds of traffic.

- ☑ *Ipsoinfo* is used to generate a detailed system summary, which can be useful to your support provider.

- ☑ *Dmesg* shows you recent console errors and boot-time messages.

- ☑ The *ps* and *vmstat* commands can be used to troubleshoot memory or swap space problems.

Frequently Asked Questions

The following Frequently Asked Questions, answered by the authors of this book, are designed to both measure your understanding of the concepts presented in this chapter and to assist you with real-life implementation of these concepts. To have your questions about this chapter answered by the author, browse to **www.syngress.com/solutions** and click on the **"Ask the Author"** form.

Q: My SCP transfers still don't work, even though I followed your instructions. What can I do?

A: Pass the *−v* option to SCP. Try forcing one particular version of SSH with *−oProtocol=1* or *−oProtocol=2*. If you use strict mode checking in your SSH server's configuration file (usually in /etc/ssh/sshd_config), try restricting access to your SSH server's ~/.ssh/authorized_keys file with *chmod 0600 ~/.ssh/authorized_keys*.

Q: Why does my Nokia reboot itself after a "Fatal Trap 12" error message?

A: This message indicates that the IPSO kernel can't continue operating because a serious error has occurred. A *watchdog* timer present in all Nokia appliances causes an automatic reboot of the device if the kernel is unresponsive for any length of time. These errors can be caused by hardware (memory or disk) failures, misbehaving application programs, or even IPSO kernel bugs. In any case, these errors are worth a call to Nokia or your support provider.

Q: Can I increase the amount of kernel memory IPSO allocates to the FireWall-1 connection tables?

A: Yes, although this is rarely necessary in IPSO versions after 3.4. You need to use the modzap utility, which can be downloaded from Nokia's support site. See Nokia knowledge base Resolutions 1261 and 1325 for details and download links.

Q: I have an old version of IPSO and I want to upgrade, but I lost my admin password. Why doesn't /etc/overpw work?

A: IPSO versions 3.1.3 or before had a nonfunctioning *overpw* command. You have to call Nokia support to get an internal-only resolution for this problem.

## Chapter 9

Advanced Routing Configuration

Solutions in this chapter:

- **RIP**

- **OSPF**

- **BGP**

- **Logging**

- **VLAN-Aware Routing**

☑ **Summary**

☑ **Solutions Fast Track**

☑ **Frequently Asked Questions**

Introduction

As we saw in the "Understanding Configuration Options" section of Chapter 4, the NSP supports quite a few different dynamic routing protocols. Nokia developed its own code base for most of the various routing protocols (that were not licensed from other vendors) and bundled their functionality together in the *IPSO routing daemon*, or *ipsrd*.

The most commonly used of those dynamic routing protocols are RIP (v1 and v2), OSPF, and BGP (v4), all of which are supported by ipsrd. In this chapter we talk about each of these protocols in detail, first by going over the basic theory and functionality offered by each protocol, then by showing how it can be configured in Voyager. In the "Logging" section we talk about how to log various routing events and how to monitor dynamic routing protocols using the command-line tool *iclid*

Finally, we discuss the theory and implementation of a new feature in IPSO 3.5: VLAN-aware routing, otherwise known as *VLAN tagging* or 802.1Q.

RIP

RIP, which stands for *Routing Information Protocol*, is a very commonly used interior gateway protocol (IGP). IGPs, as opposed to exterior gateway protocols, distribute routing information within one autonomous system, such as your LAN.

RIP is a distance-vector protocol, meaning that it determines distance to other network devices by hop count. Hop count, which is stored in each TCP packet header, is simply the number of routers (or other devices, in some cases) a packet must traverse before reaching its final destination.

The distribution of routing information from one RIP router to another is accomplished when each RIP router sends its routing table to all neighboring routers. This transmission occurs on a regular interval, usually every 30 seconds, and whenever a router receives an update to its routing table.

When a router receives an update from another router, it increments the hop count by one. It then adds the route to its routing table and sets the gateway to the router from which it received the update. The update is then broadcast to all neighboring routers. This process of route transmission continues from router to router until the network reaches a state of convergence, when all routers have been updated with the latest routes. Refer to Figure 9.1.

To avoid routing loops, in which a group of routers update each other continuously about the same route, RIP considers any hop count above 15 to be invalid, and a route with such a hop count will not be retransmitted.

Figure 9.1 RIP Data Flow

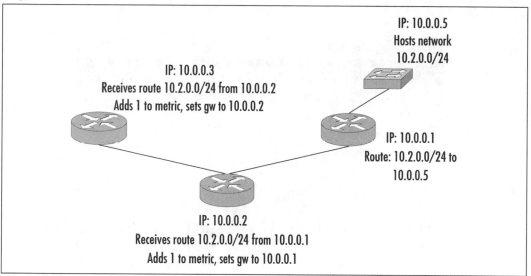

There are two versions of RIP: 1 and 2. RIP v2 provides several enhancements over v1, including authentication and additional amounts of information to be transferred per packet, such as subnet mask, which is not included in a RIP v1 packet.

Configuration

To configure RIP, open and log into your Nokia Voyager Web interface and click **Config**. On the right side of the screen, under "Routing Configuration," you will see the various routing protocols available. Click **RIP**, and you will see the RIP configuration screen as shown in Figure 9.2.

Here, you can enable or disable RIP for each interface and set the RIP version number, also per interface. It is important to set the RIP version number to match the configuration of the other RIP device(s) to which your Nokia will be speaking.

Additional general options you can configure come next. These include the *update interval*, which specifies how often, in seconds, your Nokia will broadcast its routes to its neighboring RIP routers. The *expire interval* specifies the number of seconds that must elapse without the Nokia receiving an update for a particular route before that route is removed from the Nokia's routing table.

It is important not to set this value too low, since you need to account for the fact that all routing updates might not arrive successfully—network problems could result in dropped packets. A good expiry interval is at least five or six times your update interval.

Figure 9.2 RIP Configuration

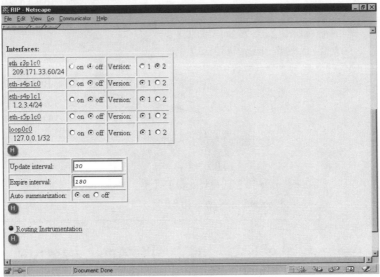

The final general configurable option for RIP is the Autosummarization setting, which can be set to *On* or *Off*. When turned on, this setting causes the Nokia to aggregate and redistribute nonclassful routes when you are using RIP v1. A nonclassful route does not include information about the size of the network; no subnet mask is specified. Because RIP v1 does not transmit subnet mask information, it is able to handle networks of varying sizes. As a result, this option is useful because it will combine your smaller networks into aggregated blocks before redistributing them to other RIP routers. Although RIP v2 is a cleaner solution when dealing with networks of various sizes, this option does give you the flexibility to work with these types of networks when RIP v2 is not available.

Now we will enable RIP v2 on interface eth-s3p1c0. Set this interface to **On**, set the version to **2**, and click **Apply**. You will see a variety of additional interface-specific options appear, as in Figure 9.3.

Options available here include Metric, which allows you to specify an additional metric to be added to all routes before sending them to other RIP routers on this interface. You should leave this set to 0 unless you are trying to manipulate router preference; another router broadcasting the same route will be preferred if this router broadcasts the route with a higher metric.

Figure 9.3 RIP Interface Configuration

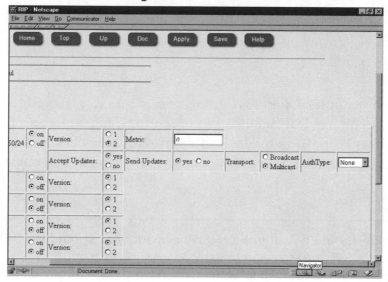

The Accept Updates option determines whether or not the Nokia will accept routes through this interface or only broadcast them. In some cases you might want your Nokia to act as a "send-only" router, so that you can update other devices with your routes but not have your routing table affected by RIP.

Similarly, Send Updates specifies whether the Nokia will transmit routing updates via RIP or simply act as a "receive-only" router.

The Transport option, when set to Broadcast, sends RIP v1 updates out to other routers, so long as these updates are compatible with RIP v2. Multicast is the default option, which uses multicast to distribute routes. *Multicast* means that the single RIP transmission can be heard by multiple listening RIP routers. Finally, we have the option to enable authentication of the RIP session between your Nokia and its neighboring RIP routers. AuthType allows you to set up authentication between the Nokia and other RIP routers. Options for authentication are None, meaning no authentication takes place; Simple, which matches a password string to authenticate; or MD5, which authenticates with an MD5 key. Enabling any authentication option besides None allows you to configure the additional parameters required, such as the password or MD5 key. One additional option available for MD5 authentication is Cisco Compatibility, which allows the Nokia to authenticate with Cisco routers running RIP. Note that even when this option is enabled, the Nokia is still able to authenticate with other Nokia devices running RIP on this interface, as long as their authentication is configured identically.

Once you have configured all these options, be sure to click **Submit** and then click **Save**, and you will have turned your Nokia into a fully functional RIP router.

OSPF

OSPF, which stands for *Open Shortest Path First*, is a more advanced interior gateway protocol than RIP and that allows you to design a more sophisticated local network. OSPF works on the basis of dividing your network into areas. An *area* consists of network nodes and routers that can logically be grouped together.

> **NOTE**
>
> When designing or adding to your network, you should keep OSPF areas in mind. OSPF areas are a convenient way of ensuring that your network is organized into manageable groups, each of which has a clean and straightforward design and clear purpose and benefit to the network as a whole.

In addition to areas, OSPF also consists of a *backbone*, also referred to as *area 0*, which transmits routes between all other areas. Other terminology that is important to OSPF is *area border router (ABR)*, which is simply a router with connections to multiple areas via multiple interfaces.

Unlike RIP, which is a distance-vector protocol, OSPF is a link-state protocol, which means that it transmits information about the state of its *links*, or connections. These transmissions, called *link-state advertisements (LSAs)*, are used to determine the short path from one router to another. This determination is accomplished via an algorithm called the *shortest path first (SPF)* algorithm, for which OSPF is named. (The *Open* in OSPF means that the source code used to write the protocol is freely accessible in the public domain.)

OSPF routers routinely send LSAs to routers in the same area, to provide information about state changes. Then, each router uses the LSAs it has received to generate a routing table based on the SPF algorithm. Due to the nature of OSPF, it is able to detect failed routers very quickly, which results in minimal network disruption in case of failure.

Figure 9.4 illustrates a typical OSPF network. Here, LSAs will be transmitted within each of areas 1, 5, and 10, but these announcements will not leave the confines of the area in which they originate. For example, the first router in area 1 will not receive LSAs from any of the routers in areas 5 or 10. However, each router in areas 1, 5, and 10 that is connected to the ABR router in area 0 does transmit LSAs to the ABR. In turn, the ABR retransmits each update from one area to the two others.

Figure 9.4 OSPF Network with Areas

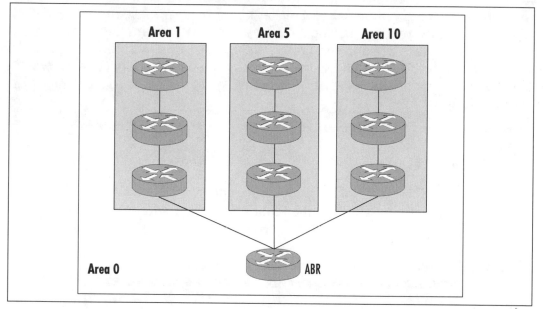

In this way, every router on the network will continue to be able to reach all other parts of the network while eliminating unnecessary LSA traffic between areas.

A key advantage of OSPF over RIP is a significantly reduced amount of network traffic required to keep routing tables up to date. This is the case because routing information within each area is restricted to that area; routers in other areas do not receive these updates. In addition, if there are more than two routers in an area, one router is elected the designated router (DR), while another is elected the backup designated router (BDR), and only the active designated router transmits LSAs. This is possible because all routers within an area contain the same routing table, so it is not necessary for all of them to be transmitting updates.

Designing & Planning...

RIP vs. OSPF

Since RIP and OSPF perform the same basic function—they are both IGPs—it is sometimes difficult to know which to use. One easy determining factor is network size: Smaller networks can make do with RIP's chatty nature without having to worry about significant excess traffic, whereas larger networks are better suited to OSPF's more efficient and organized configuration. However, compatibility of legacy network devices must also be taken into account, as some older routers might only support RIP v1.

Configuration

To configure OSPF on a Nokia, open and log into your Nokia Voyager Web interface and choose **OSPF** from the Routing Configuration section. The first items to configure appear in Figure 9.5.

Figure 9.5 OSPF Router ID and Interface Configuration

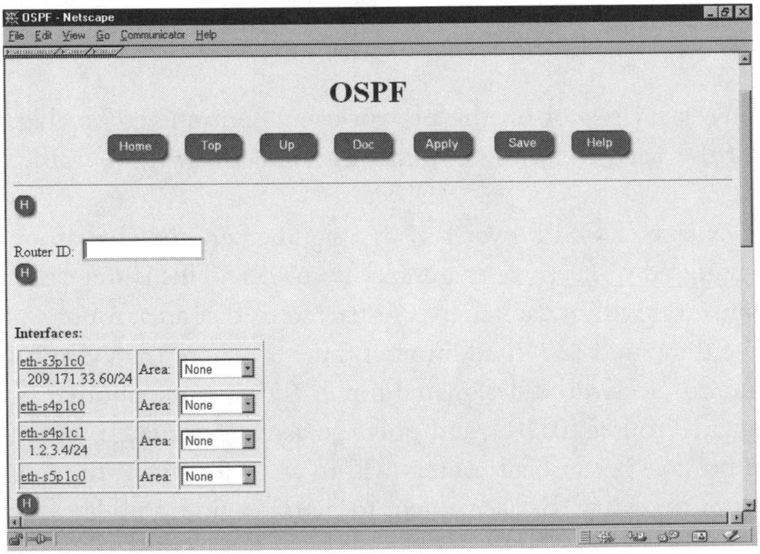

The first option you need to configure to set up OSPF is the Router ID. This should be set to a valid IP address you have configured on one of your Nokia interfaces. Next, you will see a list of interfaces, with the option to set an area for each. At this point, the only options for area will be None or Backbone, but additional areas will be available after you add them later on, as shown in Figure 9.6.

Figure 9.6 OSPF Area Configuration and Global Settings

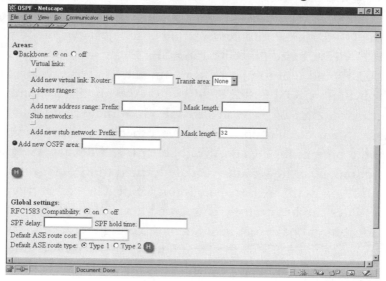

The Areas section allows you to enable or disable the backbone area. You would only disable the backbone area if your Nokia does not have an interface in area 0; otherwise, leave it enabled. Virtual links can be configured in cases in which the network that hosts the backbone area is not contiguous. In this case, virtual links allow you to bridge the gaps between one backbone network and another so that your backbone area can function normally.

If you enable a virtual link, you will be presented with additional options for this link: Hello Interval, Dead Interval, and Retransmission Interval, which should all be set the same for the routers at both ends of the virtual link. You can also configure the Auth Type as either None, Simple, or MD5, which allows for virtual link authentication between routers.

The next configurable area option is Address Ranges. An *address range* is a manual way of aggregating networks within an area so that when routing updates are sent to the backbone and other areas, only the larger aggregate is transmitted rather than the smaller network blocks.

Finally, you can configure stub networks. *Stub networks* are networks that are not running OSPF but whose routes you still want to distribute.

To add a new OSPF area, simply enter an area ID in the *Add new OSPF area* box and click **Apply**. OSPF area IDs are formatted like IP addresses—so, for area 5, for example, you would specify 0.0.0.5. Once you add an area, you will then be able to configure address ranges and stub networks for the new area. Also, you can specify whether the area is a *stub area*, meaning it has no routes that are external to your local network.

Also in Figure 9.4 are the global OSPF settings. RFC1583 Compatibility means that the Nokia's OSPF implementation will be backward compatible with an older OSPF release, based on RFC 1583. SPF Delay indicates how many seconds the Nokia should wait to update its routing table after it receives new routing information via OSPF. SPF Hold Time is the minimum number of seconds before the routing table is recalculated. Both of these SPF timer settings should be left at their defaults unless you have a specific reason to tweak them.

Next are the options for default ASE route cost and default ASE route type. Both these options affect how routes that are learned from other routing protocols (such as RIP or BGP) are distributed into OSPF. The cost and type of these redistributed routes can be manually configured here, although the default of 1 for both options should be appropriate for most configurations.

Once you have completed all these configurations, be sure to assign your interfaces to the appropriate areas you have configured. Then click **Apply** and **Save**, and your OSPF router will commence operation.

BGP

Border Gateway Protocol (BGP) is the most popular exterior gateway protocol (EGP) in use on the Internet today. As an EGP, BGP is used to transmit routing information between autonomous systems (ASs). This contrasts with RIP and OSPF, which are both generally used as IGPs and therefore only transmit routing information within an AS.

An AS is simply a collection of network devices that are controlled by one network administrator or group. There is a common network and routing policy in place in an AS, and it is has controlled ingress and egress points where traffic flows to and from other ASs in a controllable fashion.

Unlike RIP or OSPF, BGP does not transmit routing updates at any scheduled interval. Instead, BGP routers only transmit routing information to other routers when their routing table has changed. Initially, when a BGP router starts up, an entire routing table is transmitted to it, and this routing table contains information on how to connect to literally every reachable network on the Internet.

Then the router receives incremental updates to this routing table as other BGP routers' tables are updated.

The metric used for BGP is not based on distance vector or link state. Instead, the metric is a number based on a variety of factors, such as speed, number of ASs traversed, stability, and others. As a network administrator, you also have the ability to affect this metric through manual configuration of your router so that you can fine-tune route preference.

Every BGP router has neighbors, which are simply other BGP routers that communicate with it. Communication sessions between neighbors can be *internal*, meaning the two routers are within the same AS, or *external*, meaning the two routers are in two different ASs. Figure 9.7 illustrates a typical BGP network, with two ASs, each with IBGP connections internally, and an EBGP connection between them.

Figure 9.7 A BGP Network

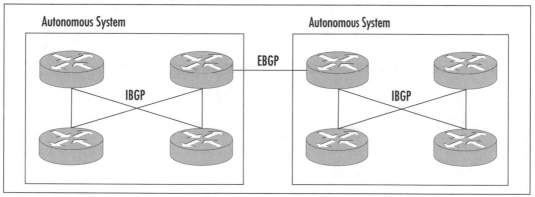

Configuration

Before you can configure BGP on a Nokia device, you need to purchase a BGP license that allows you to use this functionality. To install the license, open and log into your Nokia Voyager interface and click **Config**. At the bottom of the list of options, click **Licenses**, and you will see a list of features that require licensing, including BGP, as shown in Figure 9.8.

Enter the license key you obtained from Nokia under **BGP**, and click **Apply** and then **Save**. Then click **Up** to return to the main Configuration screen, and you will notice that under Routing Configuration, BGP now appears.

Click **BGP**, and you will see the main BGP configuration screen, as shown in Figure 9.9.

Figure 9.8 Software Licenses

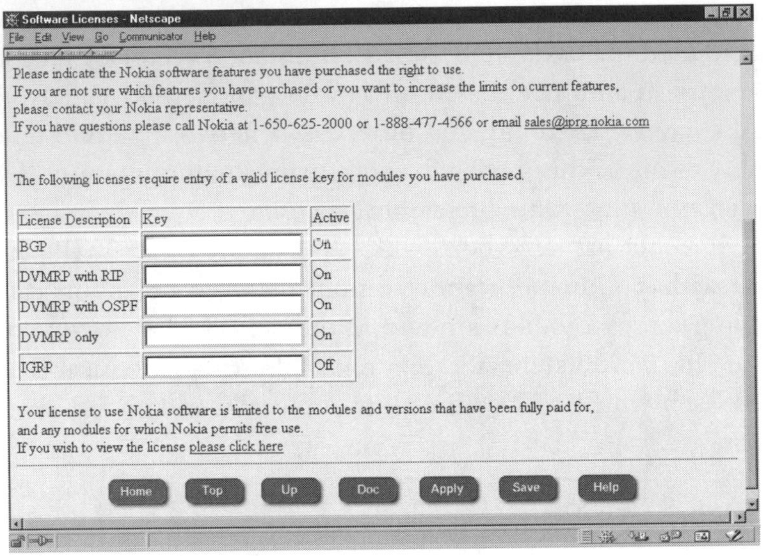

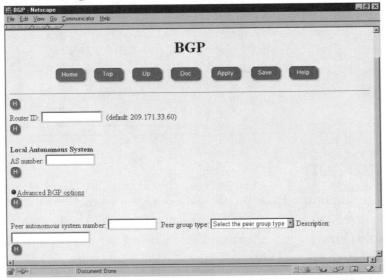

Figure 9.9 BGP Configuration

Here, set the Router ID to a valid IP address you have configured on your Nokia. This can be an address from any interface. Even better, you can configure a loopback interface via the Interface Configuration section (don't use 127.0.0.1— you will need to add another IP to the loopback interface that is routed to the Nokia), and use this loopback address as the router ID. The advantage to this approach is that even if one interface goes down, as long as the Nokia is still reach-able via another interface, the loopback address should still respond.

Next, set the Local Autonomous System to a valid AS number. To obtain an AS number, you can apply to an AS authority such as ARIN, or you have the option of using a private AS number. Private AS numbers, like private IP blocks, are reserved for internal use, so there is no risk of AS number conflict. Using a private AS assumes your service provider, with which you will establish a BGP session, has a public AS, which is what will actually be used to distribute your routes to the rest of the Internet.

We will look at the advanced BGP options later, but first let's skip to the peer settings. Set the peer autonomous system number to the AS number of the BGP router with which you are peering or establishing a session. For peer group type, select **Internal** if the peer is within the same AS as your Nokia or **External** oth-erwise. The *Description* field is a convenient place for you to enter a brief descrip-tion of this peer.

Now let's go back and click **Advanced BGP Options**, which will bring you to the screen shown in Figure 9.10.

Figure 9.10 Advanced BGP Configuration

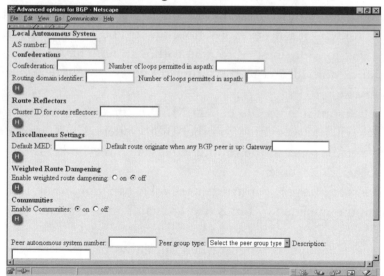

Here, you have the option to set up a number of interesting BGP features. You will see that you again have the option of setting your local autonomous system number. This field will already be populated if you entered and applied this information on the previous screen. Note that if you are using confederations, you should not set the AS number here.

Next is the Confederations section. A *BGP confederation* is a method of reducing the need to have all routers within an AS connected to each other. That is, normally in order for BGP to function, all routers within an AS must connect to all other routers—this is referred to as a *fully meshed configuration*. With a confederation, routers within an AS are subdivided into additional ASs, and then all these sub-ASs are assigned to one confederation. All routers within a sub-AS are fully meshed, and each sub-AS has a connection to each sub-AS. Confederations are not visible to outside ASs—they are an internal function.

To configure a confederation, first enter the confederation ID, which should be your AS number as it appears to your BGP peers. *Number of loops permitted in aspath* is simply a method of avoiding routing loops; if the local AS number appears more than the specified number of times, the route in question is discarded. *Routing domain identifier* is the internal AS number that will be used within the confederation. Be sure this is different from the confederation ID set earlier. Finally, the *Number of loops permitted in aspath* option is, again, a method of avoiding routing loops, but this time it relates to the confederation ID.

Next is the Route Reflectors section. A BGP route reflector is simply a BGP router that sends routes it learns from one internal BGP router to another internal BGP router—it reflects routes from one to the other. This further reduces the need for fully meshed routers within an AS. The *Cluster ID for route reflectors* option is normally set to the router ID, unless you have a specific reason to set it otherwise.

Under Miscellaneous settings, the default MED is the default metric to be used for routes that will be transmitted to other BGP routers. The *Gateway* option adds the specified default route to the routing table when the Nokia is connected to at least one other BGP router.

Weighted Route Dampening instructs the Nokia to ignore route updates and not transmit route updates for routes that constantly move from being reachable to unreachable. Such a route is said to be *flapping*.

The *Communities* option, when turned on, allows you to configure options in groups rather than per individual peer.

Next, we will look at the options that are available when you add an internal and external peer. Enter a peer autonomous system number, select **External** for peer group type, and click **Apply**. You will see the peer group options appear as shown in Figure 9.11.

Figure 9.11 External BGP Group

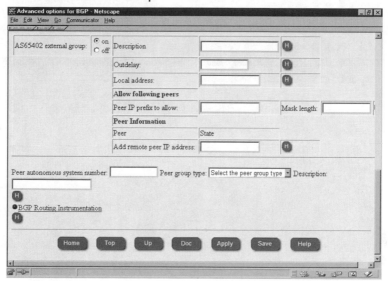

Here, *Outdelay* is the number of seconds a route must remain in the routing table before your BGP router distributes it to its peers. Setting this option to a number higher than 0 is an effective way to prevent flapping routes from being redistributed to other routers.

Local Address is an IP address on your Nokia that is on the same interface that connects to this peer. *Peer IP prefix to allow* is how you control what BGP routers within the remote AS can connect to your Nokia. For example, if you set the mask length here to 24, all routers within the subnet you specified will be allowed to establish BGP sessions.

You can also configure peers individually, by adding them under *Add remote peer IP address*. Once you do this and click **Apply**, you will see the peer listed, along with its state, and have he ability to turn it off. Click the IP address of the peer, and you will see the peer configuration screen, as shown in Figure 9.12.

Here, *MED sent out* is the metric to be set for all routes sent to this peer. *Accept MED from external peer* determines whether your BGP router will accept metric settings from this peer. *EBPG Multihop* is an option that allows you to establish a peering session with a BGP router that is not directly connected to an interface on your Nokia. *No Aggregator ID* is an option used to prevent aggregate routes with different AS paths.

There are two timers that you can configure: Holdtime, which specifies the number of seconds that can elapse with no activity over a BGP session before it is closed, and Keepalive, which sends a keepalive message to BGP peers at the interval you specify and closes the connection if no response is received.

Figure 9.12 Peer Options

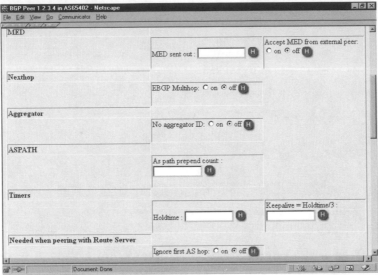

Configuring & Implementing…

EBGP Multihop

In some cases, it is not possible to connect your BGP peer directly to an interface on your Nokia. This is because you generally do not control your external peers—they belong to a third party with whom you have a peering agreement. In this case, you must be sure to enable *EBGP multihop*, which allows BGP to function even if there are two or more hops between your Nokia and your peer. However, for optimal performance you should ensure there is as little latency between the two as possible.

Ignore first AS hop instructs the Nokia to discard the first AS number on routes it receives from this peer. This option is not normally used, but it can be useful in cases when your BGP peer is a router that you want to be transparent. *Do Keepalives Always* instructs the Nokia to always send keepalives, even if not required. This option is primarily included for compatibility with devices that always expect keepalives.

In the Routes section, you can set the Nokia to either accept all or none of the incoming routes from this peer by default. Your local routing policy can then further determine what to do with incoming routes.

Setting the Passive option to On causes the Nokia never to try to initiate a BGP session with this peer. In this case, it simply waits for the peer to initiate a BGP session.

AuthType can be set to MD5 in order to enable authentication with this peer, which is recommended if security is an issue. If this option is set to None, you should be confident of the security of network between your Nokia and the BGP peer you will be connecting to. If this network is not secure, someone could maliciously "break in" to your BGP session and inject unwanted and disruptive routes into the routing table of your Nokia.

You can set a throttle count in order to limit the number of routing updates sent to this BGP peer at one time. Since routing updates can use a significant amount of bandwidth, it might be necessary to limit the number of updates sent at once, especially if you have a large number of peers.

The *Default Originate* option determines whether a default route will be added to the routing table when there is at least one operational BGP peer.

In the Logging section, you have the option to log both BGP peer transitions and warnings. The Traceoptions enable various debugging outputs that can be used to troubleshoot a BGP connection.

Once you have configured all these options, click **Apply** and then click **Up** to return to the previous screen. Go back to the Advanced BGP Configuration and you will see the options available for configuring an internal peer group. Enter another AS number under *Peer autonomous system number*, and for *Peer group* select **Internal**. You will see a variety of options, as shown in Figure 9.13.

Here you can set the protocols that will be redistributed into BGP, including IGP protocols, BGP, directly learned routes, RIP, static route entries, OSPF, and OSPF ase-type routes. This allows you to control exactly how your various routing protocols and manual routes interact.

Next you can set which interfaces are to be used for this peer group. Restricting the group to only the interfaces on which the BGP peers will connect is recommended and is also a good security precaution.

You can also set the MED, or metric, that is used for routes sent to this peer; the outdelay, the local address, and the allowed peer lists, just as with an external peer. A unique option for internal peers is *Nexthopself*, which transmits the Nokia's own IP address to peers as the gateway to be installed in the routing tables of the peers.

Figure 9.13 Internal Peer Group Options

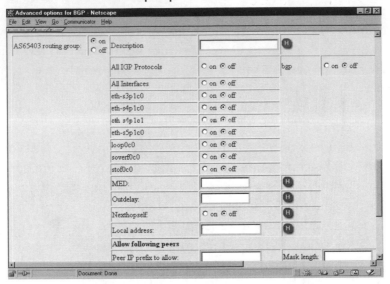

Now that we have gone through all the options available when configuring the Nokia as a BGP router, you can click **Apply** and **Save** these settings, and you are ready to establish BGP sessions with other routers.

Logging

Through the Nokia Voyager interface, you have the ability to enable logging for each of the routing protocols. A variety of logging levels are available for each protocol, so you have the ability to log only as much information about that protocol as required.

To configure logging, open and log into the Voyager interface and click **Config**. Then, under Routing Configuration, click **Routing Options**. The Trace Options section, as shown in Figure 9.14, is where you configure the customized logging options.

First, you can configure the maximum file size for each trace file. It is important to set this option to a reasonable size, related to how much disk space you have available on your Nokia, or your disk could become full due to excess logging. Once a trace file reaches the specified size, it is renamed and logging continues to a new file. The second option, the maximum number of trace files, determines how many of these files may exist before they are deleted.

Figure 9.14 Routing Trace Options

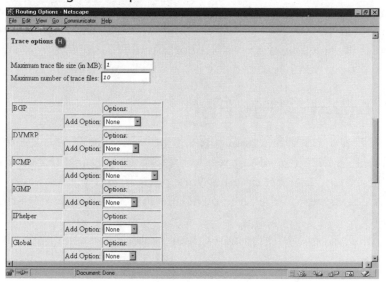

These log files are located on your Nokia in the /var/log directory. The current log file is called ipsrd.log, and previous log files are named numerically—ipsrd.0, ipsrd.1, and so on.

For each protocol, such as BGP, for example, you can enable any of the listed trace options. For example, if you wanted to enable logging of keepalive requests for BGP, you would select **Keepalive** from the drop-down menu and click **Apply**. Then you will notice that the Keepalive option is listed, with the option to turn it off, and you are free to add an additional trace option for this protocol.

This process may be repeated for any number of protocols and any number of options per protocol. Be aware of the large number of log entries that could occur if you enable too many trace options. If the trace file size and file number limits are set too small, the system could delete the trace information before you have a chance to view it.

Another way to monitor routing protocols in real time is to use the Iclid monitoring program. Refer to Chapter 7 for detailed information on this program, but we also discuss it briefly here. Iclid is a command-line program, so you need to connect and log into the command-line shell of your Nokia. Once logged in, simply type **iclid** and press **Enter**.

Once you are in Iclid, the two main commands are *show* and *get*. These commands can be used to view information on all the various routing protocols. To see the options available, type **show** and then press **?**, which will display a list of command completions. For example, you will see *bgp* as a possible command completion, so a valid command would be *show bgp*, which will show you general BGP information. If you enter another **?** after typing **show bgp**, you will see that additional completions are possible. For example, *show bgp errors* shows you any errors that occurred between your Nokia and your BGP peers.

VLAN-Aware Routing

A *virtual LAN*, or *VLAN*, functions just as a normal LAN does. What makes a VLAN "virtual" is that it need not reside on its own physical network device. That is, a VLAN can span multiple network devices, and you can even have multiple VLANs coexisting on the same ports and cables without interfering with each other.

For example, Figure 9.15 illustrates three switches on which six different VLANs reside.

Figure 9.15 VLAN Environment

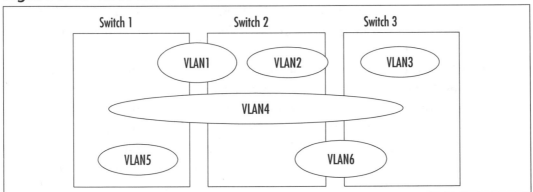

Because VLANs function equivalently to a normal LAN, all the normal behavior you would expect of a LAN also applies to VLANs: ARP entries of two devices on a VLAN are visible to each other, and no routing is required for these two devices to communicate, even if they are connected to separate network devices.

To accomplish this functionality—spanning a VLAN across multiple network devices—extra information is added to each packet that identifies the VLAN to which that packet belongs. As packets belonging to multiple VLANs are received across the same network cable and to the same network interface, the end device is able to read the VLAN tag in the packet and deliver the packet to the specified VLAN.

The protocol used to mark VLAN information in a packet is called 802.1q, and Nokia fully supports this protocol. What this means is that you can even span a VLAN between your Nokia and another non-Nokia device, such as a router, without compatibility concerns.

VLANs are useful because they allow for increased flexibility; there are fewer physical restrictions as to where network nodes on the same LAN must be located. VLANs are also extremely helpful in conserving physical interfaces on network devices, since a new physical interface is not required to set up a subsequent network segment. Finally, VLANs can be an important part of how you add redundancy to your network, since you can host a network segment on multiple devices, thereby avoiding an outage if one device fails. (Full redundancy assumes that end devices are connected to both network devices hosting the VLAN and other factors.)

Configuration

To configure VLANs on a Nokia device, open and log into your Nokia Voyager and click **Config**. Go into the **Interfaces** section, and choose the physical interface to which you want to add a VLAN. Near the bottom of the Physical Interface configuration screen, you will see an option to *Create a new Vlan ID*, as shown in Figure 9.16.

Figure 9.16 Physical Interface Configuration of VLAN ID

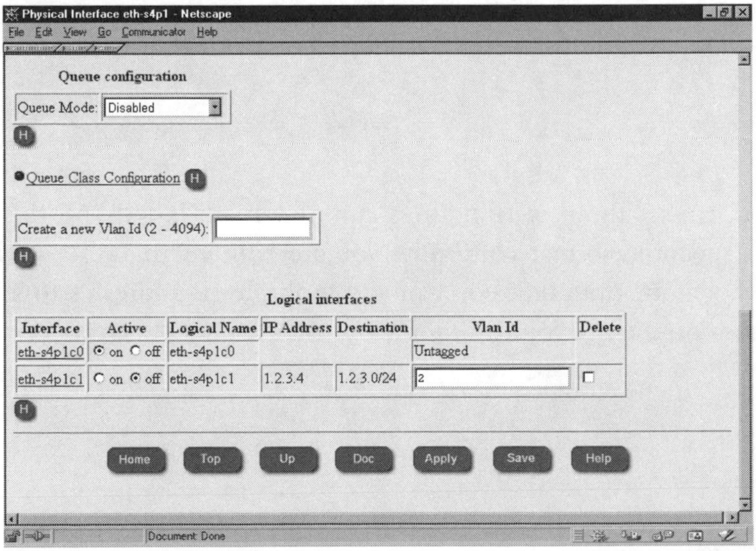

Under *Create a new Vlan ID,* enter any ID between 2 and 4094 that you have not previously assigned to a VLAN, and then click **Apply**. Remember this VLAN ID, since you must set the same ID to other devices to which you want to span this VLAN—that is how the end devices know what VLAN each packet belongs to.

Once you apply this setting, you will see that a new logical interface is created. The Nokia links VLAN IDs to logical interfaces so that it knows where to direct incoming tagged packets. You can configure the IP address for this interface just as you would for any other logical interface: Click the name of the logical interface (in this case eth–s4p1c1), and you will see the configuration screen shown in Figure 9.17.

Figure 9.17 Logical Interface Configuration

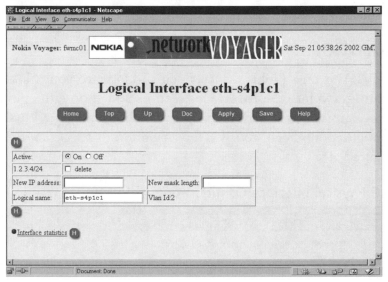

Here you can set the new IP address and new mask length. Notice that the VLAN ID is specified so that you know you are configuring a network for a VLAN. Furthermore, note that you can add multiple IP addresses to a VLAN just as you can to a nontagged logical interface.

Summary

Now that we have gone through the theory and configuration of several routing protocols, you can see that the Nokia is not only a firewall platform, but it can also act as a fully functional router.

Whether you use your Nokia as a RIP, OSPF, or BGP router, you are taking advantage of additional functionality that can result in decreased complexity in your network, since fewer devices are required as tasks are integrated on to increasingly versatile devices. You are also able to configure these dynamic routing protocols through the Voyager interface, with which you are already familiar from having configured the rest of the features for your Nokia.

Detailed information about all these protocols can be obtained using the Iclid command-line program. This information is especially useful when you're troubleshooting issues related to routing protocols gathering statistical information on various aspects of RIP, OSPF, and BGP.

The VLAN tagging feature is an extremely useful one, as you have seen. Spanning a VLAN across multiple devices, especially across multiple Nokia routers, opens up a wide variety of additional redundancy options that were not previously available. In addition, since the Nokia implementation of VLAN tagging conforms to the 802.1q standard, you have the flexibility to span VLANs to other compatible devices.

All these features add to the core functionality of the Nokia as a security platform, allowing for increased flexibility, compatibility, and functionality.

Solutions Fast Track

RIP

- ☑ RIP is a distance-vector protocol; it uses hop count to determine distance to other routers.

- ☑ RIP works by sending routing updates to all neighboring routers on regular intervals.

- ☑ You can configure RIP to either send routing updates, receive routing updates, or both.

OSPF

☑ OSPF is a link-state protocol. It uses information on interface status to determine available paths via the SPF, or the Shortest Path First algorithm

☑ The local autonomous system (AS) is divided up into areas. Routing updates are contained within the area, and routers that exist in two or more areas are called area border routers (ABRs). ABRs transmit routes between areas.

☑ There is always one backbone area, area 0, and it must either be contiguous or you must use virtual links to mesh the backbone area together.

BGP

☑ BGP is an external gateway protocol (EGP) used to transmit routes between ASs as well as within ASs.

☑ Local routers in a BGP network need to be fully meshed, unless you use confederations or route reflectors.

☑ The metric used to determine route preference in BGP is based on a number of factors, including speed, stability, number of traversed ASs, and manual operator settings.

Logging

☑ You can log a number of parameters for each routing protocol.

☑ To prevent your disk from filling up with logs, you can set the maximum size of each trace file and the maximum number of trace files.

☑ The Iclid command-line program can be used to obtain real-time data on each routing protocol.

VLAN-Aware Routing

☑ A VLAN functions just as a normal LAN does but without the same physical restrictions.

☑ A VLAN may span multiple network devices through tagging. A tag adds information to each packet, so that the packet may be recognized when it arrives at the end device and directed to the correct VLAN.

☑ VLANs are useful for reducing the number of physical ports required, increased flexibility, and redundancy.

Frequently Asked Questions

The following Frequently Asked Questions, answered by the authors of this book, are designed to both measure your understanding of the concepts presented in this chapter and to assist you with real-life implementation of these concepts. To have your questions about this chapter answered by the author, browse to **www.syngress.com/solutions** and click on the **"Ask the Author"** form.

Q: Do I need a dynamic routing protocol?

A: Dynamic routing protocols are only required when your routing table requires automatic updating based on a number of particular factors. If your routing table always remains the same, you might not need a dynamic routing protocol and can use static routes to direct traffic.

Q: Should I use RIP, OSPF, or BGP on my network?

A: Each has its advantages. RIP is very simple to set up because it does not require much configuration. If your network has a relatively small number of nodes, RIP is a good choice. With a larger number of network nodes, RIP might use up too much bandwidth, and so OSPF is a better choice, since you can divide your network into areas and enjoy faster convergence. BGP is used as an external gateway protocol, so you would not usually use it within your local network, although that is also an option in some cases.

Q: With BGP, should I set up my routers in a fully meshed configuration or use confederations or route reflectors?

A: If your network is small enough, the simplest option is to fully mesh. However, as your network grows you might find it more difficult to do this, so you can move to a confederation or route reflector setup. Confederations are best suited to networks that are easily subdivided into subgroups, whereas route reflectors are more suited to a network that is in a tree type of formation.

Q: If I have two Nokias, can I use VLANs to set them up for redundancy?

A: Yes, spanning each VLAN across both Nokia devices can help you attain redundancy. But you will also have to configure VRRP so there is a virtual gateway for the end devices to use and consider factors involved in setting up FireWall-1 in a redundant configuration.

Q: Should I use RIP v1 or RIP v2?

A: If all devices on your network that are going to take part in RIP support RIP v2, that is the version you will want to use. The main advantage to RIP v2 over v1 is that v2 transmits subnet mask information with each update, so you are able to advertise networks of varying size.

Q: If I am using OSPF, how many devices should be in each area?

A: There is no set limit or rule as to how many devices should be in each OSPF area. However, it is best to keep areas relatively small to cut down on unnecessary LSA communication between devices, which conserves bandwidth. More than 100 routers in an area are probably too many, and even that number could be a high limit in many cases, especially if bandwidth is at a premium.

## Chapter 10

High Availability

Solutions in this chapter:

- **Firewalls and High Availability**

- **Understanding Nokia's VRRP Implementation**

- **Configuring VRRP Monitored Circuit**

- **Configuring Check Point Gateway Clusters for Use in VRRP**

- ☑ **Summary**
- ☑ **Solutions Fast Track**
- ☑ **Frequently Asked Questions**

Introduction

This book's introduction mentioned the fact that many businesses today demand 24 x 7 uptime from the hardware that makes up their network infrastructures. The corporate firewall is one of those essential pieces of hardware that cannot "go down" and is frequently called on to perform flawlessly. This demand is not that unreasonable when you consider that most corporate firewalls are a weak link in their network infrastructures. All mail and Web traffic (possibly outbound as well as inbound) typically flow through a firewall before entering or leaving the network, and a malfunctioning or nonfunctioning firewall will either stop all traffic flow or allow all traffic through unfiltered, performing nicely as a router.

Nokia provides three solutions to this problem:

- An *active/passive* high-availability (HA) system known as Nokia VRRP HA; this option is described in detail in this chapter

- An *active/active*, load-balanced firewall solution that utilizes an external load balancer (such as BigIP)

- A new feature in IPSO 3.6 called *Nokia IP Clustering*

Nokia's most popular, widely deployed offering uses the Virtual Router Redundancy Protocol (VRRP) to provide an active-standby resilient firewall. IPSO uses VRRP (RFC 2338 dynamic routing protocol) to provide failover to a backup router in case of a primary failure. Additionally, Nokia has added an extension to VRRP, called *VRRP Monitored Circuit*, which handles both a total firewall failure as well as interface failures.

Another newer, slightly immature, but promising HA solution is Nokia's IP Clustering technology. Borrowing clustering technology from a previous product, the "ahead of its time" but now defunct VPN Cryptocluster series, Nokia provides a true active/active dynamically load-balanced firewall solution natively built into IPSO OS version 3.6 or greater.

We begin by discussing high-availability concepts, followed by a sample active/passive implementation, taking you through the configuration step by step. Finally, we show you how to complete the implementation by setting up a Check Point gateway cluster.

Firewalls and High Availability

There are two major components to Nokia HA solutions. First is the firewall synchronization process. Second is handling the IP address failover. Let's take a look at firewall synchronization.

At any given time on a production Check Point firewall, the machine is constantly inspecting the stream of packets passing through it and tracking authorized TCP and UDP sessions. This information is kept in a connection table. The connection table is an integral part of Check Point's stateful inspection process, which is used to increase the speed at which packets can flow through the firewall. Once a session has been authorized by the kernel's inspection engine, subsequent packets associated with that session are passed through without being evaluated by the rule base. This greatly reduces the amount of work a firewall has to perform, thus increasing performance and throughput. It also introduces a problem when you want to implement a highly available firewall solution.

Consider a case in which Johnny initiates as session from the corporate network through the firewall to his online banking Web site, as shown in Figure 10.1:

1. Firewall Snoopy inspects the outgoing packets.

2. It then writes it to the connection table. If Firewall Snoopy fails, Firewall Pepe takes over.

3. Meanwhile, Wells Fargo returns the response to Johnny via Firewall Pepe. The incoming packets are examined by Pepe's inspection engine. The packets appear to be from an already established session, of which Pepe has no record, so Pepe drops and logs the packet. This is not surprising, since the session was authorized by Snoopy, not Pepe.

To ensure that previously established sessions are not dropped when backup firewalls take over as primaries, it is essential that their connection table is copied from the active firewall to all the backups. This is done by Check Point's *state-synchronization protocol*. Now let's look at a configuration that is synchronizing its connection table, shown in Figure 10.2:

1. Firewall Snoopy inspects the outgoing packets

2. It then authorizes the session, and writes it to the connection table.

3. Snoopy then copies the new connection table entry over to Pepe's connection table via the Check Point Synchronization protocol.

4. Now, if Firewall Snoopy fails, Firewall Pepe takes over and Wells Fargo returns the response back to Johnny via Firewall Pepe. This time, Pepe has been informed that another firewall has already authorized the session, so incoming packets are allowed in without any notice to the user.

Figure 10.1 A Dual Firewall Without State Synchronization

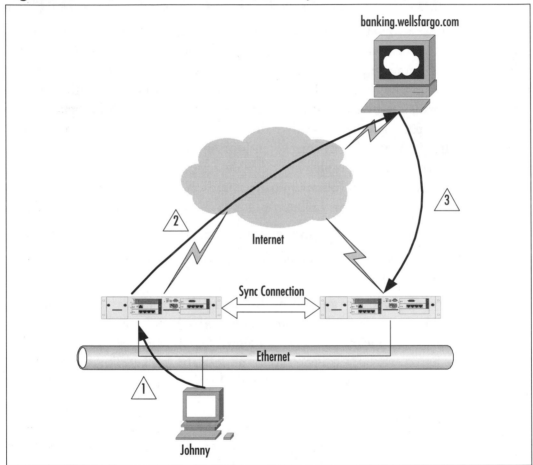

The second part of Nokia's HA solution is IP failover. You might have noticed that in the previous figures, we mentioned that Snoopy fails and Pepe takes over. What that means is that after a failure, the backup firewall assumes all functions and responsibilities of the primary firewall. In order to make this transition seamless and invisible to users and adjacent network devices, when a primary firewall fails over, its identity or IP address is actually picked up by the backup. Take a look at Figure 10.3.

Figure 10.2 A Configuration Synchronizing Its Connection Table

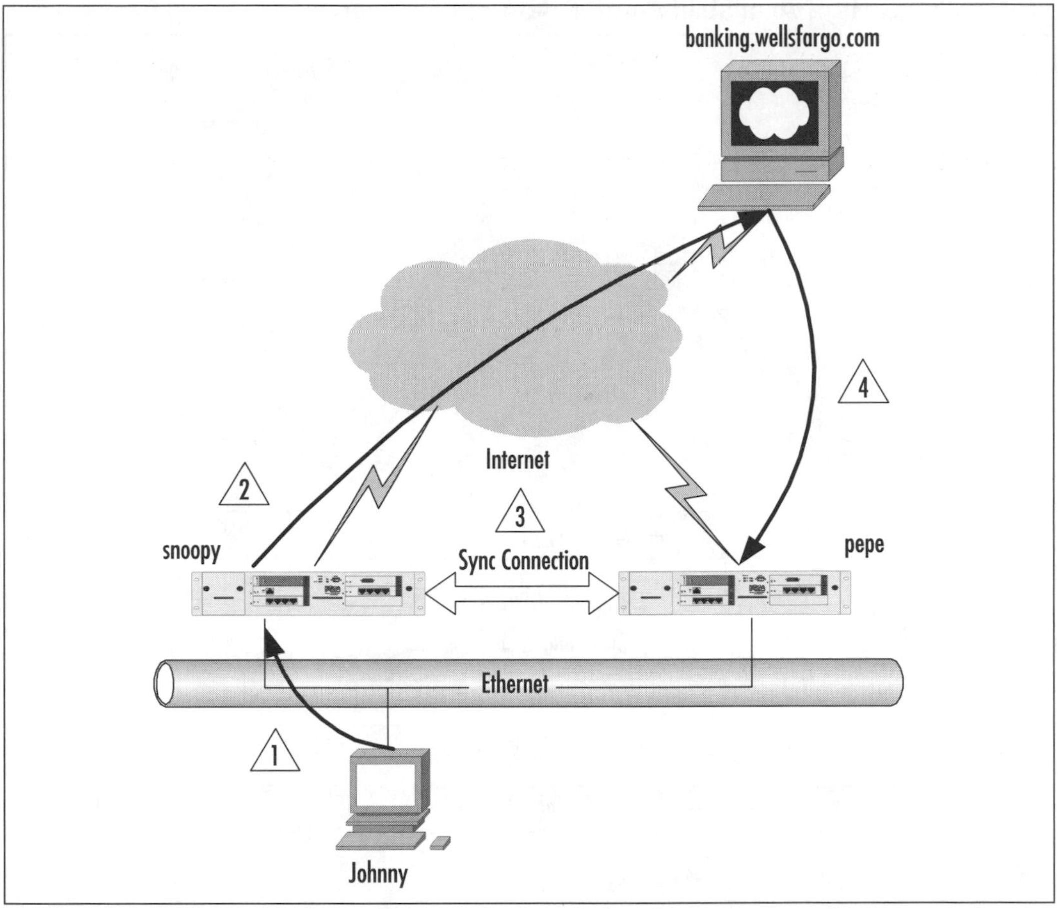

Designing & Planning...

Firewalls and State Synchronization

When firewalls are *stateful*, they are aware of the state of the connection. If you are using one firewall for outgoing traffic and another for incoming traffic, the normal latency associated with synchronizing the connection table can cause packet rejection. Check Point NG takes a minimum of 55 milliseconds to mirror its connection table. If a packet goes out and back through separate firewalls in less than that time, it will be dropped because it will appear as an unestablished TCP packet.

Figure 10.3 High Availability and IP Address Failover

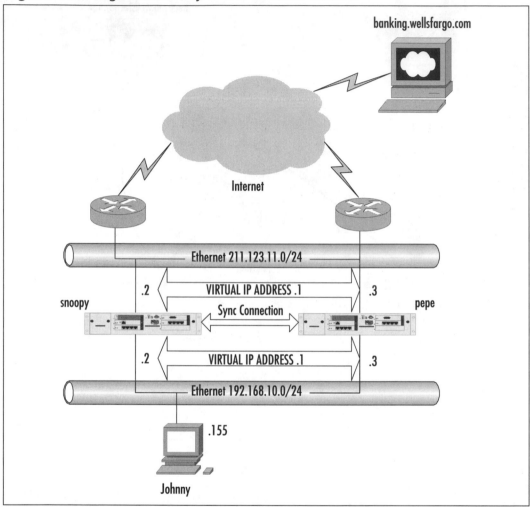

In Figure 10.3, the firewalls have two sets of addresses: one for administration and a second for routing. The figure shows firewalls Snoopy and Pepe with addresses .2 and .3, respectively. The .1 addresses are shared by the two and used as the next-hop addresses. For example, if Johnny wanted to Telnet to Snoopy, he would connect to the .2 address, but if he wanted to connect to his bank, his machine would pass the packets to the .1 address as the gateway.

The handling of these virtual IP addresses, along with their ownership and failover, differs depending on your Nokia HA implementation, but they all work essentially the same way. The virtual address is used as a next hop, and the other (real) addresses are used for administration and maintenance.

Each of the highly available solutions uses a combination of Check Point's gateway clustering feature and a mechanism for providing IP address failover. The IP failover method depends on whether you are using VRRP, an IP cluster, or an external load balancer.

Designing & Planning…

Sync Networks

When designing your network, you should plan to use a separate network to handle the firewall sync traffic. It is not necessary to do so, but it will improve your firewall's performance and reliability.

Understanding Nokia's VRRP Implementation

As mentioned in the previous section, Nokia has endorsed three solutions to provide highly available firewall and VPN solutions: VRRP Monitored Circuit, IP Clustering, and BigIP load balancers. VRRP and IP Clustering are a function of the IPSO operating system; the BigIP solution requires additional hardware. This section discusses the most common and widely deployed HA solution: VRRP Monitored Circuit.

Basic VRRP Configurations

In the all VRRP configurations, you will designate a primary router (called the *master router*) and one or more backups (called the *backup routers*). The master is responsible for forwarding packets sent to the *virtual IP address(es) (VIPs)* it owns and providing the services for that address, such as ARP, ICMP replies, and IKE or VPN connections.

An election process determines the master and is used to elect a new master should it become degraded or unavailable. The virtual address owned by the master is used as the default gateway for any of its adjacent LAN devices. In Figure 10.4, all the internal LAN hosts on 192.168.10.0/24 will use 192.168.10.1 as their default gateway. Snoopy, as the master (M), will answer all requests for that address, while Linus stands by. On the external side of the firewall, the

Internet–side routers will use 221.0.1.1 as their gateway to 192.168.10/24 and all other LAN segments on the inside of the firewall.

Figure 10.4 Basic VRRP Diagram

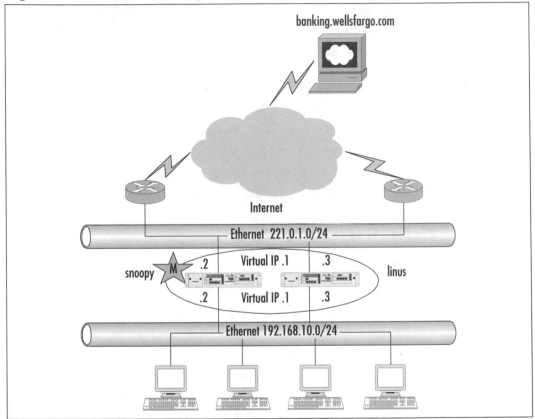

Configuring & Implementing…

Basic VRRP Configurations: The Master's Responsibilities

Nokia's IPSO implementation allows for the master to accept connection to the virtual address it owns, but the default configuration only accepts traffic that is to be forwarded, not connections terminating on the virtual address. If you are going to be configuring VRRP HA with VPNs, you need to enable the Accept Connections to VRRP IP option in Voyager. This step facilitates IKE key exchange between VPN endpoints.

Life continues with Snoopy doing all the work, but upon a failure condition, Linus takes over the ownership of the virtual IP addresses, and connections continue through Linus with no interruption to users of those connections. This exemplifies the usefulness of VRRP and the main advantage of using it: VRRP provides router resiliency in a statically routed environment without requiring configuration of dynamic routing or router discovery protocols.

The VRRP Protocol

In order to understand how VRRP handles IP address failover, let's look at the parameters that are used to implement this functionality.

As you can see in Figure 10.5, VRRP has a variable-length header, composed of many fields.

Figure 10.5 A VRRP Packet Header

0	1	2	3	4	5	6	7	8	9	10	11	12	13	14	15	16	17	18	19	20	21	22	23	24	25	26	27	28	29	30	31
Version				Type				VRID								Priority								IP Address Count							
Authentication Type								Advertisement Interval								Checksum															
IP Addresses																															
Authentication Data																															

Let's take a look at the definition and use of each:

- **Version (4 bits)** This field must be set to 2. This field specifies the VRRP protocol version that is being used. Currently, only version 2 is in use. The parameter is set by IPSO and is not user configurable.

- **Type (4 bits)** This field designates the message type, but currently, only message type 1 is used, meaning *advertisement*. The message type is set automatically by IPSO and is not configurable (see Table 10.1).

- **Priority (8 bits)** This field is used during the election process to determine who will be master. The node with the highest priority will be the master. According to the RFC, the master of the VIP should have its priority set to 255; but in IPSO, the master is just the node with the highest overall priority. The priority value of 0 has special meaning. It indicates that the current master has abdicated its ownership of the VIP. IPSO uses this special message to trigger a new election process to decide on a new master, thereby decreasing the failover time.

- **IP address count (8 bits)** The number of IP addresses contained in this VRRP advertisement.

- **Authentication type (8 bits)** Identifies the authentication method being utilized for this VRRP advertisement. Currently, three authentication types are defined in the RFC (see Table 10.2). Nokia has only implemented types 0 and 1. Type 1 is similar to the OSPF text-based authentication protocol, where advertisements are not accepted unless they have the proper shared secret. The downside to this type of authentication is that it is not encrypted, so anyone using a packet sniffer on this network is able to see the authentication string.

- **Advertisement interval (8 bits)** Sets the time interval (in seconds) between VRRP advertisements. If the backup routers miss three of these "Hello" advertisements, they consider the master down. The minimum setting here (as well as the default) is 1 second, which means that the minimum failover time for a completely crashed Nokia box is 3 seconds .(Faster failover times are possible using the *Priority =0* message, but a master cannot send out that message if it has lost power.)

- **Checksum (16 bits)** This is a simple error-checking mechanism that detects errors in the entire VRRP message, starting with the version field.

- **IP addresses** This is the list of VIPs owned by the master. The number of addresses included is specified by the *IP Address Count* field.

NOTE

Because the IP address count field is limited to 8 bits, the maximum number of virtual routers on one network segment is 255. This figure might seem small, but it is more than adequate for production environments. We have never seen more than four backups for one master in the field, and that was at a site providing online banking services.

- **Authentication data (variable length, 0 to 64 bits)** This field may contain up to an eight-character alphanumeric string. If a VRRP advertisement is received with the incorrect authentication string, it is discarded and the incident logged in the /varlog/messages file. The authentication strings are set on a per-interface basis. That means that all the virtual router IDs (VRIDs) participating on an interface use the same authentication string.

Table 10.1 The VRRP Type Field

Type	Description
0	Not used
1	Advertisement
2-15	Not used

Table 10.2 The VRRP Authentication Type Field

Type	Description
0	No authentication
1	Simple text password
2	IPSEC AH (authentication header)
3-255	Not used

Scenario: VRRP on the Whiteboard

Now that you have read about VRRP parameters, let's take a look at how to implement them in a standard VRRP firewall deployment at a fictitious company, ACME Corn, Inc. (see Figure 10.6). Uptime is very important to ACME, so the company chooses to have three firewalls, A, B, and C, ready to go. The company wants to establish a cascading failover such that if A fails, B takes over, and if B fails, C takes over. This is an active/passive setup, so there is no load balancing. The company also wants less than a 10-second failover time in the event of a failure.

NOTE

It is not a requirement that backup routers be the same model or have the same hardware specifications as the master. However, when designing your network, you must plan for potential problems. Make sure that any backup routers can handle the traffic you plan to send through them if the master fails.

Figure 10.6 ACME Corn's Network Setup

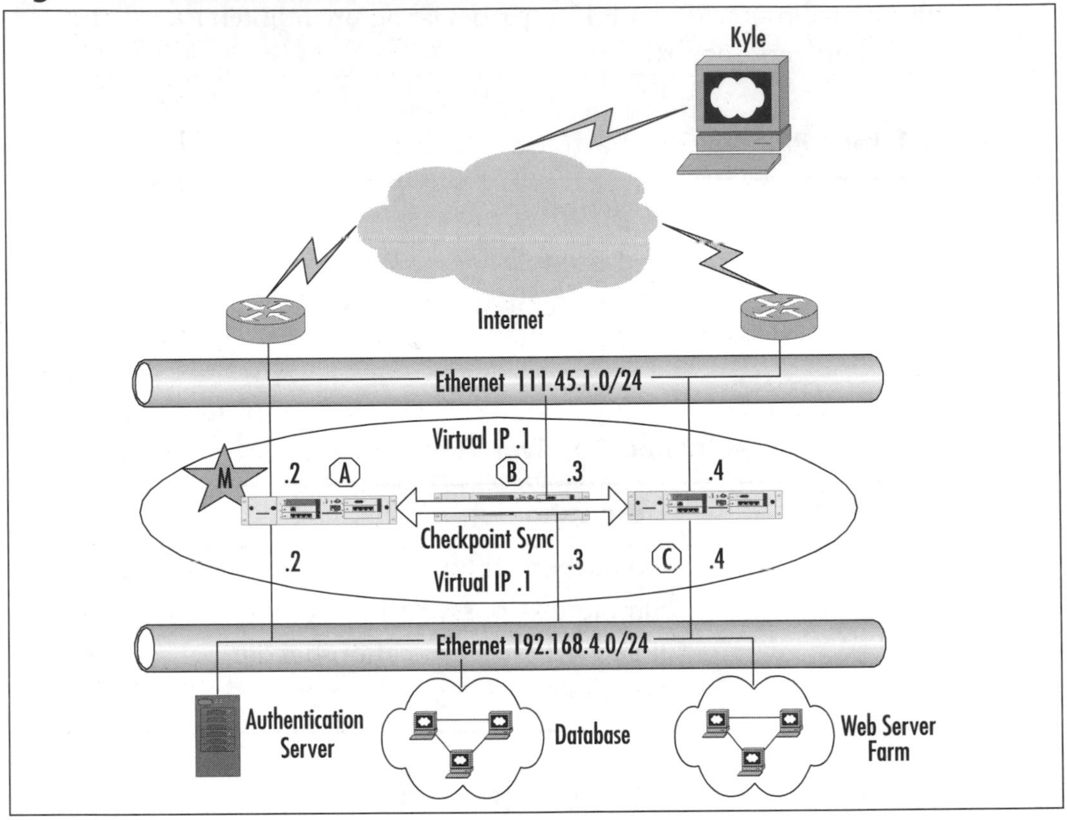

The three firewalls are all have identical network connectivity, and all have the same hardware and throughput specifications. The settings shown in Tables 10.3 and 10.4 will be made on each interface.

Table 10.3 Inside Interface

VRRP Setting	Firewall A	Firewall B	Firewall C
VRID	192	192	192
Virtual Address	192.168.4.1	192.168.4.1	192.168.4.1
Priority	254	234	214
Hello Interval	2	2	2

Table 10.4 Outside Interfaces

VRRP Setting	Firewall A	Firewall B	Firewall C
VRID	111	111	111
Virtual Address	111.46.1.1	111.46.1.1	111.46.1.1
Priority	254	234	214
Hello Interval	2	2	2

These settings will successfully satisfy the stated requirements. Two networks are running VRRP, one on the inside and one on the outside. Firewall A starts off as the master since its priority is highest at 254. If Firewall A goes down, it stops sending VRRP Hello advertisements. After the backups miss three consecutive advertisements, the backups elect a new master. In our example, the process elects B as the master, which takes 6 seconds (three times the 2-second Hello interval). Note that the VRID, which uniquely identifies a virtual router, is the same for each virtual "segment," so the inside virtual router at 192.168.4.1 uses one ID (192), whereas the outside virtual router at 111.46.1.1 uses another (111). Also note that this configuration is not complete, because we have not set up the firewall synchronization yet; this setup is covered in later sections of this chapter.

NOTE

If a failed master becomes healthy again, it resumes ownership of the virtual router, just as thought another machine had come online with a higher priority.

VRRP Monitored Circuits

Nokia has improved standard VRRP by adding some functionality. In the previous example, we showed how VRRP can be used to handle system failures or power outages. Consider what would happen if Firewall A's internal interface were to go down. In the previous example, it would continue to be master of the external VIP, but it would relinquish its ownership of the internal VIP. It would be unable to advertise through its internal network, causing a timeout, and eventually (after three missed Hello packets) it would fail over to Firewall B. This would cause the external routers to continue to use Firewall A's external interface as the gateway to the internal network, resulting in reachability failures.

To solve this problem, Nokia added a VRRP feature called *Monitored Circuit (VRRPmc),* whereby a firewall can monitor the link state of its interfaces so that if an interface fails, the priority in the advertisements of its other interfaces is degraded. To do this, Monitored Circuit uses some additional fields not implemented in the VRRP standard, called *Monitored Interface* and *Priority Delta.*

So, with Monitored Circuit, a list of interfaces and their corresponding delta values is added into the VRRP configuration. If a monitored interface goes down, the priority of the master is decremented by the interface's associated delta value. This new priority is known as the *Effective Priority* (EP).

For instance, using the previous example, if we were configuring the internal interface of Firewall A, we would have it monitor the link status of its external interface. If the external interface goes down, the internal's priority will be affected. The external interface's delta value will be subtracted from the overall priority to yield a new priority.

Let's take a look at another example that serves to illustrate a VRRP monitored circuit. Virgin Blue Airlines wants to create a highly available firewall network (see Figure 10.7). The airline has a screening router that connects an external network (5.29.66.32/27) to the Internet. Its two firewalls, Fred and Barney, are using VRRPmc to provide high availability, and it protects a DMZ network that contains the company's public online booking Web cluster as well as a mail server and an FTP server. The company uses a separate interface for FW-1 synchronization. Fred is the master firewall, but if any of Fred's forwarding interfaces go down, Fred will fail over to Barney.

In the network example shown in Figure 10.7, we use the basic VRRP settings but add monitored interfaces and delta values to handle an interface failure. When choosing which interfaces to monitor, *the interface we are configuring should monitor all other interfaces that are passing "important" traffic.* An example of an "unimportant" interface is your synchronization interface or any interface for which failover doesn't make sense, such as your own interface. (In the case of a sync interface, if one of the sync interfaces fails, the sync traffic will never be able to pass between the firewalls, regardless of failover.) Delta values should be chosen carefully to ensure that when an interface fails, its effective priority (after subtracting the delta of the failed interface) is lower than that of the backups (see Tables 10.5 through 10.7).

Figure 10.7 Virgin Blue's VRRP Monitored Circuit Configuration

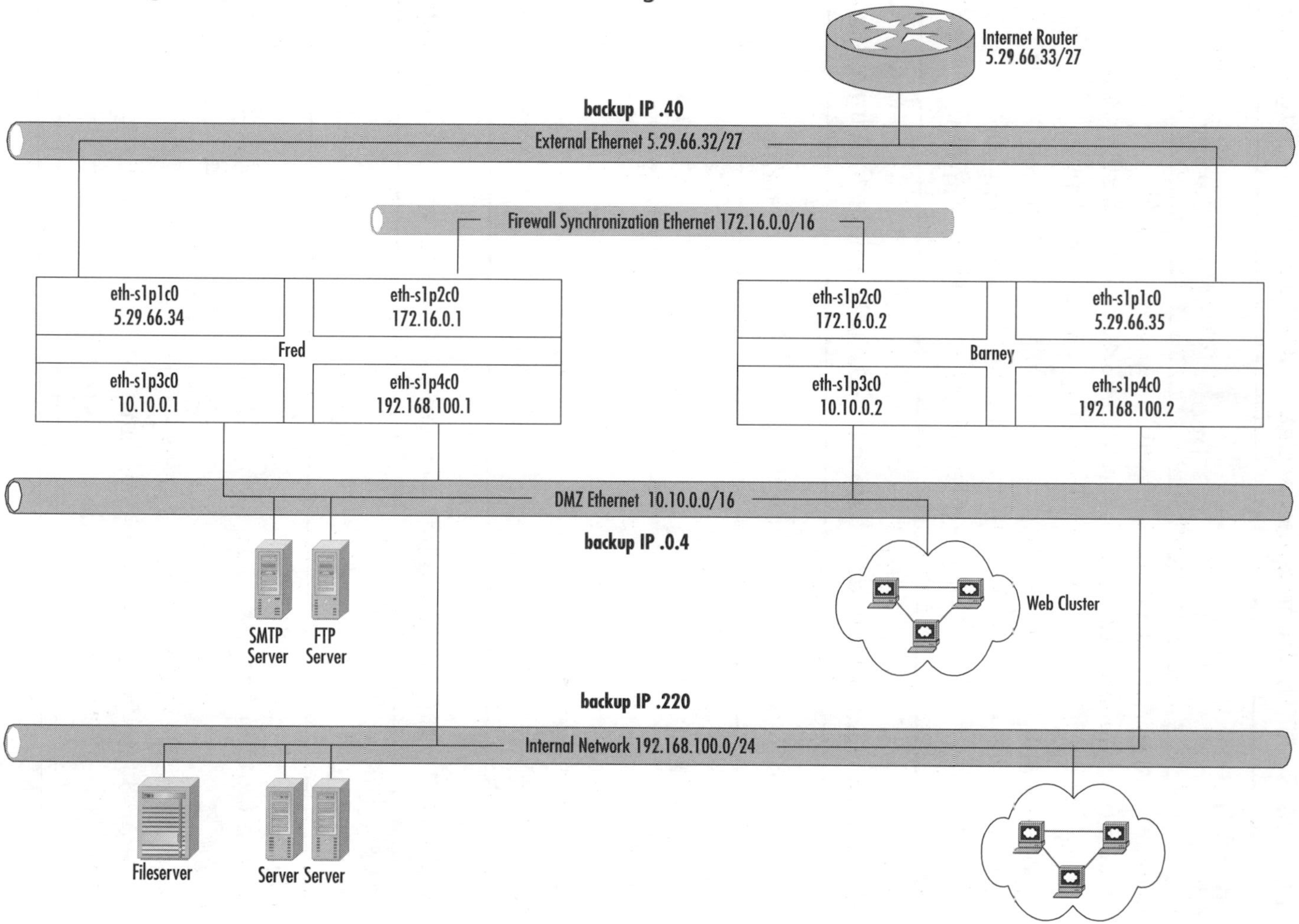

Table 10.5 VRRP Monitored Interface eth-s1p1c0 Settings for Virgin Blue

VRRP Settings: eth-s1p1c0		Fred		Barney	
VRID		40		40	
Backup (Virtual) Address		5.29.66.40		5.29.66.40	
Priority		254		244	
Hello Interval		1		1	
Monitored Interfaces		eth-s1p3	20	eth-s1p3	20
	Deltas	eth-s1p4	20	eth-s1p4	20

Table 10.6 VRRP Monitored Interface eth-s1p3c0 Settings for Virgin Blue

VRRP Settings eth-s1p3c0		Fred		Barney	
VRID		4		4	
Backup (Virtual) Address		10.10.0.4		10.10.0.4	
Priority		254		244	
Hello Interval		1		1	
Monitored Interfaces		eth-s1p1	20	eth-s1p1	20
	Deltas	eth-s1p4	20	eth-s1p4	20

Table 10.7 VRRP Monitored Interface eth-s1p4c0 Settings for Virgin Blue

VRRP Settings: eth-s1p4c0		Fred		Barney	
VRID		220		220	
Backup (Virtual) Address		192.168.100.220		192.168.100.220	
Priority		254		244	
Hello Interval		1		1	
Monitored Interfaces		eth-s1p1	20	eth-s1p1	20
	Deltas	eth-s1p2	20	eth-s1p3	20

In this example, Virgin Blue uses two Nokia IP 530 boxes to create the HA firewall network. Fred is the master for all three VRRP circuits, so for each VRID, Fred has a higher priority than Barney. For each interface Fred and Barney share, they must have the same backup IP address and VRID. You should try to choose values that make it easy for another person to understand the setup. For example, on the external network, Fred and Barney are using the 5.29.66.40 backup address and using VRID 40, the last octet of the address. We'll keep this convention for the rest of the VRRPmc interfaces.

> **NOTE**
>
> A configuration in which a single firewall has responsibility for inspecting all traffic and passing all responsibility over to a backup is known as an *active/passive configuration*. In such a configuration, the backup firewall only handles traffic when the master fails; otherwise, it sits idle. This type of configuration is most common in today's Nokia HA networks.

VRIDs, deltas, and priorities are arbitrary values, but you must choose values within their defined ranges. It is always a good idea to pick sensible values for these fields so that someone else could understand your setup should you win the lottery and not come back to work.

For priorities, it is recommended that your intended master start off as the master of all VRRP addresses and have his priority set to 254 (the maximum setting). All other firewall priority settings should be unique and lower than the master's. In the event of a tie, the ownership is awarded to the machine with the highest IP address. The tie-breaking mechanism is there for robustness, but having machines with equivalent priorities is considered a configuration error.

The priority settings are set up so that Fred is the master of all three addresses, but if any of Fred's interfaces fail, Fred should fail over to Barney. In our example, Fred's base priority is 254, which is lowered to 234 if an interface goes down (254 − 20 = 234). Barney takes over in that case, since Barney has a base priority of 244—now greater than Fred's.

Properly configured, this solution provides Virgin Blue with a failover service if Fred sustains a total system failure or has even one of its interfaces fail.

VRRPv2

VRRP version 2 (VRRPv2) is an older, less functional way of providing firewall resiliency. In a VRRPv2 configuration, firewalls do not use a virtual IP address, as they do in VRRPmc. VRRPv2 masters use dynamic routing protocols, such as OSPF, to advertise network reachability to adjacent routers. When a master firewall fails, the backups will notice the absence of the master's VRRP advertisements and go into an election process to decide on a new master. Once elected, the new master begins advertising itself (via dynamic routing) to the adjacent routers as the new gateway, thus causing the adjacent routers to switch over to the new master instead of the old "deceased" one.

VRRPv2 does have some drawbacks and one major shortcoming when implemented on Check Point firewalls. A condition can occur when a VRRPv2 master has an interface failure rather than a total system crash. It causes the downed interface to fail over, but the remaining working interfaces stay in the master state. As a result, it is possible to have an asymmetric routing condition that will cause problems for Check Point firewalls.

The problem exists because the master's downed interface no longer broadcasts VRRP advertisements, causing the backup on that network to take over. The master's other interfaces continue to broadcast VRRP advertisements, so it stays the master on the "up" interfaces. This causes one of the master's interfaces, but not the rest, to fail over to the backup. In a router-only environment, asymmetry is no trouble; routers are designed to handle changing network topology. The problem occurs in the Check Point state table synchronization process.

As discussed in the previous section, Check Point copies its connection table between the backups. This copy process takes around 55ms, an eternity in LAN round-trip timings. If Check Point firewalls experience asymmetric ingress and egress (incoming and outgoing) traffic, they won't have enough time to synchronize state tables and will erroneously believe they are seeing an unestablished TCP connection. The symptom of this situation in your log viewer will be drops on "rule 0," but only if you are logging implied rules.

Due to this potential Check Point problem, Nokia no longer recommends VRRPv2 for customers who want to implement VRRP HA solutions. Using VRRPmc eliminates the asymmetric routing conditions that occur in a VRRPv2 configuration.

Designing & Planning...

Summary of Differences Between VRRP v2 and Monitored Circuits

Here are the characteristics of VRRPv2 configuration:

- Backup of router interface address (real IP address)
- When an NSP is in master mode it responds to ICMP echo requests
- Requires use of dynamic routing to recover from single interface failure
- Cannot track other interface statuses (whether up or down)

Here are the characteristics of a VRRPmc Monitored Circuit configuration:

- Uses a virtual IP address (not a real address)
- Does not respond to ICMP echo request (by default, but can be overridden)
- Does not require the use of additional routing protocols
- Can monitor the state of multiple interfaces

Configuring VRRP Monitored Circuit

Now that you have seen how VRRP Monitored Circuit is configured at an abstract level, let's look at an actual configuration via the CLI and Voyager. To demonstrate, we use a dual firewall example (see Figure 10.8). We are using two IP120s with an outside, inside, and Firewall-1 synchronization interface.

In this network configuration, we create an active/passive monitored circuit HA pair. We first need to configure the individual NSP settings, much like the ones you created in the standalone mode discussed in Chapter 4. Next, we configure the VRRP settings. Finally, we need to set up Check Point to put our firewall enforcement points (FEPs) into a gateway cluster.

Figure 10.8 VRRP Monitored Circuit Diagram

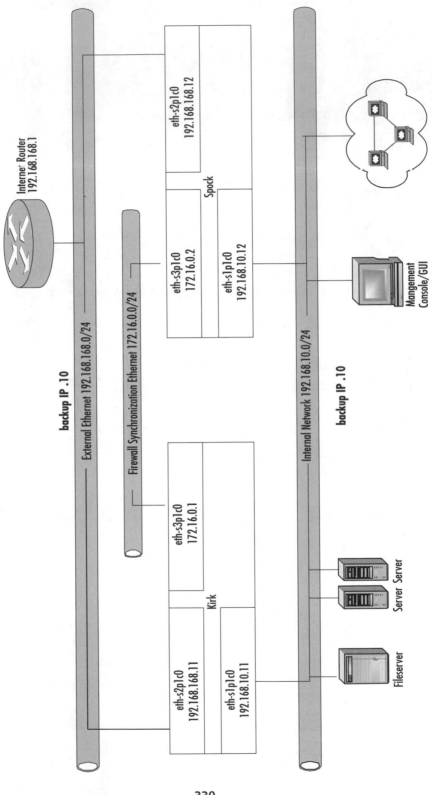

To help us with this task, let's use the following procedure:

1. Set up the network topology.
2. Configure all the gateway cluster member interfaces.
3. Synchronize the system clocks on all our cluster members.
4. Add entries to the Host table for the other cluster members.
5. Configure the Voyager VRRP settings.
6. Configure a Check Point gateway cluster object composed of our FEPs.

Set Up the Topology

You can use hubs or switches to physically connect your cluster interfaces, although switches configured with virtual LANs (VLANs) provide for the least complicated setup. Each set of interfaces with the same VRID can be placed into its own VLAN, which makes sense logically and also simplifies maintenance, since you can use one large switch instead of many separate ones. Remember that your sync interface should be a separate physical interface on each firewall in your cluster to improve performance.

Configure All Interfaces

After you have successfully created your network topology, you can configure your NSP's network interfaces. Using our diagram in Figure 10.9, Kirk and Spock's interface configurations are shown in Figures 10.9 and 10.10, respectively.

Figure 10.9 Kirk's Interface Configuration

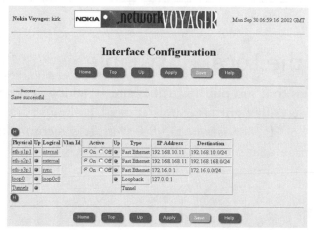

Figure 10.10 Spock's Interface Configuration

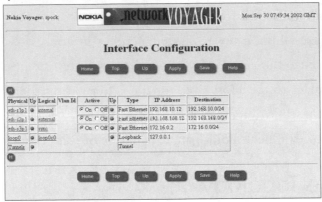

Synchronize the Time

Timing is essential in HA. Although VRRP machines can be set to different times, Check Point synchronization demands that gateway cluster members' clocks be set to within a few seconds of each other. It is best to use a time server (NTP) for consistency, but NSPs have internal CMOS clocks that can be used. See Chapter 4 for information on setting and synchronizing the NSP's time.

> **NOTE**
>
> NSPs care only about Greenwich Mean Time, or GMT. Firewall clocks can display a different time if each is in a different time zone. This is uncommon, however, since NSPs running VRRP HA must share networks and thus are typically physically close.

Configure the Local Host Table

Nokia recommends that you put hostnames and IP address pairs into each cluster member's host table. Although this is not required, it allows administrators to use hostnames instead of IP addresses or DNS servers. It is recommended that you also put your management server, GUI client, and VRRP neighbors into the host table. See Chapter 4 for instructions on entering hosts in the Host Address Assignment table.

Configure the Voyager VRRP Settings

Setting the Voyager VRRP settings takes some getting used to. Like other parts of Voyager, the configuration form changes dynamically as you fill in and apply settings. Before we start, let's make a table for our VRRP settings. We will use this table as a reference when we go into the configuration pages (see Tables 10.8 and 10.9).

Table 10.8 VRRP Monitored Interface Internal Settings for Enterprise

VRRP Settings: Internal		Kirk		Spock	
VRID		10		10	
Backup IP Address		192.168.10.10		192.168.168.10	
Priority		254		244	
Hello Interval		1		1	
MonitoredInterfaces	Delta	eth-s2p1	20	eth-s2p1	20

Table 10.9 VRRP Monitored Interface External Settings for Enterprise

VRRP Settings External		Kirk		Spock	
VRID		168		168	
Backup IP Address		192.168.10.10		192.168.168.10	
Priority		254		244	
Hello Interval		1		1	
Monitored Interface	Delta	eth-s1p1	20	eth-s1p1	20

First, let's configure Kirk (Kirk wouldn't have it any other way):

1. In Voyager, go to **Config | VRRP**.

2. Select the internal interface and click the **Monitored Circuit** radio button, then click **Apply**. You will see the Virtual Router field appear (see Figure 10.11).

3. Create the virtual router by entering the VRID field (from Table 10.8) in the interface and then click **Apply**.

Figure 10.11 Kirk's Internal VRID Assignment

4. Repeat Step 2 for the external interface using the data from Table 10.9. Figure 10.12 shows Kirk at this point in the configuration. There are a lot of blanks, but we will fill those in next.

Figure 10.12 Building Kirk's VRRP Configuration

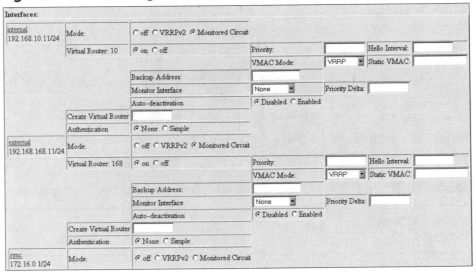

5. Set the **Backup Addresses**, **Priorities**, and **Hello Intervals** for both interfaces. Use the data from Tables 10.8 and 10.9. **Apply** your changes. Figure 10.13 shows us where we are now with Kirk's configuration.

6. Under the internal interface, select the **Monitor Interface** drop-down menu and choose the external interface. Insert the appropriate delta value.

7. Under the external interface, select the **Monitor Interface** drop-down menu and choose the internal Interface. Insert the appropriate delta value.

8. Click **Apply**.

Figure 10.13 Kirk's VRRPmc Backup IP, Priority, and Hello Settings

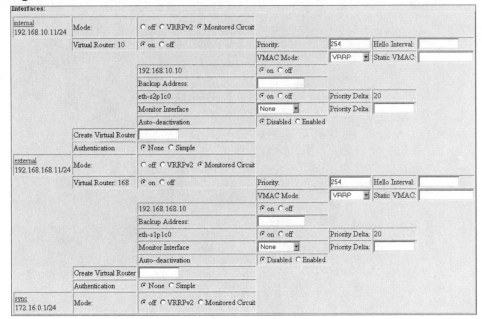

NOTE

You can add only one monitor interface at a time. To monitor additional interfaces, enter the first interface, then click **Apply**. After you apply your changes, you will see additional fields appear where you can put additional interfaces and their delta values. Notice that each monitored interface can have its own delta value. This means that it is possible to put more weight on specific interfaces should they fail. Doing so greatly complicates the VRRP configuration, and it is not recommended.

Figure 10.14 shows Kirk's completed configuration.

Then we repeat this process for Spock using our data from Tables 10.8 and 10.9. The final result for Spock is shown in Figure 10.15.

Now that Kirk and Spock have been configured, let's have a quick look to verify that Kirk is indeed the master and that Spock is the backup. We verify by looking at the monitoring information, which we can do by choosing **Monitor | VRRP** from the main Voyager Configuration screen. There, we will see that Kirk has two interfaces in master state, whereas Spock has two interfaces in backup state, just as we would expect (see Figures 10.16 and 10.17).

Figure 10.14 Kirk Is Finished

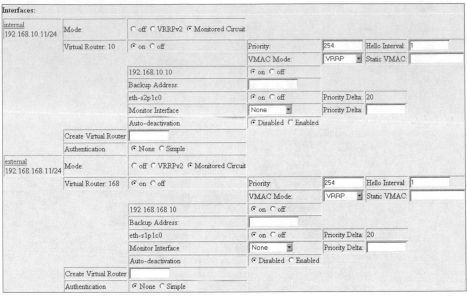

Figure 10.15 Spock's VRRP MC Is Finished

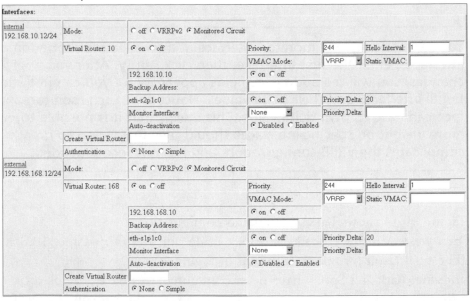

Figure 10.16 Kirk's VRRP Monitor Screen

Figure 10.17 Spock's VRRP Monitor Screen

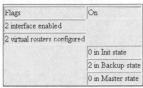

Configuring & Implementing…

Other VRRP Settings

Some additional controls in VRRP are worth mentioning:

- **Coldstart Delay** This is used to prevent your NSP from becoming a VRRP master before FW-1 state synchronization has finished. When this control is enabled, IPSO will not activate VRRP until the delay has elapsed.

- **Accept Connections to VRRP IPs** This feature allows IPSO to respond to packets whose destination address is that of the VRRP Backup IP address. It allows the NSP to respond to requests such as ping. Enabling this option overrides the RFC required behavior but is useful for detecting failures and is required if used in a Check Point Cluster VPN gateway due to IKE authentication requirements.

- **VMAC Mode** This allows you to tell IPSO how to assign MAC addresses to the backup IP address (called a *virtual MAC*, or *VMAC*). In the default setting, VRRP mode assigns an RFC2338 allocated multicast MAC address to the backup address. Since IPSO version 3.4.1 and later, three other methods have been added: *interface*, *static*, and *extended*.

Continued

- *Interface mode* has IPSO use local interface's MAC address as the VRRP MAC. This mode is useful if your network switches don't like to see packets on multiple ports with the same MAC address. The master of the VRID will use its own MAC address while it is active.

- *Static mode* allows the user to define the VMAC address.

- *Extended mode* is similar to VRRP mode except it uses 3 bytes of the VMAC address to extend the available range of unique addresses.

Configuring Check Point Gateway Clusters for Use in VRRP

Remember that any Nokia HA solution incorporates two parts: IP address failover and Check Point gateway clustering/synchronization. IP address failover allows nodes to use a virtual IP address that will be serviced by the master of that IP address, failing over to a backup if the master dies or loses an interface. The main purpose of Check Point clustering is to allow the individual firewalls to synchronize their connection tables. Check Point has its own HA solution, which must not be enabled if you are using Nokia and VRRPmc.

When installing your firewall modules, make sure you install them as enforcement modules only; your management station cannot be a member of your gateway cluster. You also need to enable the State Synchronization option. In this section we assume that you have standard gateway objects already defined for the individual gateways that will be participating in your gateway cluster and enabled Secure Internal Communications (SIC) on each cluster member. In order to complete the Nokia HA solution, you need to create a Check Point gateway cluster object and add your Nokia firewall modules to it.

Gateway Clusters

Before creating your cluster object, you need to make sure that **Enable Gateway Clusters** is checked off on the management server. This is simply done from within the Global Properties in the Policy Editor. Figure 10.18 shows you how to enable HA on your management server object.

You can then go ahead and create a new gateway cluster object with a unique IP address that should be the virtual or backup address of your external virtual router. You can then add the individual cluster firewall objects by clicking **Add** on the **Cluster Members** tab, once for each cluster member. Remember to enable SIC on each firewall module before you add it to the cluster (see Figure 10.19).

Figure 10.18 Enabling Gateway Clusters

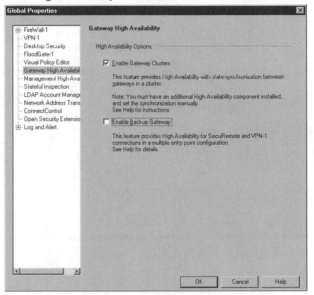

Figure 10.19 Gateway Cluster Members Tab

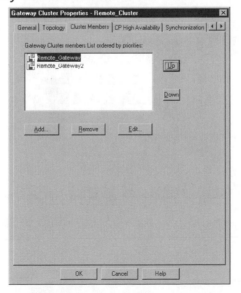

The last step in configuring your gateway cluster is to enable state synchronization. You do this by checking off **Use State Synchronization** on the **Synchronization** tab of your cluster object, then adding a synchronization network by clicking **Add** on the same tab and entering the network parameters. This should be the network address and netmask of your dedicated sync interface (see Figures 10.20 and 10.21).

Figure 10.20 Gateway Cluster Synchronization Tab

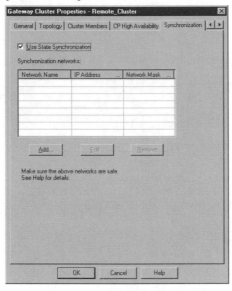

Figure 10.21 Add Synchronization Network

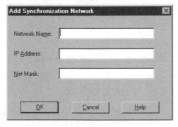

Configuring Your Rule Base

Here are the steps to follow to allow the VRRP multicast traffic to flow among your cluster members:

1. Create a new workstation object with the name **cluster–all–ips**. Use your external VRRP address for the IP address of this object. It should be a gateway, with no products installed.

2. On the cluster–all–ips object's Topology tab, add *all* the cluster member's physical IP addresses and all the virtual addresses.

3. Create a new workstation object named **mcast–224.0.0.18** with the IP address **224.0.0.18**.

4. Add the rule shown in Table 10.10 (make sure it is above your stealth rule, if any), where *cluster-object* is the gateway cluster object you created previously.

Table 10.10 VRRP Rule Base Configuration

Source	Destination	Service	Action
cluster-all-ips	cluster-object mcast-224.0.0.18	vrrp igmp	Accept

That's all there is to creating a gateway cluster for use with Nokia's VRRP. Just push your new policy to the gateway cluster you just created, and your cluster members should start communicating and sharing state information. You can use *tcpdump* to verify the traffic flow across your sync network (see Chapter 8). For more detailed information on setting up highly available VPNs or for instructions on how to use SecuRemote and Secure Client with gateway clusters, see *Check Point NG Next Generation Security Administration* by Syngress Publishing, ISBN: 1-928994-74-1.

Summary

Nokia offers several solutions for implementing highly available firewall and router solutions. The most common method uses a so-called active/passive failover, in which one Nokia is an established master and one or more others are idle and considered backups. This is implemented using an RFC-standard protocol called VRRP, for Virtual Router Redundancy Protocol. Other methods of implementing HA with Nokia include using VRRP with external load-balancing solutions as well as IP clustering, which is new in IPSO 3.6.

Nokia's IPSO supports VRRPv2 and VRRPmc, or VRRP Monitored Circuit. Of the two, VRRPmc is the recommended way to implement HA because it is simpler, solves some asymmetric routing problems, and can be used to fail over an entire firewall on a single interface failure. In VRRPmc, each interface has a delta value that is subtracted from its router's global priority in the event of an interface failure. If the delta values and priorities on the virtual routers are set up correctly, the interface failure will force failover to the backup router.

System time must be synchronized somehow between members of your HA setup, before VRRP with Check Point state synchronization can be implemented. The best way to do this is to use NTP. You should also add host table entries for the other members to each member of your gateway cluster. VRRPmc can then be implemented and monitored in Voyager.

The final step to enabling a highly available firewall solution is to configure your Check Point gateway cluster object. Individual cluster members are added to the cluster object one at a time, and the cluster object itself is given the IP address of your external virtual router. Finally, state synchronization is enabled on the cluster object, which should be functional after a policy is installed on it.

Solutions Fast Track

Firewalls and High Availability

☑ Nokia offers three different HA solutions with IPSO 3.6: VRRP active/passive, VRRP active/active, and IP clustering.

☑ The use of VRRP in an active/passive configuration is one of the most commonly implemented methods of HA with Check Point on Nokia.

☑ State synchronization solves asymmetric routing problems with HA firewalls.

Understanding Nokia's VRRP Implementation

☑ Basic VRRP configurations have a master router and one or more backup routers.

☑ VRRP is an RFC proposed standard, number 2338.

☑ Nokia's VRRP implementation chooses the router with the highest effective priority to be the master.

☑ VRRPmc, or Monitored Circuit, is a Nokia extension to VRRP that allows an interface to monitor other interfaces and respond should they go down.

☑ VRRPv2 is supported by Nokia but is not recommended; Nokia favors VRRPmc.

Configuring VRRP Monitored Circuit

☑ VRRPmc can be configured and monitored entirely through Voyager.

☑ System time must be synchronized among all the members of an HA setup.

☑ You should enter all members of your HA setup into their respective host tables.

Configuring Check Point Gateway Clusters for Use in VRRP

☑ You must create a gateway cluster object after enabling clusters on your management station.

☑ Your cluster object's IP address should be the same as the external virtual router address.

☑ You add cluster members one at a time to the Cluster Members tab of your gateway cluster object.

☑ You can enable state synchronization from the Synchronization tab of your gateway cluster object.

Frequently Asked Questions

The following Frequently Asked Questions, answered by the authors of this book, are designed to both measure your understanding of the concepts presented in this chapter and to assist you with real-life implementation of these concepts. To have your questions about this chapter answered by the author, browse to **www.syngress.com/solutions** and click on the **"Ask the Author"** form.

Q: Can I configure VRRP through CLISH?

A: Yes. You can use the *set vrrp interface* command—just ask for help in CLISH after typing this prefix. Additionally, *show vrrp summary* or *show vrrp interfaces* will give you statistics of your running VRRP implementation.

Q: Does VRRP support failover for multicast traffic, like that used in PIM or DVMRP?

A: No, VRRP only supports failover for unicast traffic. Both of those protocols should work independently of VRRP.

Q: Are there problems using VRRPmc in a switched environment?

A: Yes, there could be. To minimize the risks or avoid problems, disable the spanning tree protocol if possible, or disable MAC address caching on the ports connected to your VRRP devices.

Q: The VRRP monitor in Voyager shows one of my interfaces in the *initialize* state. Is this a problem?

A: Yes. This means that the IP address used as the backup address on that interface is invalid or reserved.

UNIX Basics

Solutions in this appendix:

- **Understanding Files and Directories**
- **Understanding Users and Groups**
- **Using the Shell and Basic Shell Utilities**
- **Using Vi**

Introduction

For readers who have little or no experience with UNIX, this appendix explains the basic concepts and commands to quickly get you up to speed with Nokia's (or any UNIX, for that matter) command-line interface. This foundation will also help you when you read some of the chapters in this book, most notably Chapter 8, "Advanced System Administration."

Here you will learn the basic form of the UNIX file system and how files and directories are a part of that system. We make our examples Nokia-specific where appropriate. You will also learn about the UNIX user and group permission concept and the commands that manipulate file ownership and access permissions. We round out this appendix with some sections on shell usage and basic shell utility commands and conclude with a section on Vi editor basics.

Understanding Files and Directories

When working with UNIX-based systems, you must understand the concepts of files and directories. This is no easy task, especially if you do not have a background or substantial training with UNIX or Linux. In this section, we look at the fundamentals you need to know to operate within the UNIX environment and demonstrate how to navigate through the file and directory structure. Let's begin with the basic concepts of the file and directory system.

The UNIX Directory Hierarchy:

With UNIX, the main concept of understanding files and directories is understanding their *hierarchy*. The hierarchy system is based on a tree. A tree has roots on the bottom that go into the ground, and its branches stretch out at the top. The easiest way to see the UNIX file system hierarchy is to take this concept of a tree and flip it upside down. Now, your roots are on top and the branches reach downward. With UNIX, just think of the roots of the tree as a single root.

Figure A.1 shows a simple diagram of the root with its branches flipped upside down.

With Figure A.1 in mind, consider this concept from a more technical perspective. If you understand this concept, all you have to do is start naming your branches. The first thing we have to name is the root itself. In Figure A.1, it is simply called *Root*. The root directory is represented by a slash (/) when we use it in a command or pathname.

Figure A.1 The Basic UNIX Hierarchy Concept

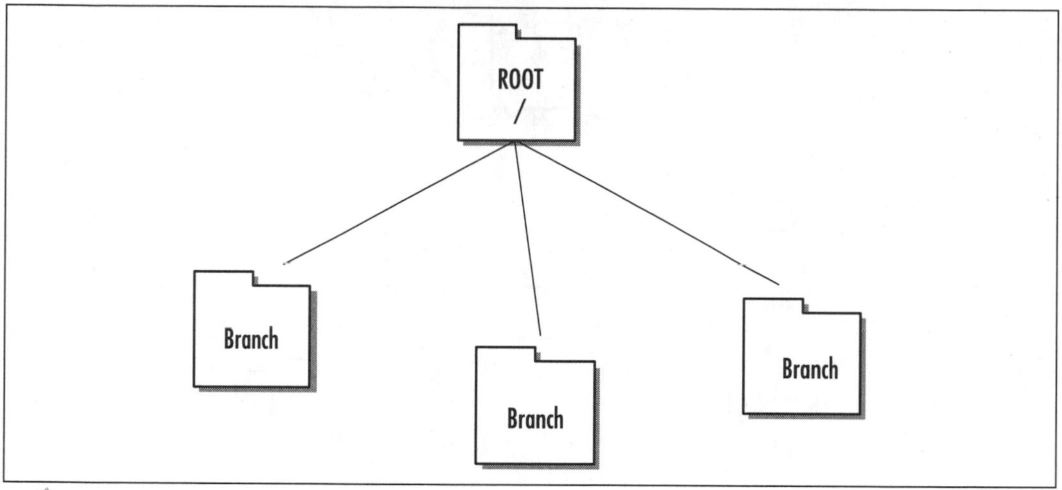

> **NOTE**
>
> It is very important that you know immediately that the UNIX-based operating system is case sensitive and anything you do must be in the proper case. If you make a case-based mistake, you will not be able to get your commands to work. So, for example, the command *ls* will give you a directory listing when typed in lowercase but a syntax error if you type it in uppercase (*LS*).

With UNIX, data, disk and program information are all stored as files organized within this tree. You cannot get very far without knowing the location of what you need and how to find it. Let's now look at where exactly everything is in the system and start giving these branches of the tree some logical names.

In Figure A.2, you are shown the actual layout of the UNIX hierarchy, with the root at the top and the tree expanding downward. For now, don't be concerned with what each branch represents; we will explain that in a moment. Familiarize yourself with the idea of how the hierarchy is laid out. You must remember this layout because, when you log in to a UNIX-based system via the command line, you need to have this information memorized to quickly find your way around.

Figure A.2 Viewing the UNIX-Based Hierarchy

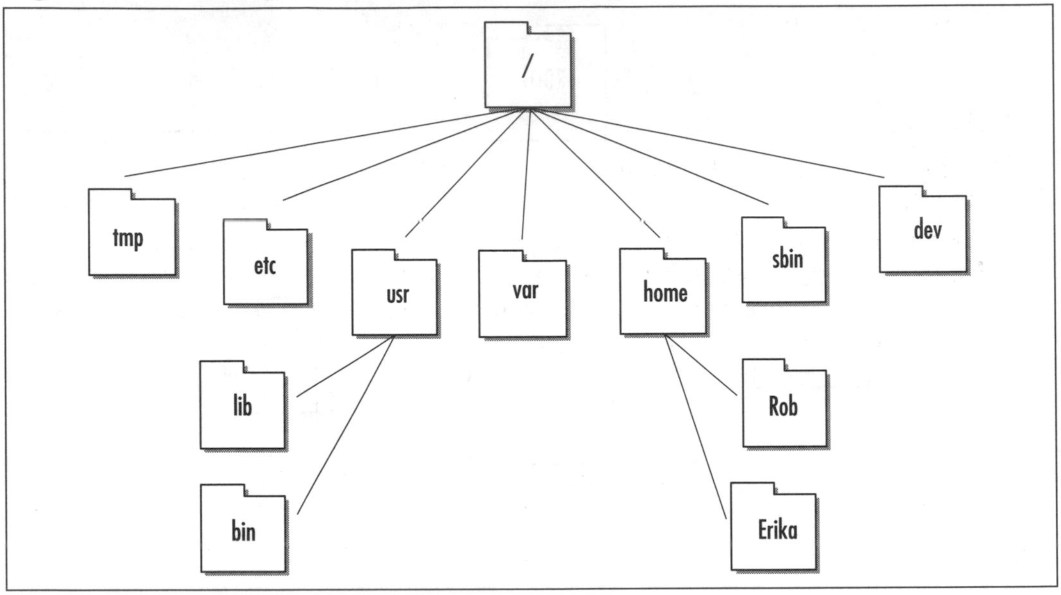

A *directory* is a special type of file that contains information about other files. You can also make directories within other directories (as long as you have the right permissions to do so). This means that the fundamental layout you see in Figure A.2 can actually change and become very deep. For instance, in the home directory, Rob and Erika have their own home directories on the system. What if you had more than just root, Rob, and Erika? What if you have 20 users? The point here is that you need to master the fundamental layout quickly or you could become lost or confused as the system grows.

NOTE

There is no theoretical limit the number of levels you have within your hierarchy. Therefore, if your directory is heavily populated, you will want to know the location of the root of the hierarchy and how to navigate from it as your starting point. The system can become very populated and quickly get very deep.

To add to the confusion even more, you must understand that when working with UNIX-based operating systems, *everything appears as a file*. A good example of this concept is when you want to look at running processes and system memory; this information is accessible through various files in the file system.

> **NOTE**
>
> Depending on your terminal type, it might be possible to "colorize" your directory listing output so that, for example, directory names are displayed in a different color than regular filenames. When you use your Nokia system, however, connecting from a console will not normally display colorized directory outputs. A good tip is to use *ls –F*, which makes directories stand out on any terminal by appending the directory name with a forward slash.

We will look at an example of this idea in detail. You might think that this information would be difficult to remember. It really isn't once you know what each directory contains. Table A.1 lays out the fundamentals as to what each directory does and its most important features.

Table A.1 The UNIX Hierarchy in Detail

Directory Name	Function
/	This is the system root directory.
tmp	This is the directory used for creating system temporary files. Many systems delete the contents of this directory during the boot process.
etc	This is the directory that contains global system configuration files.
usr	This is the directory that contains a majority of your system files and typically is broken down into the lib and bin directories. Program libraries and executable binaries are stored here.
var	This is the directory responsible for holding most of the volatile system information such as logs and print spooling that are constantly in a state of change.
boot	This is the directory that holds system startup files as well as the kernel image itself. On some other systems, you might also see these files in /stand or even just /.
home	This is the main directory that holds the user's home directories. On Nokia systems, /var serves this purpose.

Continued

Table A.1 The UNIX Hierarchy in Detail

Directory Name	Function
sbin	This is the directory that is responsible for holding system files and programs such as mount and fdisk.
dev	This directory contains many special files that allow access to physical devices such as your hard disk or diskette drive.

Depending on which flavor of UNIX you are working with, you might find other directories visible, but Table A.1 shows the most common directory layout that you will encounter. Other directories you could see include /opt (for optional software) and /proc (for specialized runtime kernel information).

Basic Directory Commands

Before you begin working with a UNIX system, you need to know some basic commands. Again, remember that everything is case sensitive when you work with UNIX. This is the biggest problem people face in learning UNIX basics. You have to be very conscious of the fact that a capital *S* is not the same as a lowercase *s*, for example. The case of a letter you use as a command-line argument could mean very different things, depending on whether it is upper- or lowercase.

UNIX commands will be easy to master if you have a command-line background (DOS, Cisco IOS, and so on), as it's only a matter of memorizing new commands and relating them to what you already know. Let's take a look at some of the most common UNIX commands used to navigate the file and directory system.

Command: cd

The *cd* command is used to change directories. If you are used to the old DOS command, this command will be easy to remember. However, there is one major difference between UNIX and DOS: With DOS, you don't leave a space between the command and the directory you want to switch to, whereas with most UNIX systems, you have to leave a space. Let's look at the actual command syntax to change to the directory one level up. In this example, we look at the mild differences between working with UNIX and DOS.

Open a UNIX session and log in. After logging in, try changing to the /home directory (which should be one level up) using the *cd* command. The syntax for this command is *cd* with a space and two dots following it. It looks like this:

```
cd ..
```

Remember that there is a space between the *cd* and the two dots. If you do not include the space, you will not execute the command but will instead generate a syntax error.

Here, you can see that when you try to use the *cd* command with the two dots directly adjacent to the *cd* command, it turns up an error and a suggestion. You can use the suggestion from the system to use the *cd* command with two dots placed correctly:

```
rshimonski@BEAST:~> cd..
Error: Try: cd ..
rshimonski@BEAST:~> cd ..
rshimonski@BEAST:/home>
```

The problem that most administrators run into is that they learn DOS before they learn UNIX commands and therefore get into a habit of doing a certain thing a certain way. UNIX can be unforgiving when it comes to errors like this!

Command: pwd

The *pwd* command is used to print the working or current directory. The *pwd* command is often mistakenly referred to as the *primary working directory,* but it really stands for *print working directory.* You can use whatever mnemonic device helps you to remember the command.

The commands are used as follows: Open a UNIX session and log in. After logging in and moving up one level with *cd* .., type **pwd** at the prompt:

```
rshimonski@BEAST:/home> pwd
/home
rshimonski@BEAST:/home>
```

By using the *pwd* command, you have printed to the console the directory you are currently working within. This directory was of course listed as part of the prompt itself, but if you were unsure, this is the command you would use. Not all UNIX prompts will show you what directory you are currently in.

Let's get a little more creative and use the *cd* command with the *pwd* command. Change directories from /home to your current user (in our case, rshimonski) directory. Here is the syntax you would use:

```
rshimonski@BEAST:/home> cd ~
rshimonski@BEAST:~> pwd
/home/rshimonski
rshimonski@BEAST:~>
```

The most important thing to remember here is that you are learning how to navigate through the hierarchy and to see where your place is within it.

Command: ls

The *ls* command is also heavily used within the UNIX system. This command will probably become one of your most used commands when you work within the directory structure. The *ls* command lists filenames, sizes, modification and access times, and file types for you. There are many options you can use with it as well. Pay attention to the fact that when you use *ls,* the default sort order of the directory listing will be alphabetical by name. You can, however, use options like *–t* to change the sort order to list files by time instead of by name. Table A.2 shows some of the more common options you will most likely use with the *ls* command:

Table A.2 ls Command Options

Option	Description
-l	This option provides for a longer listing or a full listing.
-a	This option shows all files, even hidden ones.
-t	This option sorts the output by time instead of by name.
-d	This option lists only directories.

Note that you can use options together for more flexibility. In other words, you can use the *–l* and *–d* options together, as shown in the following commands:

```
rshimonski@BEAST:~> ls -d
.

rshimonski@BEAST:~> ls -ld
drwxr-xr-x   12 rshimons users        1208 Sep  2 13:37 .
rshimonski@BEAST:~>
```

Working with and navigating around the directory structure and UNIX-based system hierarchy are not really that difficult; it just takes a little knowledge and patience. Now let's look at the file structure.

UNIX File Basics

In this section we look at the fundamentals of UNIX-based files and how to work with them. There are a few important things you need to remember about working with the file system. First, you should know that an *inode* is a data structure used by the file system to uniquely represent a file and its associated attributes. An inode contains the file type (for example, plain file, directory, symbolic link, or device file); its owner, group, and public access permissions; the owner and group ID numbers; its size in bytes; the number of links (directory references) to the file; and the times of last access and last modification to the file. In addition, there is a list of data blocks claimed by the file. It is critical that you understand the fundamentals of an inode when learning the UNIX system. Other items to note are:

- UNIX file systems will support long filenames (more than eight characters and typically much longer). Filenames are also case-sensitive.

- Only one file system is allowed per disk partition, although one physical disk can have many different partitions and hence many different file systems on it.

- Each file system has its own inode table.

- The file system uses inodes to uniquely identify files with the system.

- Files are referenced internally by inode number, not names (although you see names in an *ls* output).

That's it! This is the most important information you need to know about UNIX files and how they are managed in your UNIX system.

Symbolic and Hard Links

Before we work directly with the file structure and look at what you can do with it, let's examine links. *Links* are references to either a file or a directory and can be very useful. There are two link types: *symbolic* (sometimes called *soft*) and *hard*. You can use links for filename aliasing purposes because sometimes filenames can be hard to remember. The *ln* command creates hard or symbolic links. Here is the syntax of the *ln* command (your command-line options might be slightly different, depending on what flavor of UNIX you are using):

```
rshimonski@BEAST:~> ln --help
Usage: ln [OPTION]... TARGET [LINK_NAME]
or:    ln [OPTION]... TARGET... DIRECTORY
or:    ln [OPTION]... --target-directory=DIRECTORY TARGET...
```

You can also remove a link or a file with the *rm* command, as shown in this syntax:

```
rshimonski@BEAST:~> rm --help
Usage: rm [OPTION]... FILE...
Remove (unlink) the FILE(s).
```

Hard Links

Hard links are used only on files, not on directories, and are created using *ln <target file> <link>*. When you create a hard link, both the source and target of the link must be provided and must be within the same file system. A hard link always refers to the same inode number, so you can have many hard links to a file, but each link really points to the same underlying inode. (Use *ls −i* to see inode numbers.)

Symbolic Links

Symbolic links are created with the *ln -s* command. When you create a symbolic link, you create a link to the path of a source file, but in this case, the link has its own inode. So you can delete the link without deleting the file that it points to, much like a Windows shortcut.

Working within UNIX

To get to a UNIX-based system, you will most likely make a remote connection to it. In this section we look at what we have learned by connecting to a remote system and manipulating files and directories so that we can tie all our knowledge together.

Let's now bring all this information on using directories and files together by connecting to a remote UNIX system and manipulating it. First, you need to have a UNIX-based system to connect to. If you do, you can follow along with these steps:

1. Open a UNIX session and log in. You can see in Figure A.3 that I am using SSH.

Figure A.3 Viewing the Console with SSH

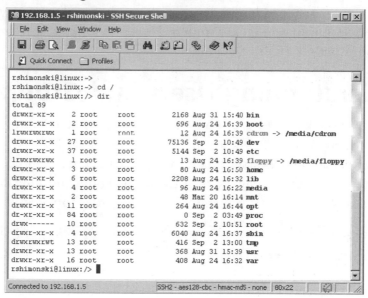

2. After opening a connection and logging in, I decided to change from my home directory to the root directory, or /. To do this I simply typed **cd /**.

3. I then typed **dir** to see what was in the root directory. I could have just as easily typed **ls −l** (*dir* is an *alias* for *ls −l*).

Designing & Planning...

Telnet vs. SSH

As a security professional working on Nokia appliances, you should use SSH rather than Telnet for remote login sessions. You should use SSH as an alternative to Telnet because SSH uses encryption between the client and the remote device that you are trying to connect to. Telnet transmits all its data unencrypted, so that when you Telnet to a device, your authentication credentials (username and password) are susceptible to eavesdropping or capture. Using SSH eliminates this problem. Chapters 2 and 4 discuss the use and configuration of SSH on Nokia devices in detail.

It's that simple. You have just looked at the entire hierarchy, and you can move between any parts of it. If you decide to view the usr directory, you now know how to switch to it and look within it. Now let's look at how to work with users and groups within a UNIX system.

Understanding Users and Groups

Once you now know how to connect to a UNIX system, you need to know how to log in, who to log in as, and what control over the system you have. Most of this information is not very hard to understand, but it can be a little complicated due to UNIX's highly flexible use of the command line. Let's take a look at all the basic fundamentals you should know in order to work with users and groups on a UNIX-based system.

Users and Groups

To log into the system, you need a user account, which has its own password. The UNIX system employs user accounts to keep the system secure from unauthorized access. The user is authenticated to the system via a certain process:

1. You must first be at the console of the system or use a remote access protocol such as SSH or Telnet. Once you connect to the system, you will be prompted with a banner:

```
Red Hat Linux release 6.2
Kernel 2.4.12 on an i686
login:
```

2. Once prompted, you can type in the user account you have configured on the system—for example, **rshimonski**.

3. Once you type in an account name, the system will ask for the password with the password banner prompt.

4. If you enter the proper credentials, you are authenticated and now have access to the system. If you do not enter the proper credentials, you are prompted to re-enter your username. Once you are authenticated, you should see the prompt at which you can begin working:

```
Red Hat Linux release 6.2
Kernel 2.4.12 on an i686
login: rshimonski
```

```
Password:
bash$
```

That's it! So what else is there to know? Now that you know how to log in to a system, you should be aware of the various levels of systems permissions you have based on who you are logged in as. Now let's look at the two basic types of users.

User Types

When working with UNIX, remember that you can use different kinds of user accounts: privileged and unprivileged. There is what is called the *superuser*, also known as the *root user* (or the *admin user*, specific to the Nokia platform), which is a privileged user. There are also *normal users* you create, each with their own varying levels of permissions and rights, often called *unprivileged users*. Frequently, administrators log onto the system with the superuser account. This habit is problematic in a security sense for several reasons:

- The administrator gets so used to using the root account that he or she makes the password easy to log in with. The administrator usually picks a password that is quick to type and remember. This usually means that it is also easy to crack with most automated password-cracking tools.

- Administrators often use the root account over Telnet to connect to the server they want to administer, making the password susceptible to capture with any standard packet-capture device.

- Because it is constantly used, the root password is not changed often enough. This opens up the possibility that the password can be gained through some form of social engineering (*shoulder surfing,* for example).

The list goes on, but you must remember that the root account is in fact a superuser account. It has more rights and permissions to the system than any normal account; for this reason, you should not take its security lightly. Remember, a superuser has full access to the system and can damage it very easily. The recommended way to administer a system is to log in as an unprivileged user and use the *su* command to become root as necessary.

As a Nokia administrator, you should consider the following information as well. Nokia has parted from the long-standing security mantra not to log in directly as the root user. Nokia takes the view that you should have only one user on a system, and that user is admin and has root privileges. Not having other users in a system prevents other users from logging in and gaining some privilege that they don't have. Both views have some merit, but I still recommend the *su* method, especially since Nokia has taken strong measures to prevent the types of local root exploits that would give unprivileged users root access. (See Chapter 2 for details on Nokia's security measures.)

UIDs and GIDs

UID is the abbreviation for *user identification* or *user ID*. *GID* stands for *group ID*. When you log on, your account is given a numerical ID number that is known as the UID. The rule of thumb is that the lower the number, the more privileged the account. The superuser (root) has a UID of 0, whereas ordinary users typically have a UID greater than 100.

More detailed information about UIDs and GIDs can be helpful to your overall understanding of the UNIX system. UIDs are uniquely indicated within the */etc/passwd* file. You can view this password file by navigating to the /etc directory and using the Vi editor on the file.

NOTE

In your Nokia box, you can view usernames and UIDs in the /etc/master.passwd file.

You will learn how to use the Vi editor at the end of the appendix. You can view the file by issuing the following commands:

```
rshimonski@BEAST:/etc> vi passwd
root:x:0:0:root:/root:/bin/bash
bin:x:1:1:bin:/bin:/bin/bash
daemon:x:2:2:Daemon:/sbin:/bin/bash
lp:x:4:7:Printing daemon:/var/spool/lpd:/bin/bash
```

The third field in the preceding file view is the UID. So the bin user has UID 1. Also specified in the system password file are the user's home directory and login shell (/bin and /bin/bash, in this case). The GID is also indicated, but it is located within the file /etc/group. Here is the view of a standard group file:

```
rshimonski@BEAST:/etc> vi group
root:x:0:root
```

```
bin:x:1:root,bin,daemon
daemon:x:2:
sys:x:3:
tty:x:5:
disk:x:6:
lp:x:7:
wwwadmin:x:8:
kmem:x:9:
wheel:x:10:
mail:x:12:cyrus
```

The GID is the third field in the preceding file view. Adding a user to a group is just a matter of appending the username to the appropriate line in /etc/group. In the preceding example, you can see that the users root, bin, and daemon are all members of the bin group, which has GID 1.

Wheel Group

The *wheel group* is a group that exists for added security. Only users in the wheel group can execute commands such as *su* (or *superuser,* which we look at in the next section). Most standard UNIX systems already have this group added by default, so you only need to edit the group file to add your username to the wheel group. Nokia systems do have the wheel group already created for you.

To add a user to the wheel group, edit the /etc/group file and add the username to the line that begins *wheel:.* This is not overly difficult, but make sure you remember that commas delimit the list of login names:

1. Open the /etc/group file again with the *vi* command. (If you are having problems using Vi, skip to the last section of the appendix to read up on how to use it.) You can now add the users to the wheel group as follows:

```
rshimonski@BEAST:/etc> vi group
root:x:0:root
bin:x:1:root,bin,daemon
daemon:x:2:
sys:x:3:
tty:x:5:
wheel:x:10:root,rshimonski
```

2. Now you can *su* to root using the user you just added to the wheel group in /etc/group:

```
rshimonski@BEAST:/etc> su
Password:
BEAST:/etc #
```

File Access Permissions

When you look at the output of the *ls –l* command, you will see a group of letters or characters along the left side of your screen (refer back to Figure A.3). They specify the type of file and how it can be accessed. Here is the first line of the preceding figure:

```
drwxr-xr-x    2    root    root    2168    Aug 31    15:40    bin
```

The first letter, *d*, indicates that this file is really a directory. Other characters you will see in this position are *l* for symbolic links and – for a regular file. The next nine characters specify the file's access rights. These rights are divided into three groups: owner, group, and world, for the owner of the file, the primary group of the file, and everyone else, in that order. Each group has three *access specifiers*, which can be present or not. These are read, write, and execute—the *rwx* you see in the example line. Any specifier that is not present is represented by a dash, which means that group of users does not have that access right. So the permissions string *rwxr-xr-x* means that the owner of the file has read, write, and execute permissions on it (the first *rwx*), that the members of its primary group have read and execute permissions on it (the next group of three, *r-x*), and everyone else has read and execute permissions on it (the last group of three, *r-x*). Some terminology that you often see used is that each access specifier is a *bit*, so you can say "That file has its execute bit set."

Table A.3 shows what the various permissions mean when they refer to regular files or directories:

Table A.3 Permissions and Their Meanings

	Read	**Write**	**Execute**
Regular files	Read permission	Modify, rename, or delete permission	Execute permission
Directories	Directory list permission	Create, rename, or delete permission	Permission to *cd* into directory

The file's owner and group are also in the *ls −l* output. In this case, we see that the bin directory is owned by the root user and groups, so only the root user has permission to list the contents of the bin directory, *cd* into it, or delete it. All other users can *cd* into the bin directory and list its contents, but they cannot modify it in any way.

File access specifiers are modified using the *chmod* and *chgrp* commands. There is much more to learn regarding permissions, so see your system's man pages for details if you are interested.

Setuid and Setgid Binaries

Executable files in a UNIX system (which we now know must have one of their execute bits set) can sometimes assume the identity of their owner or primary group when they are executed. This is different from the way UNIX processes normally decide what access rights they have; usually, a file assumes the permissions of the user who executed it.

Files that take on the permissions of their owner or group are termed *set UID* or *set GID* files, respectively. You will often see them called simply *setuid* or *setgid* files. An example will probably make this clearer. On my Linux workstation, the su binary looks like this when I type **ls −l /bin/su**:

```
-rwsr-xr-x    1 root      root        23176 Apr  7 11:59 su
```

Notice the *s* in the string *-rwsr-xr-x*. This letter means that this executable file is setuid. When I run it as an unprivileged user, it would normally (if it were not setuid) take on the permissions and access rights of whomever I was logged in as; instead, it assumes the permissions of the root user, since it is owned by root. Because su is designed to give unprivileged users root access (after entering the root password, of course), this works nicely. There is a potential security problem here, though. A malicious user can sometimes take advantage of poor programming practices in setuid or setgid files to obtain privileges that they would not normally have—what security professionals call an example of a *local root exploit*. For this reason, more modern or security-conscious Unices attempt to reduce the dependence on setuid or setgid files or at least audit the source code of binary files that must have these special permissions.

Using the Shell and Basic Shell Utilities

This section looks at the fundamentals of a shell and how to use it. It also takes a look at a few of the more common commands. The term *shell* is a UNIX term that stands for the user interface that you use to interact with the system. The shell is also called the *command interpreter*. It is the layer of programming and the code with which you interact and is highly modifiable in a UNIX-based system. The shell can be considered the skin that surrounds the core of your operating system and interacts with it. There are many types of shells, but for now we take a look at one in particular: *csh* or *C-shell*, which just happens to be the default shell used by Nokia.

C-Shell

The C-shell (csh) is a command interpreter with syntax similar to the C programming language; since most UNIX gurus are (or were) C programmers, they feel right at home with the advanced features of this shell. The C-Shell was created by Bill Joy at the University of California at Berkeley as an alternative to the original UNIX shell, the Bourne shell. Table A.4 looks at some of the options available with csh. Also, Appendix B discusses optional Nokia shell packages such as Bash and ksh.

Table A.4 csh Options

Option	Description
-b	Forces a "break" from option processing. Subsequent command-line arguments are not interpreted as C-shell options. This allows the passing of options to a script without confusion. The shell does not run set-user-ID or set-group-ID scripts unless this option is present.
-c	Executes the first argument (which must be present). Remaining arguments are placed in argv, the argument-list variable, and passed directly to csh.
-e	Exits if a command terminates abnormally or yields a nonzero exit status.
-f	Fast start. Reads neither the .cshrc file nor the .login file (if a login shell) upon startup.
-I	Forced interactive. Prompts for command-line input, even if the standard input does not appear to be a terminal (character-special device).
-n	Parses (interprets) but does not execute commands. This option can be used to check C-shell scripts for syntax errors.
-s	Takes commands from the standard input.

Continued

Table A.4 csh Options

Shell Prompt Options	Description
!!	Repeats the last command.
!<text>	Repeats the most recent command that begins with *<text>*.

NOTE

The Tab C-shell (tcsh) is an enhanced but completely compatible version of the Berkeley UNIX C-Shell, csh. Tcsh is a command language interpreter usable both as an interactive login shell and a shell script command processor. Some of tcsh's added features are:

- Enhanced history substitution
- Spelling correction
- Word completion

Configuring & Implementing...

Man Pages

Most of the information in the next section comes directly from the UNIX-based help system called *man*. *Man* is short for *manual pages*. To use your manual pages, just type **man <command>** and press Enter. For example, to find out about the use of the *mv* command, you can simply type **man mv**. Typing **man man** at the console gives you an overview of the *man* command itself.

You can also use a command called *apropos*, which searches a set of database files containing short descriptions of system commands for keywords and displays the result on the standard output. Both commands are very helpful in navigating a system. Type **man apropos** for details.

Command: mv

The *mv* command is used to rename a file or move it from one directory to another directory. You can do this by typing the following at the console prompt:

```
mv file.txt directory/
```

This command moves the file *file.txt* to the directory named *directory*. Table A.5 shows the options available for use with the *mv* command.

Table A.5 mv Options

Option	Description
-f	Moves the file(s) without prompting, even if it is writing over an existing target. Note that this is the default if the standard input is not a terminal.
-i	Prompts before overwriting another file.

Command: cp

The *cp* command is simply used to copy files:

```
cp file.txt dir/
```

This command copies the file *file.txt* to the *dir* directory. Table A.6 shows the options available for use with the *cp* command.

Table A.6 cp Options

Option	Description
-i	Prompts you before replacing a file.
-r	When a directory is copied, copies the subdirectories within the directory and creates the directories if they do not exist.

Command: cat

Using the *cat* command allows you to look at, modify, or combine one or more files in your UNIX system:

```
cat fileA.txt fileB.txt > fileC.txt
```

This command reads fileA.txt and fileB.txt and combines (concatenate) the files to make fileC.txt. Table A.7 lists the options available for use with the *cat* command.

Table A.7 cat Options

Option	Description
-n	Precedes each line output with its line number.
-b	Numbers the lines, as -n, but omits the line numbers from blank lines.
-u	The output is not buffered. (The default is buffered output.)
-s	*cat* is silent about nonexistent files.
-v	Visibly prints nonprinting characters (with the exception of tabs, new-lines, and form feeds).
-e	Prints an $ character at the end of each line (prior to the new line).

NOTE

Note that if -v is used, -e and -t will be ignored.

Command: grep

The *grep* command is used to find text within a file. In other words, if you *grep* for something, UNIX searches for that something. For instance, if you are interested in finding every occurrence of *index.html* in a large number of files in your current directory, you could *grep* for it:

```
grep * 'index.html'
```

This command searches all the files in the current directory for any reference of *index.html* and prints results to the console. Table A.8 lists the options available for use with the *grep* command.

Table A.8 grep Options

Option	Description
-b	Precedes each line by the block number on which it was found.
-c	Prints only a count of the lines that contain the pattern.
-h	Prevents the name of the file containing the matching line from being appended to that line. Used when searching multiple files.

Continued

Table A.8 grep Options

Option	Description
-I	Ignores case.
-l	Displays the files that have the text, not the text within the file.
-n	Precedes each line by its line number in the file (first line is numbered starting at 1).
-s	Suppresses error messages about nonexistent or unreadable files.
-v	Specifies that you are looking for files that don't contain the text.
-w	Searches for the expression as a logical word.

Command: more

The *more* command displays blocks of text one screen at a time. The following command would begin displaying the file file.txt at line 4:

```
more +4 file.txt
```

Just press Spacebar to page through the file on screen, and type **q** to quit. This very simple command allows you to display a number of different things with the available options listed in Table A.9.

Table A.9 more Options

Option	Description
-c	Clears before displaying.
-d	Displays error messages rather than ringing the terminal bell if an unrecognized command is used. This is helpful for inexperienced users.
-e	Exits immediately after writing the last line of the last file in the argument list.
-f	Does not fold long lines. This is useful when lines contain non-printing characters or escape sequences.
-I	Performs pattern matching in searches without regard to case.
-l	Ignores form-feed characters (Ctrl + L starts the new page).
-n	Specifies the number of lines per screen. The number argument is a positive decimal integer.
-r	Displays control keys.
-s	Doesn't display extra blank lines.

Command: tail

The *tail* command displays the last few lines of the file given to it as an argument. Performing this command lists the last lines of the file file.txt:

```
tail file.txt
```

The default number of lines to display is 10, but with the options listed in Table A.10, you can specify otherwise.

Table A.10 tail Options

Option	Description
-l	Units of lines.
-b	Units of blocks.
-c	Units of bytes.

Command: head

The *head* command displays the first 10 lines in a file given to it by default. The *head –n* command displays the first *n* lines in a file to the screen. The following example specifies that we want to see the first 12 lines of the file file.txt:

```
head -12 file.txt
```

NOTE

This discussion provides merely a sampling of the many, many UNIX-based system commands you can use. I recommend you visit the man pages for more information. You can also visit the following link to get more information on the various commands you can use:

www.bsd.org/unixcmds.html

For Nokia-specific commands, you can go to freebsd.org and check version 2.2.6 of the man pages if you need to do further research. They are located at www.freebsd.org/cgi/man.cgi?manpath=FreeBSD+2.2.6-RELEASE.

Table A.11 shows the options available for use with head.

Table A.11 head Options

Option	Description
-n	Indicates the number of lines you want to display.
filename	Indicates the file of which you want to display the first *n* lines.

Using Vi

Vi is a very flexible and powerful editor, but it can also be very confusing. The Vi editor is invoked on the UNIX system console with the following command:

```
rshimonski@BEAST:/etc> vi
```

Figure A.4 shows the opening screen of the Vi editor once it has been invoked.

Figure A.4 The Vi Editor's Opening Screen

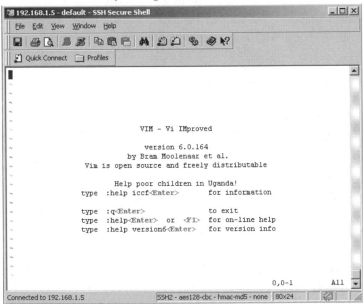

In Figure A.4, I am using Vim, a more feature-rich (and in some ways easier to use) version of Vi. Vim acts just like Vi by starting up in Vi compatibility mode by default.

Vi is a *modal* editor, which means that it uses one mode for entering editor commands and another for actually editing text. You can always go back to command mode by pressing the **Esc** key. The Vi editor lets you edit files by using simple mnemonic keystroke combinations while in command mode.

> **NOTE**
>
> Emacs is another editor you can use. Some people prefer it because it is nonmodal. (It has one mode for entering text and uses special keystrokes preceded by Alt and Ctrl to execute editor commands while you are entering text.) Most people find Vi faster and less complicated than the Emacs editor, but be warned: This is a subject of many historic e-mail flame wars!

Table A.12 shows many of the command-line options you can use with the Vi editor.

Table A.12 Vi Options

Option	Description
-l	Sets up for editing LISP programs.
-L	Lists the name of all files saved as the result of an editor or system crash.
-R	Read-only mode; the read-only flag is set, preventing accidental overwriting of the file.
-r	Edits filename after an editor or system crash.
-v	Starts up in display editing state using Vi. You can achieve the same effect by simply typing the Vi command itself.
-wn	Sets the default window size to n. This is useful when using the editor over a slow speed line

To get around in Vi, you need to know a few basic commands. Here are some of the easiest to remember to get you started navigating and using the Vi editor:

- **Arrow keys** Moves the cursor (*h, k, j,* and *l* movement keys will also work in case you are at a terminal that doesn't recognize arrow keys).
- **x** Deletes a character.

- **dw** Deletes a word.

- **dd** Deletes a line.

- **u** Undoes previous change.

- **yy** and **pp** Useful to cut and paste lines.

- **Ctrl–u (page up) Ctrl–d (page down)** Useful for screen movement.

- **H** Moves to the top line of the screen.

- **L** Moves to the last line on screen.

- **M** Moves to the middle line on screen.

That's it! With a little work and patience, you will be a UNIX pro in no time. Here are a few other commands you can use to exit your Vi session:

- **ZZ or :wq** Used to quit, after saving the current file.

- **:q!** Used to quit while making no changes.

Appendix B

Additional Packages

Solutions in this appendix:

- Perl v5.005_02
- Netcat
- MRTG
- Bash
- Other Useful Utilities

Introduction

In general, it is not possible to run binaries from FreeBSD or other versions of UNIX under the IPSO operating system. Although IPSO is based on FreeBSD, it has diverged enough in recent years that most third-party binaries either won't run or make the system unstable. It is also not possible to compile binaries from source code (unless you work for Nokia), because the IPSO operating system has no compiler and no shared libraries.

After enough people asked, Nokia released some "unsupported" third-party packages for IPSO that can be downloaded from Nokia's Web site, including Perl, the Bash shell, netcat, MRTG, and a few other useful shells and tools. If you already have familiarity with UNIX-based systems, you're probably familiar with these tools.

This appendix reviews some of the more useful utilities and discusses their installation and usage.

Designing & Planning...

Is Installing Extra Software on the Firewall a Good Idea?

Before heading down the road of installing these additional packages on your firewall, consider the purpose of the firewall itself. It's a security device designed to protect your network from intrusion. Technically, it shouldn't be doing anything else, because each service you add will consume some of its packet-processing resources. Additionally, extra software you add could technically be used against you should an attacker compromise your firewall. Think very carefully before adding any of these packages, and make certain that you really can justify their use on your firewall.

Perl v5.005_02

Perl is a very powerful scripting language that can be made to do almost anything. Perl scripts can range from the incredibly simple to the fiendishly complex. You need only look the annual Perl Obfuscation Contest (www.samag.com/

tpj/obfuscated/) to see a demonstration of this power and range. Nonetheless, Perl can be very helpful on a Check Point firewall in helping sift through log files and processing other files to make them more readable. In this section, we discuss how to install Perl on the Nokia appliance, how to run Perl scripts, and some links to useful Perl scripts.

Installation

You must initially download the Nokia Perl package from Nokia's support site. Searching for Perl on the Nokia support site will take you to the Perl discussion and download page. Click the link and save it to disk. Once it's on disk, you can get it to your firewall for installation in a number of ways. Burning all the useful packages to a CD-ROM can be particularly easy, but this method requires physical access to the device. Since only the 400 series has CD-ROM drives, this is not always an option. Other installation methods include FTPing the software to the firewall and installing from a local directory. Installation of packages is done via the *newpkg* command.

If you're looking to install any of the other unsupported packages, it is important to install Perl first, because it is required for several of the other packages. Installing the packages is fairly simple. The *newpkg* command, which is used for installing, is detailed more thoroughly in Chapter 7. Here is a screen capture of the actual install process for Perl 5.005_02 for Nokia IPSO:

```
firewall1[admin]# newpkg


1.   Install from CD-ROM.
2.   Install from anonymous FTP server.
3.   Install from FTP server with user and password.
4.   Install from local filesystem.
5.   Exit new package installation.
Choose an installation method (1-5):   4
Enter pathname to packages [none]:   /var/admin


Found packages:
Perl.tgz


Package Description:   Perl 5.005 - Unsupported


Would you like to :
```

```
1.   Install this as a new package

2.   Skip this package


Choose (1-2):  1


Installing perl.tgz
     Extracting Package
Done installing perl


firewall1[admin]#
```

That's all there is to it. Installation via the *newpkg* command is very quick and convenient. The Perl package is now ready for use and installed under the /opt directory. Don't forget to set your path or links to include Perl, if you want to do so. Additionally, with any Perl script you use, don't forget to update the location of Perl from the standard UNIX /usr/bin/perl to reflect the location on your NSP, /opt/perl/bin/perl.

Useful Scripts

There are numerous useful scripts for Check Point, but because of their length, it's not practical to include any in this section. The idea of having to type in 400 lines of code from a book isn't the most appealing, so instead we've included links to the most useful scripts. Looking at how these scripts operate should give you an idea of how you can use Perl within the IPSO environment. One thing to keep in mind when getting scripts from the Internet is that you must make sure that you change the location of Perl at the start of the script to /opt/perl/bin/perl.

There are two very useful scripts, with the same name, *fwlogsum*. The two scripts have similar functionality, but they have a slightly different execution. The first one, found at http://fwlogsum.sourceforge.net/, allows you the flexibility to create custom reports but modifying the configuration. Although it's not necessary to do so, you can get a great deal more mileage from this script by making changes to capture data that's important and suitable to your own environment. It's also important to note that the author cautions that, as the script is quite processor intensive, it's not a good idea to run it on a busy firewall.

The second *fwlogsum* can be found at www.ginini.com.au/tools/fw1/. Although it's very similar to the first script, it offers a slightly different output format, has been around longer, and is available for older versions of Firewall-1.

Its output is also done in HTML, but it can be also be generated in 80- or 132-column text, which can be a bit easier for viewing with lynx.

A number of other scripts can be found at www.phoneboy.com/sw/. The variety of scripts on this site can help you get an idea of doing something with Perl other than log manipulation and processing. For example, adtr.pl and fwobjects.pl can help give you an idea of how to parse and poll the Objects.C file on your firewall. When you're looking at the scripts found on the Internet, it is important to realize that the scripts are all freeware and are generally unsupported. It's also important to note that some of them might not even work as expected without modifications. However, they still offer insight into how Perl can be a useful tool on Check Point.

Configuring & Implementing…

Use Caution!

Because most firewalls are considered production devices, adding unsupported software might not be permissible within your company's security policy. Many organizations have strict guidelines regarding production hardware, and they might not be particularly forgiving should a problem arise. Additionally, any changes made to production firewalls should be done first in a test lab. Causing an outage on a test firewall will only cost you a few hours of time in troubleshooting, but an outage on an enterprise-critical firewall will cost you more.

Netcat

Netcat is basically the Swiss Army knife in a hacker's toolkit. On one hand, netcat is a tool that can be used to read and write data across a network using both TCP and UDP. On a firewall, it can be used to test connectivity to certain ports, since it can be set up as a listener. It can also be used to make connections, similar to Telnet. Another useful function of netcat is that it can be used to do port scanning, which could be used to diagnose connectivity issues, or simply test the security of your own firewalls.

On the other hand, as useful as it is for the administrator, netcat is also attractive to an attacker. Were an attacker to compromise your firewall, having netcat will certainly make the attacker's job of exploiting additional hosts on your network much easier. Additionally, netcat would allow an attacker to set up tunnels through your firewall. If you're not familiar with netcat, learn how to use it on another machine on your network rather than your firewall.

The following sections discuss how to install and use netcat—but make certain you absolutely require it on your firewall before proceeding, because netcat is an extremely powerful tool for both administrators and attackers.

Installation

Installing netcat is most easily done via the *newpkg* command. Once you've decided from where you'd like to install, launch *newpkg* and begin the installation. What follows is a screen capture of the actual installation process for this procedure:

```
firewall1[admin]# newpkg



1.   Install from CD-ROM.

2.   Install from anonymous FTP server.

3.   Install from FTP server with user and password.

4.   Install from local filesystem.

5.   Exit new package installation.


Choose an installation method (1-5): 4

Enter pathname to packages [none]:   /var/admin

Found packages:

netcat11.tgz


Package Description:    netcat 1.1 - Unsupported


Would you like to :


1.   Install this as a new package

2.   Skip this package


Choose (1-2):   1
```

```
Installing netcat11.tgz
        Extracting Package
Done installing netcat
```

Again, this process is very simple. Netcat installs into the /opt directory; you don't have to worry about adding it to your path, because the installation procedure adds */opt/netcat/bin* to the $PATH environment variable.

Basic Usage

Using netcat is pretty simple. It includes a small help file accessed with the *–h* option. Since netcat is basically a socket tool, it's fairly easy to do all kinds of things. The easiest and most basic use of netcat is as a Telnet replacement. By typing **nc <hostname> <port>**, you create a connection to that host on the port you've specified.

A more complex example involves copying data through netcat from your firewall to another host on your network, 10.10.0.1, using the command sequence that follows.

On the host you're sending data to, establish a listener on port 5555 (this can be any unused port higher than 1024 unless the user has root privileges) with netcat by typing:

```
nc -l -p 5555 | tar xvfp -
```

Now you need to send the data from your firewall, so type:

```
tar cfp - /your/directory | nc -w 3 10.10.0.1 5555
```

That's it. You've moved files from one host to another by piping it through standard input with *tar*. Traditionally, functionality like this is done with *rsync* or *rsh* (or securely using *ssh*), but netcat bypasses any type of authentication and creates a direct pipe. Of course, in order to use this method, you need to have an open port on your firewall.

Netcat can also be used as a "poor man's port scanner" by entering the following command:

```
echo QUIT| nc -v -w 5 <target> 20-400
```

This command port-scans the target on ports 20 through 400 and returns you a list the successful TCP connections.

These examples should give you an idea of the more likely uses for netcat on the Nokia firewall, but there are many more functions for which netcat could be useful. Be sure to look at the netcat README file that is installed in the directory with netcat for more usage ideas. In addition, many Web sites contain comprehensive netcat usage ideas, some of which you could find useful and some you might find downright shocking.

MRTG

MRTG is the multirouter traffic grapher. It's a tool that will monitor the load on your routers and other network devices and generate easy-to-read graphs on an HTML page. It also auto-updates the pages so that the statistics are always current In order to work, MRTG reads the SNMP data on your routers and network devices, using a Perl script to collect the data. Once the data is collected, a C program sorts the data and generates the graphs. Using MRTG, logs can be kept and seen visually, charting an entire history of a router's usage. However, do keep in mind that MRTG output is ultimately in HTML format. The output needs to be sent to a Web server directory either on your firewall or replicated to a different host in your environment. Remember that running software like MRTG can be somewhat processor intensive, and serving up Web pages on your busy firewall can also put a strain on it.

We cover the installation of MRTG in this section, followed by a discussion of how it can be configured. Because MRTG is such a flexible tool, it can be configured in literally thousands of ways. Because this is the case, we discuss the most common configurations and provide reference to information detailing more complex configuration scenarios. A very common configuration for MRTG is shown in Figure B.1.

Figure B.1 MRTG's Web Output

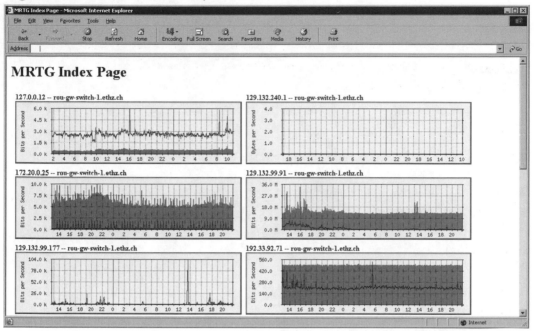

Installation

To install MRTG, use the *newpkg* command. The installation example assumes the files are located on a CD-ROM:

```
firewall1[admin]# newpkg

1.   Install from CD-ROM.
2.   Install from anonymous FTP server.
3.   Install from FTP server with user and password.
4.   Install from local filesystem.
5.   Exit new package installation.

Choose an installation method (1-5):   4

Enter pathname to packages [none]:   /var/admin
Found packages:
mrtg.tgz
netcat11.tgz
```

```
perl.tgz
shells11_ipso3211.tgz
squid.tgz
unsupported.tgz
webtools.tgz


Package Description:   Multi Router Traffic Grapher MRTG - Unsupported


Would you like to :


1.   Install this as a new package
2.   Skip this package


Choose (1-2):  1


Installing mrtg.tgz
Extracting Package
        Running Post-install script
Done installing mrtg


firewall1[admin]#  cd /opt/mrtg
firewall1[admin]#  perl INSTALL.pl



You can find documentation at http://xx.xx.xx.xx/admin/mrtg_docs
Read NokiaReadme.txt to get mrtg running


firewall1[admin]#
```

Once MRTG has been properly installed, it must be configured to run properly with any devices you want to monitor.

Configuration

The first step in running MRTG is to generate a configuration file. This is generally done with the cfgmaker file. On the Nokia installation, cfgmaker is found in /opt/mrtg/bin. Here's an example of how cfgmaker is used to build an initial config file:

```
firewall1[admin]# cd /opt/mrtg/bin
firewall1[admin]# ./cfgmaker public@10.10.0.1 >> mrtg.cfg
```

This code creates a configuration file called *mrtg.cfg*, using the SNMP string *public* on the 10.10.0.1 device. Make sure that the 10.10.0.1 device is configured to allow the firewall to read SNMP data. Once this has been done, you've created your first mrtg.cfg file. Rerunning the command with a different host IP address will append to the existing configuration file (indicated by the >> in the code) and allows you to monitor multiple hosts. Now you'll need to edit the file to tell it where to write its log and HTML data. Bring the file up into your text editor and search for the *WorkDir:* line, and uncomment it if it's commented. Edit the path to reflect where you'd like the data stored, and save the file. You've now built your first working MRTG config file.

With the configuration file built, you'll need to put MRTG into admin's crontab to have it run automatically. Edit admin's crontab by typing **crontab −e**. This brings the cron configuration file up into your editor (defaults to the environment variable $EDITOR, usually *Vi* by default). You'll now need to add the following line to the bottom of the file:

```
0,5,10,15,20,25,30,35,40,45,50,55 * * * * /opt/mrtg/bin/mrtg_run
```

This code runs MRTG every five minutes. (More details on editing the crontab can be found in Chapter 5.) You might want to run it more or less frequently, although the documentation recommends running it every five minutes. Next, you'll need to let MRTG run for a few iterations, so it can collect some data. It might give a few errors, since it does not have any existing data. Once it has run and collected some data, you'll need to run the indexmaker program to generate your HTML. To better understand the options of indexmaker, run it by itself. A good starting point for indexmaker is found in the NokiaReadme.txt file in the MRTG installation directory, which suggests the following.

```
Firewall1[admin]# ./indexmaker −t 'All Firewalls' −1 −r '.' −o \
    /var/admin/stats/index.html /opt/mrtg/bin/mrtg.cfg
```

Additional Options

You can graph a number of additional things with MRTG. Anything that can output data of any kind can be graphed. Nokia has included a couple of programs that you can use to generate useful firewall stats. *Fwstat* allows you to graph the number of accepted and rejected packets on a specified firewall. Adding the following code to your mrtg.cfg file will get you started:

```
Target[firewall1]: `/opt/mrtg/bin/fwstat 10.10.0.1 1`
Title[firewall1]: FireWall-1 Statistics for firewall1
 PageTop[firewall1]: <H1> FireWall-1 Stats for firewall1</H1>
 MaxBytes1[firewall1]: 100000
 MaxBytes2[firewall1]: 100000
 YLegend[firewall1]: Packets
 Legend1[firewall1]: Accepted Packets
 Legend2[firewall1]: Dropped/Rejected Packets
 LegendI[firewall1]:  Accepted:
 LegendO[firewall1]:  Drop/Rej:
 ShortLegend[firewall1]: pkt
```

In the first line, specifying the firewall to query, you need to pass an option to the *fwstat* program. The command is set up in the format of *fwstat firewall_ip option_number*. The option numbers are listed here:

1. Accepted + Rejected + Dropped

2. Accepted + Dropped

3. Accepted + Rejected

4. Rejected + Dropped

5. Logged + Total packets

So, for example, if you used the command line *fwstat 10.10.0.1 4,* you would be getting stats on all Rejected + Dropped packets. Of the five options, you can select the one that best serves your needs, or you can choose to graph them all by adding the preceding code an additional time in your MRTG configuration file.

You can choose to graph just one of them, or you can duplicate the preceding code in your mrtg.cfg file to have it run all the options, if you desire. Once you feel comfortable with MRTG's configuration, you'll want to explore adding more programs to the graphing. You can add monitors using the preceding config sample as a template. The nokiareadme.txt file also contains more useful information about adding monitors to the MRTG config file.

Bash

Bash is an enhanced command-line shell. If you've never used bash, you'll be in for a pleasant surprise because it offers many additional features from the standard csh. You'll immediately notice the command completion and command-line editing features. With command completion, you need only enter a few characters, and with the press of the Tab key, Bash will find the closest filename match for you. The ability to set an editor allows you to use a familiar editor such as Vi or Emacs within the command line. The familiarity of having Vi or Emacs editing capabilities available from the command line can be particularly useful when you're dealing with long or complex entries. Users of Vi will find commands such as *dw* and *x* helpful at the command line, whereas Emacs users can use key bindings such as Ctrl + A, Ctrl + E, Ctrl + K, and so on.

Bash also supports command history and command re-entry. This basically keeps a log of all commands entered and makes it easy to recall any of those commands in the future. Although convenient, this particular feature of Bash might not be desirable on a firewall, because it usually contains sensitive information and is generally a first target for potential intruders. It can be disabled by adding *export HISTCONTROL=ignorespace* to the user's profile. If the user then types a command beginning with a single space, the command will not be entered into the command history. If you still want to have command history logging enabled, proceed with caution when using this feature on your firewall.

Some of the more advanced features of Bash, such as arrays and arithmetic, make possible the ability to create advanced shell scripts. Shell scripts in Bash are quite powerful and can make system administration tasks much less complex. Be mindful to change #!/bin/bash to #!/opt/shells/bin/bash when creating your own scripts with Bash. For more advanced information on bash, be sure to visit its homepage at http://cnswww.cns.cwru.edu/~chet/bash/bashtop.html, and for more detailed information on scripting in Bash, read the *Advanced Bash Scripting Guide* found at www.tldp.org/LDP/abs/html/.

This section details downloading and installing Bash and lists a few tips on how to get up and running with bash.

Installation

Installing Bash is simple with *newpkg*. This example assumes that the reader is installing from CD-ROM. Other methods are identical, but obviously they require the files to be in different places such as a local FTP server or directory:

```
firewall1[admin]# newpkg
```

1. Install from CD-ROM.
2. Install from anonymous FTP server.
3. Install from FTP server with user and password.

```
4.   Install from local filesystem.
5.   Exit new package installation.


Choose an installation method (1-5):   4


Enter pathname to packages [none]:   /var/admin
Found packages:
shells11_ipso3211.tgz


Package Description:   Unix Shells {bash-2.05,tcsh-6.10.00,pdksh-5.2.14,
    zsh-3.0.0} for IPSO-3.2.1.1-FCS5


Would you like to :


1.   Install this as a new package
2.   Skip this package


Choose (1-2):   1


Installing shells11_ipso3211.tgz


        Running Pre-install script
        Extracting Package
        Running Post-install script
System-V style /bin/{bash,tcsh,zsh,ksh} shell links inserted...
Done installing shells


firewall1[admin]#
```

The quickest way to get started with Bash is to simply run it. From there, you will have all its functionality available to you and can begin exploring its features.

The other shells that are installed can be deleted if you are not planning to use them, because it's always a good idea to remove unused programs from your firewall. Should you decide you'd like to use another in the future, it's a trivial matter to reinstall them all.

Other Useful Utilities

Some of the other useful programs Nokia offers are found in the iprgdev.tgz and unsupported.tgz packages. Nokia has labeled the latter package unhelpfully, but the message that it is unsupported is adequately conveyed. To get started with these packages, install them as we've done with the earlier examples, using the *newpkg* command. After they're installed, we'll discuss the useful utilities included in each:

```
firewall1[admin]# newpkg


1.   Install from CD-ROM.
2.   Install from anonymous FTP server.
3.   Install from FTP server with user and password.
4.   Install from local filesystem.
5.   Exit new package installation.


Choose an installation method (1-5):   4


Enter pathname to packages [none]:   /var/admin
Found packages:
iprgdev.tgz
unsupported.tgz


Package Description:   IPRG Development Tools


Would you like to :


1.   Install this as a new package
2.   Skip this package


Choose (1-2):   1


Installing iprgdev.tgz
        Extracting Package
Done installing iprgdev


Package Description:   IPRG Unsupported tools
```

```
Would you like to :

1.   Install this as a new package
2.   Skip this package

Choose (1-2):  1

Installing unsupported.tgz
        Extracting Packages
Done installing unsupported

firewall1[admin]#
```

Programs from the iprgdev.tgz Package

The iprgdev.tgz package contains a few programs that might be of some use to you. It also contains bash, so if you're looking to install bash and iprgdev.tgz, you can save yourself a download. The tools in this package are geared more for development on the machine, because it contains *ktrace*, a kernel tracing program; *dmalloc*, a debug malloc library; and *kdump*, which displays kernel trace data. These might or might not be of particular use to a firewall administrator, but they could be nice to have handy if you're trying to diagnose a complex problem with the actual firewall programs. Some of the more useful tools in this package are *fstat*, which could be useful in diagnosing certain network or file problems on the firewall. The *less* command, although not essential, certainly makes the viewing of large text files much easier. This archive also contains a great FTP client replacement called *ncftp*, which is also included in the unsupported.tgz program, which we discuss next. The following sections contain some command-line usage examples for each of the programs mentioned previously.

ktrace and kdump

This example starts a ktrace on process number 34;

```
firewall1[admin]# ktrace -p 34
```

This code places the trace output in the file ktrace.out. Once you feel you've run the process long enough, you can cancel it with the −C option:

```
firewall1[admin]# ktrace -C
```

The data from the ktrace program is not in a readable format, so the kdump program is used to read the output. kdump looks in the file ktrace.out by default:

```
firewall1[admin]# kdump
34 fw       RET       select 0
34 fw       RET       gettimeofday(0xefb7e44,0xefb7ddc)

firewall1[admin]#
```

NcFTP

Using NcFTP is really easy—much easier, in fact, than the standard FTP. The interface is very intuitive, and anyone familiar with the traditional FTP client will be up and running in no time. The lines that follow show what NcFTP looks like after it has run and are a listing of the commands offered from the main menu:

```
firewall1[admin]# ncftp
[NcFTP 1.9.4 (April 15, 1995) by Mike Gleason, NCEMRSoft
Tip: Have you tried typing 'open' by itself lately?
ncftp> ?

Commands may be abbreviated.  'help showall' shows aliases, invisible and
unsupported commands.  'help <command>' gives a brief description of
<command>.

!          help       mls        predir      rename      user
$          lcd        modtime    put         rmdir       type
cd         lookup     mput       pwd         show        verbose
cdup       ls         open       quit        set         version
create     macdef     passive    quote       site
delete     mdelete    page       redir       size
dir        mget       pdir       remotehelp  system
get        mkdir      pls        rstatus     unset

ncftp>
```

fstat

fstat is a tool that can be used to glean loads of information from your Nokia appliance. It shows you information on all open files, similar to lsof. Run by itself, *fstat* shows you information for the entire system, but if you want to limit your search to a specific directory, the *–f* option can be used to do so. For example, *fstat –f /usr/bin* would only show you information about open files in the /usr/bin directory. Here is a sample showing partial output from the *fstat* command:

```
firewall1[admin]# fstat
USER       CMD         PID    FD MOUNT        INUM MODE          SZ|DV R/W
root       fstat       361    wd -               -       ?(10)      -
root       fstat       361    0  /           69780 crw-------    ttyv0 rw
root       fstat       361    1  -               -       ?(10)      -
root       fstat       361    2  /           69780 crw-------    ttyv0 rw
root       fstat       361    3  /           69280 crw-r-----     mem   r
root       fstat       361    4  /           69279 crw-r-----     kmem  r
root       fstat       361    5  /           69278 crw-r-----     drum  r
root       fstat       361    6  /           46137 -rwxr-xr-x   1527510  r
root       bash        265    wd -               -       ?(10)      -
root       bash        265    0  /           69780 crw-------    ttyv0 rw
root       bash        265    1  /           69780 crw-------    ttyv0 rw
root       bash        265    2  /           69780 crw-------    ttyv0 rw
root       bash        265    63 /           69780 crw-------    ttyv0 rw
root       netsod      216    wd /               2 drwxr-xr-x     512   r
root       netsod      216    0* internet stream tcp 0
root       netsod      216    1* internet stream tcp 0
root       netsod      216    2  /var       115211 -rw-rw-r--     418   w
root       netsod      216    3  /opt       199731 -rw-rw----   28673 rw
root       netsod      216    4* internet stream tcp 0

firewall1[admin]#
```

Programs from the unsupported.tgz Package

As mentioned previously, the *ncftp* program is a much nicer and friendlier FTP client than the standard UNIX version. It is useful to have on your firewall if you do a lot of FTP transferring. It provides an easy-to-read progress bar for your transfers, displaying file upload or download completion as a percentage. It also features a nicer batch uploading and download interface.

A couple of good firewall management tools are included in this package. The addstatic program, which requires Perl, makes adding and removing static routes much faster than the conventional method. Use of addstatic is fairly straightforward. Simply running the command takes you to the main menu, which gives you the option to add or remove static routes and the option to view what's currently configured. Also useful is the fwtable program, which dumps the firewall connections table and converts the output to decimal. Although it does not need to be run with any options, the –h option provides you with a list of some options, which follow:

```
firewall1[admin]# fwtable -h
fwtable by Lance Spitzner <lance@spitzner.net>
Usage: fwtable -L -c <# of connections> -i <infput file> -t <target>


       fwtable converts a FireWall-1 connections table to readable
       format. It can be ran without any options.  By default,
       fwtable queries the local machine for the FireWall-1
       connections table, and converts the first 500 connections.
       This information is then sent to STDOUT.  You have the
       following options.


       -c: Number of connections you want to query from the
           Firewall.  The default is 500. This option dos NOT work
           with the '-i' option.


       -i: Instead of querying a Firewall for the connections
           table, convert an existing file <input file>.


       -t: Query a remote Firewall for the connections table.


       -L: Loop until interrupted


       -s: Seconds to sleep between loops (default of 5)


firewall1[admin]#
```

Finally, one of the not-so-necessary, but nice-to-have programs is *clear*, which quickly clears your screen. This could be useful if you're concerned about others walking up behind you while you're editing sensitive firewall data. The cut and paste programs are somewhat useful if you're interested in doing string manipulation within shell scripts on your firewall. Lastly, the dos2unix program is quite useful in that it strips out annoying ^M characters from text files. If you've ever downloaded scripts or config files from Web sites using lynx, you've probably encountered the ^M issue. Using dos2unix strips out the offending bits in a matter of seconds, preparing your scripts or other essentials for use.

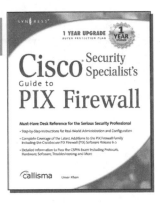